WRITERS REPUBLIC

PRODIGAL
PARISH

Revised Edition

Leo F. White

WRITERS REPUBLIC L.L.C.
515 Summit Ave. Unit R1
Union City, NJ 07087, USA

Website: *www.writersrepublic.com*
Hotline: *1-877-656-6838*
Email: *info@writersrepublic.com*

Ordering Information:
Quantity sales. Special discounts are available on quantity purchases by corporations, associations, and others. For details, contact the publisher at the address above.

Library of Congress Control Number:		2020949705
ISBN-13:	978-1-64620-668-1	[Paperback Edition]
	978-1-64620-669-8	[Digital Edition]

Rev. date: 11/11/2020

Dedicated to:

Abigail, David, Andrew, Jonathan, Suzanne, Jessica, Caroline and Catherine

My eight newest and closest friends

PROLOGUE

It was one of those days which made living in New England sheer misery. It was the middle of March—a time for the changing of the seasons—and Mother Nature wasn't sure as to which season to favor, winter or spring, so, as a result, she was attempting to accommodate both. The day had started with wet snow falling from the heavens. The elements soon turned to sleet and by the time the afternoon had arrived, it had become a cold and piercing rain. Combined with the raw wind blowing in off the nearby Atlantic Ocean, the effect was of bone chilling dimensions.

The scuttlebutt on the streets was that someone of importance was coming to see Father Coniglio, the pastor and only priest serving the Church of St. Theresa. The rumor in the neighborhood had the person in question as being the archbishop of the diocese of Boston, Carroll Cardinal Burke. This was the day which many who called themselves parishioners of St. Theresa's rued. It was to be the day their little church on Everton Street ceased to exist.

The small church was known to its faithful as the *Poor People's Parish*. Standing in the shadow of the more opulent St. Matthew's, St. Theresa's had been built in the 1930s to accommodate the city of Paine's swelling Catholic population. In the beginning the unpretentious church catered to the large French and Italian cultures which populated the area. But with the passage of time the littoral base which gave St. Theresa's life moved onto the more attractive suburbs and the old neighborhood became the haven of ethnic minorities. What was left from the old contingent of the French and Italian population was that of the hardliners and the indigent. In place of those who left were

African Americans, Brazilians and Asian refugees from Cambodia and Vietnam. Those people presented a different look but they, too, were God's children and welcomed to worship at St. Theresa's.

St. Matthew's, however, was operated differently. Unlike St. Theresa's which had only one prelate to administer its day-to-day operation, St. Matthew's was manned by a staff of three: Monsignor Peter Cosgrove and two assistants. St. Matthew's also had a musical director and several lectors, whereas St. Theresa's had none. It was an affluent church which trumpeted the designs of Vatican II and profited from it. St. Theresa's, by comparison, looked as though it had been excluded from the changes directed through Vatican II. It had long ago ceased to operate in the black.

The structures of the two churches were also quite different. St. Theresa's was a modest stucco house of worship built flush against Everton Street. It had been constructed on a small parcel of land, so small that the rectory had to be built so the side of the house faced the street. The church had just one altar for its three masses on Sunday. Most of the parishioners walked to services, for there were limited parking spaces around the church, restricted to what could be found on the streets.

St. Matthew's was a church devoid of such problems. Although an older church than St. Theresa's, St. Matthew's legacy had proven to be a more prosperous one. Built on a large tract of land, the church was of cathedral proportions and featured a 250 foot high belfry. The rectory and a function hall abutted the side of the church, and the entire area was surrounded by a parking lot which could accommodate 200 automobiles for the seven masses held each weekend in the upper and lower church.

The parishes were also run on a different basis when it came to monetary concerns. At St. Matthew's the churchgoers were urged to dig deep into their pockets for the collection plate, almost shamed into it. Also, heavy stipends were asked for when it came to such sacred rituals as baptism and marriage. As a result St. Matthew's financial take for any given week was much greater when compared to the paltry collection St. Theresa's was mustering.

Now the archdiocese was downsizing and some churches had to go. St. Theresa's was on that endangered species list. The church was expected to be closed with the parishioners becoming part of an expanded St. Matthew's. It was a situation the faithful of St. Theresa's felt was intolerable.

Two churches established for the same purpose. Two churches meant to be a temple for the faithful and a sanctuary of comfort for the desperate and confused. Two churches now being told they can no longer co-exist. The prosperous one stays, the poor one goes. All because of the greed and ambition of one man.

CHAPTER
ONE

The rain continued to fall and it chilled to the bone. Antonio Grimaldi, the sixty-eight-year-old caretaker of the grounds of St. Theresa's, was busy removing what remained of the sleet covering the walkway leading to the rectory. Despite the cold and dismal conditions Grimaldi had managed to break a sweat with his servile duties.

A smallish man with tufts of unruly salt and pepper hair on his head, Grimaldi had been performing St. Theresa's custodial duties for the past twenty years. It wasn't, however, until his retirement two years earlier that he took the job on full time. He also performed the function on a voluntary basis; it was a way of keeping him busy, or so he told anyone who inquired as to how much such a position paid from a church so desperately strapped for cash. St. Theresa's certainly didn't have the money to pay a caretaker.

"Grimaldi," the voice shrieked through the raw atmospheric conditions. "Are you almost done?"

The darting shrill caused Grimaldi to stop what he was doing. With his back to her, Grimaldi did a slow burn. It was something about the way she expressed herself. Here he was, breaking his hump to see that the walkway and sidewalk were clear and sanded for the cardinal's visit, and she was checking on him, as if he were a small child being lax at his chores.

"Yes," he answered in an inflection which indicated he didn't care for her busybody tactics in regard to his work. "You can rest assured the cardinal will not slip and fall on his *arse* because of Grimaldi's negligence."

"Now, don't you being using that kind of language when His Eminence is here. Do you hear me?" She was doing it again and Grimaldi fumed a little more.

The *she* was Mildred Fortnat, the sixty-six-year-old housekeeper at St. Theresa's. She assumed the role of household overseer twelve years ago, and since that time, she had taken on the role of *Girl Friday* in all matters concerning Father Coniglio. She was the nerve center of St. Theresa's. Unlike Grimaldi, she was paid for her services.

Mildred had poked her head out the front door of the rectory to check on Grimaldi, careful to see she didn't get wet in the process. Satisfied with the progress the caretaker was making she returned to see how the old priest was doing. The cardinal's visit had him feeling down. He, like so many of the parishioners, believed the cardinal's forthcoming visit spelled doom for their poor but beloved church.

Mildred, however, did not share in the same despondent thought. She couldn't help but feel there was some sort of silver lining to the dark cloud hovering over St. Theresa's. The feeling she carried with her came strictly from the gut and it was strong. She was certain St. Theresa's demise was not going to happen on this day.

Mildred directed her small and rotund body to the staircase which led to the second floor of the rectory. She had been trying all day to buoy Father Coniglio's sagging spirit about the cardinal's visit but he wasn't buying into it. She was going to make one final attempt to convey what she was feeling to the old priest. She was well aware of the friendship Father Coniglio and the cardinal had once shared as seminarians. Unlike Father Coniglio she believed, because of their friendship, the hole had yet to be dug to put St. Theresa's at rest. It was the old priest's belief the cardinal was doing the job himself out of respect for the friendship they once shared. Mildred refused to buy into the priest's line of thinking. The housekeeper was certain the cardinal was coming here to put Father Coniglio's mind at rest regarding the future of his church and once the two old schoolmates reunited, St. Theresa's future would be safe and secure.

Father Coniglio was a smallish man of sixty-eight with a full head of white hair, often unkempt, which, at times, had him resembling Albert Einstein. He was now into his thirty-first year as pastor of St. Theresa's. However, the straining times St. Theresa's was now enduring was showing in his outward appearance. His weight had dropped to skeletal proportions and the stress he had been laboring under had him looking much older than his actual age. He had also become a prisoner of his domain, in the past six months, not venturing beyond the grounds of St. Theresa's. His church was dying and so was he.

The old priest had pushed his big black easy chair over to the window in his bedroom so he could peer down on Everton Street. As he did so, a great number of memories came together. It was as if the past thirty-one years were passing before him and the thoughts filled his heart with anguish, a heart the cardinal was about to put a dagger in.

As Mildred entered the room she had to stop and look at the back of the sad man who seemed beaten. It hurt her to see what a sorry sight the venerable old priest had become. She wanted to shake him and somehow restore his confidence which had taken such a hit. The fighting spirit which had been so much a part of him was now out of him. What she was witnessing was killing a part of her as well. She could see herself beginning to hate the Church because of what it was doing to this priest she admired so much. Nevertheless, she had to put up a strong façade to keep the old priest from becoming more demoralized.

"Father, whatcha doin'?" she asked upon stepping into the room.

"Visiting some old memories," he told her, remaining fixed in his position, his back still towards her.

"Well, are you ready for the cardinal's visit?" she continued. "He should be here in an hour or so."

"I'm ready," he answered. "Perfect weather for it. Don't you agree?"

"I don't understand," Mildred replied as she walked to the window so she could look Father Coniglio in the eye.

"The weather, Mildred, the weather. It's perfect weather for a burial. And that's what the cardinal is coming to do. He's going to bury us once and for all."

3

"I wish you wouldn't say such a thing." Mildred detested his frame of mind. "You don't know that for sure."

"Mildred, you are either very believing in miracles or very naïve. The truth is this: St. Theresa's is a losing proposition. One of the biggest losers the archdiocese has. Churches more prosperous than ours have been closed. What makes you think St. Theresa's is going to be spared?"

"Because of your relationship with the cardinal," she was quick to reply. "It has to stand for something."

"I'm sure it does," he answered. "But the cardinal has to do what he feels is in the best interest of the archdiocese. Besides being a priest, he also has to be a businessman. I'm afraid when it comes to the business side of doing things St. Theresa's doesn't fit into the equation. She has been a good church and parish but her time has come. Now, if you don't mind, I'd like to be alone with my thoughts."

"Understood," Mildred responded as she withdrew from the room. But as she did so she was not at ease. Over the past six months she had worried more and more about the aging cleric. There were times when his mind wandered and she wondered if he were on the verge of going senile. But now he talked so precise, very clear headed, and appeared to be giving in and ready to face the inevitable.

The clarity with which he spoke seemed to shake Mildred's belief that nothing bad was to happen on this day. His clear thinking had caught her off guard. She had to admit right now she missed the dimwitted priest she had come to know in the past half year. This dose of reality didn't set well with her. Where was the Church she had faithfully followed her entire life? Where was the Church that was long on compassion and in the business of saving souls? Mildred was becoming spiritually adrift because of what the Church was doing to Father Coniglio, and in the process was developing a tremendous amount of resentment for the men who ran it.

CHAPTER
TWO

The black Lincoln Continental made its way into the city of Paine and came to a halt at a traffic light entering Tolleson Circle. Straight ahead, in the distance, the belfry of St. Matthew's could be seen. However, the Lincoln's destination was not St. Matthew's but rather St. Theresa's.

In the rear seat of the Lincoln sat two men: Carroll Cardinal Burke and his personal secretary, Father John Moore. The cardinal was making this trip to see if the rumors he was hearing were accurate. It had been brought to his attention that his old friend, his roommate from their seminary days, Father Ronald Coniglio, was in failing health. The cardinal had been led to believe Father Coniglio's mental faculties were not what they used to be and it might be time to ask and, if necessary, force the esteemed old priest into retirement. The cardinal was open to the idea but he was not satisfied to implement such action on the sole recommendation of others. He would see his old friend first and then render his decision.

Cardinal Burke had been the archbishop of Boston for fourteen years, but this was the first time he had ventured to St. Theresa's to look in on Father Coniglio. He was feeling a tinge of guilt knowing he had neglected his old pal all these years, and it made him feel worse to know it took such rumors about Father Coniglio's mental well-being to finally force him to come here. But it gave him some solace to know he had rallied before it was too late, and thus the reason for his personal visit. Father Coniglio was to be put out to pasture only if the cardinal himself deemed it necessary.

In appearance the cardinal was an imposing figure. He stood six feet tall but weighed nearly 300 pounds. He was the possessor of a booming voice which could intimidate when required or console if needed. He had proven to be a good shepherd when it came to the overseeing of the archdiocese, but he was also a man getting a *bum rap*. The man responsible for putting him in such a position was sitting to his right.

Since his ordination the forty-five-year-old Father Moore had proven to be a whirling financial dervish when it came to the archdiocese's pecuniary matters. And since his appointment as the cardinal's personal secretary five years earlier, he now had a firm grip on the day-to-day monetary operation of the archdiocese. The cardinal relied on Father Moore's advice and usually implemented his recommendations.

Father Moore did not give the impression of being a man of power. A scrawny individual, Father Moore stood only five-foot-six and weighed a paltry 135 pounds. He had a closely cropped head of red hair which looked orange in the light. However, Father Moore may have looked like milquetoast with his emaciated features but beneath that veil of timidity was a brusque, cruel, and unnerving personality. In a surreptitious manner, Father Moore had appointed himself to be the cardinal's henchman, and he did the job well.

It had been Father Moore who convinced the cardinal the time had come for consolidation; there were too many churches in the urban regions of the archdiocese. Many of those churches had been built in the first half of the twentieth century to accommodate the burgeoning Catholic population. But since that time, many of those Catholic families had uprooted and headed for suburbia. In addition, Catholic participation in Sunday services had diminished with the passing years. Catholics, like many of their Christian counterparts of the Protestant persuasion, had become lazy and no longer considered it important to attend Sunday Mass or any other services the Church provided. It was time to allow the more prosperous parishes to take over and force the ones not pulling their weight to close their doors.

Father Moore compiled what was known as his *Hit List*. On the list were ten churches slated to be eliminated. Despite the protests of parishioners he had managed to close three. Our Lady of the Sea in Quincy was condemned. St. Kevin's in Dorchester and the Sacred Heart in Montrose conveniently burned to the ground. Then Father Moore's downsizing plan hit a snag. It came in the form of St. Theresa's.

When the ambitious priest drew up his *Hit List* he was unaware Cardinal Burke and Father Coniglio had been seminary roommates and shared a long standing friendship. When the cardinal had been notified that his longtime friend's church was about to go under, he was not so quick to approve. Father Moore tried convincing the cardinal that Father Coniglio's failing mental faculties may have him headed towards dementia if he remained responsible for the losing proposition known as St. Theresa's.

The cardinal, however, was not to be swayed so easily. He made it quite clear to his able assistant how the decision regarding St. Theresa's and Father Coniglio's fate was to be made by him. His old friend and parish were not going to be dismissed so readily. The cardinal had a sense of allegiance to his former roommate, or so he told Father Moore.

Yet, the truth be told, the cardinal made this sojourn as an act of contrition. Since his appointment as the archbishop of Boston the cardinal's correspondence with Father Coniglio had waned. In fact, he and Father Coniglio hadn't spoken in ten years. So, upon hearing the disturbing stories surrounding Father Coniglio's mental decline and the sorry plight of his parish, it was time to atone for his negligence. The cardinal was coming to St. Theresa's to set matters straight.

Cardinal Burke was scheduled to meet with Father Coniglio at two in the afternoon. As the hour approached Mildred became extremely nervous and took out her anxiety on Grimaldi. Her heart was racing and her stomach churned when she returned to the front door with an umbrella in hand.

"Grimaldi," she screamed. "Take this and greet the cardinal when he arrives." She tossed the umbrella his way and it landed on the slush covered lawn.

Grimaldi stepped on the wet grass and picked up the umbrella. "But of course," he muttered to himself. "Can't let the cardinal get wet. We need to save all the water we can so he can drown St. Theresa's in it."

The excitement of the day had aroused the curiosity of some parishioners. Word of the cardinal's visit had circulated through the streets and a small crowd had gathered in front of the church. Some of them had come to catch a glimpse of the cardinal but most had come to voice their displeasure about the impending closure of their parish. The small crowd was not an unruly one but they were not a happy lot either. Their faith had been shaken because of the cloud of doom which hovered over their little church.

As the black Lincoln made its approach and crossed over the commuter rail bridge—which served as the west boundary on Everton Street separating the parish of St. Theresa's from St. Matthew's—a pall came over the awaiting crowd. A helpless feeling engulfed their inner beings. This was it: a high noon shootout which they could not win. Well, if that were the case, they were not going to go quietly. The cardinal was going to hear of their disapproval with his decision regarding their little church. By the end of the day St. Theresa's fate would probably be official but it will not have been met without a fight.

Since parking was allowed on only one side of the street, the cardinal's vehicle was forced to park on the opposite side of Everton Street from the church. As the Lincoln came to a halt Grimaldi made a mad dash across the street to greet the cardinal. But as he arrived at the side of the Lincoln, with the open umbrella, he was hustled away by a large and muscular individual who emerged from the driver's side of the Lincoln. Rebuffed, Grimaldi backed away a few steps, and stood on the sidewalk and watched as the chauffeur opened a large black umbrella meant to shelter the cardinal from the falling rain.

The first to step out of the back of the Lincoln was Father Moore. Grimaldi had to suppress a laugh as he watched the cardinal's associate step into a puddle of slush which had yet to wash away from the curb. The incident brought a scowl to Father Moore's face as he shook the watery residue from his expensive Italian leather shoes. He did his best to show his displeasure without cursing.

Grimaldi noticed when the cardinal emerged from the Lincoln his footwear was more appropriate for the weather, although not something the caretaker expected someone such as Cardinal Burke to be wearing. His Excellency's feet were being protected by insulated *Timberland* boots.

Standing on the sidewalk, the cardinal stretched his massive frame before catching a glimpse of the sheepish Grimaldi, who was keeping his distance from him and his associate. Cardinal Burke noticed the red umbrella in Grimaldi's hand and realized the man had been dispatched to escort him and Father Moore to the rectory.

"Sir," the cardinal bellowed as he glanced in Grimaldi's direction. "Do you work here at St. Theresa's?"

Grimaldi jerked his head and looked over his shoulder to see if the cardinal might be speaking to someone else.

"Sir," the cardinal repeated. "I am talking to you."

Grimaldi, still unsure, raised his right index finger and pressed it against his chest. "Are you speaking to me?" he asked in an unsteady voice.

"Yes, my good man," the cardinal's voice boomed. "Do you have something to do with St. Theresa's?"

A smile graced Grimaldi's face as his confidence returned. "Yes, Your Eminence, I handle the odd jobs around the church…for nothing, of course," Grimaldi made sure to add, not wanting the cardinal to think Father Coniglio was spending money St. Theresa's didn't have.

"I see. And what might your name be?"

"Grimaldi, Antonio Grimaldi," he proudly proclaimed.

"Well, Mr. Grimaldi, why don't you do the honors and escort us across the street." The cardinal was well aware he was in hostile territory so it was best to turn on the charm.

Grimaldi's chest seemed to expand an inch or two as he prepared to answer the cardinal. "Yes, Your Eminence. It'd be my pleasure to escort you to the rectory."

"Fine," the cardinal responded. He then instructed the chauffeur to remain with the Lincoln. Mr. Grimaldi was going to see him and Father

Moore the rest of the way. It was then the cardinal caught a glimpse of the crowd on the other side of the street. He knew, unlike Grimaldi, they were not here to greet him in a cordial manner.

The cardinal anticipated some verbal backlash from the discordant gathering. It didn't take them long to begin voicing their displeasure over the ugly rumor they had come to accept as fact. As the three men made their way across the street, the church gathering started to make their dissatisfaction with the cardinal known.

"Save our parish!"

"Close this church and you close off our faith!"

"We thought the church was more interested in saving souls, not dollars!"

Grimaldi was embarrassed by the comportment of his fellow parishioners as he led the two priests up the walkway to the rectory. In a sudden change of heart he gave no credence to their right to dissent. He wanted to shout out to them to knock off the verbal histrionics. They were doing more harm than good. But he thought better of it, not wanting to embarrass the cardinal in the process.

Father Moore, on the other hand, took great delight in what he was witnessing. The parishioners' futile outbursts were joy to his ears. What he was observing he had seen before and it had always spelled victory for him. If the past was any indication then the doors of St. Theresa's would soon be locked, leaving what was to be done with the place his decision to make. Outwardly his face was a picture of revulsion because of the seemingly sacrilegious display being acted out. But inwardly he was aglow with satisfaction.

Then there was the cardinal. He was the target of the group's displeasure. He was the one who was prepared to do an injustice to their beloved church. Despite the ire they directed his way the cardinal remained unflustered. Being cast as the heavy didn't seem to bother him, or so it appeared to the lot gathered in front of the church. The smile he directed their way had to be considered pretentious. In the minds of the angry protesters Cardinal Burke came here as a dark prince of the Church.

Once the threesome reached the front door of the rectory, Mildred was there to greet them. She immediately dispatched Grimaldi (which infuriated the caretaker to the core) and welcomed the cardinal and his associate to St. Theresa's while introducing herself and taking care of their damp coats. If efficiency was to count for anything with the cardinal, then Mildred was shooting for a high grade.

The cardinal thanked Mildred for her help before introducing his secretary and then asked: "Where is my good friend, Father Coniglio? I've been looking forward to this day."

Mildred took that remark in a positive vein. Surely the cardinal wouldn't blatantly boast about *looking forward* to his visit to St. Theresa's just to drop the axe on the place. In the last hour Mildred had started second guessing herself and wondered if she wasn't being naïve about the cardinal's visit. Now, as she stood in his presence, she was again thinking the *Grim Reaper* of reality would not be visiting St. Theresa's on this day.

"He's waiting in the kitchen," she informed the cardinal.

The rectory kitchen was just off the living room, towards the back of the property. As the cardinal entered the area he saw Father Coniglio sitting at the kitchen table sipping on a cup of tea. The sight of his old roommate brought a worried look to Cardinal Burke's face. He did, indeed, look old and tired. Apparently the stories he had heard about Father Coniglio's health were not fabricated. The cardinal shot a glance in the direction of Father Moore. His personal secretary's face had a smug look about it. It seemed to say: *I TOLD YOU SO!*

This day was not turning out the way Cardinal Burke had hoped. Father Coniglio's feeble condition was going to have to be addressed. If it proved he was no longer lucid then there was a decision to be made. The cardinal could feel himself becoming ill with the thought.

"Ronny," the cardinal's booming voice called out as he made his way to the opposite side of the table from where Father Coniglio sat. "How have you been? It's been years."

The cardinal's attempt at being the jovial old friend did not set well with Father Coniglio. *If you have come here to snuff out the life of my church then go ahead and do so. Let's skip the dog and pony show,* was the old priest's thinking as he stared at the face of his one-time roommate. Despite his consternation Father Coniglio did understand what the cardinal was up against. What the old priest was feeling was a sense of being tired, tired of a fight which he could not win on his own. If this was to be the end then he simply wanted it over and done.

"Ronny," the cardinal continued as he sat down. "I've been hearing disturbing news about your health. How are you feeling?"

That's cute, thought Father Coniglio. *Not only have they labeled me an old man but a tired and sick one at that.* The old priest could feel Cardinal Burke making a case against him.

"I'm feeling fine, Your Eminence. I don't know who'd be spreading such rumors."

"Your Eminence! What's with this *Your Eminence* drivel? Between us it has always been Carroll and Ronny. It's been that way since our seminary days and it's the same way today."

All Father Coniglio could do was shrug and grunt. This inane banter about old times and how they should address one another really wasn't doing him any good. He wanted to skip the preliminaries and get to the heart of the matter. The cardinal was here for one purpose so why not get to it.

It then dawned on Father Coniglio that perhaps the cardinal was having trouble segueing into the task at hand. As Mildred had suggested, maybe their friendship did stand for something. If the cardinal was having a problem with the situation which had been presented to him, then Father Coniglio intended to enjoy watching his old friend squirm as he tried to find the proper time and point in their conversation in which to do his dastardly deed. Father Coniglio had tremendous respect for the cardinal and he dearly treasured their fifty year friendship. But the cardinal was going to have a church after today. Father Coniglio was fairly certain he wouldn't be able to say the same when the sun rose tomorrow.

Mildred felt the meeting between the cardinal and Father Coniglio was proceeding at an awkward pace. This was not what she envisioned. The cardinal was doing his best to be friendly while Father Coniglio was doing his best to keep him at a distance. Mildred figured a little hospitality might ease the situation.

"Cardinal Burke, can I offer you and your colleague some refreshments?" she asked.

The cardinal took a look at Father Coniglio's half-filled cup of tea before saying, "Why, Mildred, I think that's a splendid idea. I'll have the same as Father Coniglio. How about you, Father Moore?"

Father Moore! The mention of the prelate's name brought a piercing stare from Father Coniglio. He turned and glared at the man who was standing at the entrance to the kitchen. This was the priest Father Coniglio had heard so many bad things about. This was the priest who was the prime mover in seeing a certain allotment of churches closed. This was the priest who intended to toss the first shovel full of dirt on the grave of St. Theresa's. Now he was standing here in the rectory, on the grounds he intended to shut down. His mere presence solidified Father Coniglio's worst fear.

"Nothing for me," Father Moore said as he moved forward and took a seat at the kitchen table.

Father Coniglio returned his attention to the cardinal. "Well, Your Eminence—"

"No, Ronny, no," the cardinal interjected. "It's Carroll. Just like in the old days."

Father Coniglio shrugged and muffled a silent laugh. If the cardinal chose to play this silly game then so be it.

"Well…Carroll, I see you've met Mildred. She has been a godsend to me. She's been with me for fifteen years."

Mildred cringed when she heard what Father Coniglio had to say. Upon introducing herself to the cardinal she mentioned being employed at St. Theresa's for the past twelve years. The housekeeper felt any slip-up on the old priest's part might work against him and the parish. The smallest of inconsistency might weigh heavily against St. Theresa's and its struggle to survive. Hopefully, the cardinal—if he were looking for signs of his old friend's mental instability—would simply dismiss the number of years Father Coniglio recollected in alluding to Mildred's tenure at the church as a simple rounding off of the years. Too close to be splitting hairs.

The next half hour brought Mildred some piece of mind. Father Coniglio gradually seemed to become less unreceptive towards the cardinal as they traded stories about their younger days. Despite their sudden camaraderie there still remained an air of suspense hanging over the room. The cardinal had yet to indicate as to what the future held for St. Theresa's.

Whatever was taking place had Mildred feeling anxious, Father Coniglio feeling confused, and Father Moore feeling frustrated. Not one of the trio had an inkling that the cardinal was now using this trip to St. Theresa's to decide what Father Coniglio needed to make his life easier; not to shut down his church. The cardinal valued their friendship dearly. If an exception was to be made in this downsizing scheme of Father Moore, then St. Theresa's was it.

After nearly an hour the cardinal announced he had to leave and raised himself from the table. Father Coniglio and Mildred exchanged glances, both mystified at what was going on. The same could not be said of Father Moore. He feared this trip down memory lane was going to deter His Eminence from the task at hand. He was going to have to figure out another way to get his hands on St. Theresa's. The church remained high on his list of priorities.

As he and Father Moore were about to leave, the cardinal remarked to Father Coniglio how fortunate he was to have such a fine and caring housekeeper as Mildred. The old priest agreed but as he did so, he had Mildred wishing he would keep his mouth shut.

"Yes, Carroll, she has been that and more. In the ten years she has worked here she has been like a second mother to me."

Oh, no, Mildred thought. Here he goes again with the shaky math. Maybe Mildred was making too much of the issue but she needed to set the record straight.

"Twelve," she interjected.

"Twelve what?" the old priest asked.

"Twelve years, Father. We've been together twelve years." Then looking at the cardinal she said. "It's been twelve years. The father here has never been very good with his arithmetic."

"I see," the cardinal remarked while giving off a small laugh, as if to indicate that he hadn't given any thought to what Father Coniglio had said regarding Mildred's time spent as St. Theresa's housekeeper.

Once the cardinal and Father Moore had left, Mildred let out a massive sigh of relief. "No mention of St. Theresa's closing. I told you things were not going to be so bad. Your friendship with the cardinal does mean something. Do you believe it now?"

Father Coniglio separated himself from the housekeeper's side and walked over to the living room window. As he watched the cardinal's Lincoln drive away his words to Mildred from earlier in the day were ringing in his head. *She was either very believing in miracles or very naïve.* Something had happened and he wasn't sure as to what it was.

Had Mildred been right? Was the cardinal placing their long standing friendship above archdiocesan matters? It sure looked as if he did. Father Coniglio finally heaved a sigh of relief of his own, relieved to know today was not the day his church and parish ceased to exist.

Nevertheless, Father Coniglio was not without his reservations. With rumors running rampant of the impending closing of St. Theresa's, the cardinal's visit had to have more to do with it than just renewing acquaintances. The cardinal couldn't fool him; Father Coniglio knew him too well. The cardinal was up to something but what, Father Coniglio didn't know.

The venerable old priest turned and looked at Mildred. His tired eyes seemed to tell the story. "It was kind of the cardinal to come here," he told her. "But there is more to his agenda than what we saw today. I can only pray to God the decisions he is making are in the best interests of the Church."

Mildred smiled. "God's will be done," she replied, softly.

It was still gray, with lingering low clouds, but at least it had stopped raining. The cardinal's Lincoln was mired in heavy traffic as it crossed Boston's Tobin Bridge, en route to the chancery. However, the stillness was not confined to the road. In the back of the Lincoln, silence prevailed. The feeling was one of distinct discomfort.

The cardinal drummed the fingers of his right hand on the top of his kneecap. His thoughts were still centered on Father Coniglio and what he needed to do to help his old friend through his remaining years.

There was only one answer and he was gradually committing himself to it.

Meanwhile, Father Moore remained stationary as he sat next to the cardinal, his stare locked on the dark clouds hovering over Boston Harbor, trying to figure out what the cardinal was doing. When they left the chancery earlier in the day he believed he and the cardinal were on the same page. What they were to do at St. Theresa's was perfunctory.

Then, bang, with no warning, the cardinal does an about face. There could be only one answer for what he had done. Upon seeing his old roommate and friend, the cardinal had become a victim of sentimentality. His Eminence's eleventh hour change of heart angered him and he was in no mood to talk about it. St. Theresa's was at the top on his list of churches to be closed and the cardinal had taken it away from him.

Cardinal Burke was well aware of Father Moore's displeasure. He had great admiration for his private secretary's monetary and organizational skills. But he wondered if Father Moore's zeal for financial conquests had blinded him to a priest's true objective in life. The cardinal felt he did owe his secretary an explanation for his last minute decision to not close the doors of St. Theresa's. He could only hope and pray his assistant understood.

"Father, are you upset with me for not informing Father Coniglio that his church is one we would like to close?"

Normally a question such as the one the cardinal was putting to Father Moore was answered with a modicum of respect for his station in the church hierarchy. But protocol be damned, as far as Father Moore was concerned. He wasn't going to answer the cardinal's question with the pretense that he understood.

"Let's just say I was a little surprised. When we left the chancery you were committed to the agenda at hand. Then, less than two hours later, you change your mind. I think once you saw Father Coniglio, your old friend and roommate, you started feeling sorry for him. So sorry that you decided to spare your old buddy the agony of seeing his church closed down."

A slight smile creased the face of the cardinal. "You are quite perceptive," he told him.

Father Moore shook his head in disgust. "Your Eminence, I can't say I admire your allegiance to an old friendship. In fact, I believe you did your pal a disservice by keeping St. Theresa's alive."

"In what way?" the cardinal wanted to know.

"Your Eminence, we both agreed St. Theresa's was a losing proposition and it wasn't going to get any better. You were made aware of Father Coniglio's failing health, especially his mind. We came to the conclusion St. Theresa's had a lot to do with his deteriorating condition. You insisted—I assume to free your conscience—that you see for yourself just how bad his condition had become. Today you got a major league dose of it first-hand. So what do you propose to do about it? Nothing! That's what."

The cardinal's smile grew a little wider. Despite the tremendous respect he had for Father Moore's abilities, he had to admit the man was wound a little too tight when it came to official matters. He was also a little too presumptuous as to how far his powers as the cardinal's personal secretary extended. There were moments when the cardinal enjoyed antagonizing him, bringing him down a peg or two. This was one of those moments.

"Father, I don't recall, in our meeting with Father Coniglio, saying anything about whether the doors of St. Theresa's remained open or closed."

"You didn't have to. Your actions spoke for you."

"I see," the cardinal answered with a slow turn of the head so he could look directly at Father Moore.

"Damnit, Your Eminence, you saw how dimwitted Father Coniglio has become. What was the nonsense with the housekeeper? He has no idea how long she has been working for him. Did you notice how she was trying to cover-up for him?"

"Yes, I noticed."

The cardinal's remark irritated Father Moore. "You noticed. So you're admitting it. You're admitting Father Coniglio is losing some of his faculties. Do you also admit he is no longer capable of running a parish?"

"I do," the cardinal said, smugly.

"Then what in heaven's name are you doing by allowing him to continue to run that *dog* of a parish. The place is not going to generate any income. It is only going to plunge deeper and deeper into the red."

Suddenly, the cardinal's facial expression took on a haughty look. The cat and mouse game he had been playing with Father Moore was over. It was time to get serious.

"Father," the cardinal began, his eyes developing a dark and determined glare about them. "Father Coniglio will continue to run St. Theresa's, but then again, he won't."

"Just what does that mean?" Father Moore asked in an unsure voice. The cardinal's secretary didn't like what he was hearing.

"Confused, Father?"

"I am," he answered warily.

"Well, Father, here is how it goes. Father Coniglio stays on as pastor of St. Theresa's. When I saw him today I knew taking him away from his church would kill him. When we were together in the seminary, Father Coniglio was one of the brightest in our class. He could have gone a long way in the Church hierarchy but he chose not to. Ronny Coniglio had only one design in life and that was to be a dedicated parish priest. He has performed that task admirably for the past forty years. If we separate him from his church, it is as though we are divorcing him from his life. He'll just wither away and die. I don't want his soul on my head."

"Your Eminence, he is no longer capable of running a parish. You don't seem to be taking that into account. Or are you?"

Now a lecherous smile found its way to Cardinal Burke's face. "Father, that's where you come in," he told him.

A disgruntled look drifted across the face of Father Moore. He knew what the cardinal was going to ask of him.

"Father, I want you to find a priest who can serve as Father Coniglio's assistant, a priest who can settle into the community without arousing suspicion. A priest who can oversee the day-to-day operation of St. Theresa's in a clandestine manner, allowing Father Coniglio to believe his parish is safe and he is in charge. In the meantime, our covert priest will report to us—actually you—so we can protect St. Theresa's from plunging deeper into bankruptcy."

Father Moore rolled his eyes. It could prove to be difficult recruiting a priest who was willing to act as the cardinal's undercover agent. Getting a priest to blend in and not arouse suspicion in a tight knit community such as St. Theresa's was a tall order, considering the entire parish was expecting the place to close, not have a new priest move in. The problem compounded itself because Father Moore was not going to tolerate a priest who might take on the assignment only to use it as a loaded gun against the archdiocese as a means of advancement. The man the cardinal was asking Father Moore to find had to be unique. Father Moore wondered if such a creature existed.

"Your Eminence, with all due respect, you're asking me to find a *Bing Crosby* type of character, like the one he played in that old movie *Going My Way*. A humble priest committed to the Church and God's laws. Yet, a priest with just enough pretense in his soul to think what he is doing is in the best interests of the Church and Father Coniglio."

The cardinal blinked his right eye, to confirm what Father Moore was saying was in line with his thinking. The die had been cast. It was now up to Father Moore to carry it out.

"Father, you are a man of amazing attributes. What I ask of you is to be done with as much expediency as possible."

Father Moore read the cardinal's eyes. It was end of discussion. Father Moore again glanced out the window at the Boston Harbor skyline. He would find the cardinal the priest he sought. But the priest he found was also going to serve his purposes. Father Moore could feel his grip on St. Theresa's tightening once again.

CHAPTER
THREE

Father Paul Wesley made a spirited dash across the courtyard separating the church and rectory. It was eight o'clock at night and he had been out and about for several hours. He had taken an evening stroll through the neighborhood and when he returned to the church, he helped set up the tables in the grammar school's auditorium for the weekly bingo games which were to take place that evening. He continued on to the church sacristy to lay out the vestments for the next day's seven o'clock Mass. Although thirty-seven-years of age Father Wesley had the shortest tenure of the three priests in residence at St. Ann's in the Dorchester section of Boston. As a result most of the more menial tasks on the church grounds requiring a priest's touch came his way.

Father Wesley was a tall, handsome man in a rustic sense with an athletic build. He had a touch of gray starting to develop along his sideburns and wore horn rimmed glasses which gave him a somewhat distinguished look. Outwardly, he was a charmer, but inwardly he carried the baggage of a tormented soul. He was a paradox of a man whose topsy-turvy existence was going to have to survive another chapter.

He entered the rectory through the side door, which led to the kitchen, and saw Monsignor Kenneth Devine sitting at the kitchen table drinking a cup of coffee. The sight of the monsignor caught Father Wesley by surprise. You rarely saw the monsignor in the kitchen area. You, also, rarely saw the sixty-year-old prelate after seven in the evening. Something was up and the young curate knew he was involved in it.

Father Wesley was aware the monsignor had a meeting earlier in the day with Cardinal Burke. The younger priest had a checkered past until a serious auto accident—which had robbed him of his eyesight for three years—served as an epiphany to turn his life around. Nevertheless, Father Wesley couldn't help but feel that the monsignor's meeting with the cardinal had something to do with him. Because of his former lifestyle Father Wesley lacked for self-assurance since joining the priesthood. He had this constant feeling he was on probation. The feeling was quite overwhelming at this precise moment.

Monsignor Devine spotted him as he came through the door and motioned for his younger associate to take a seat at the table. The curate apprehensively sat in a chair opposite the monsignor. There was an envelope on the table before the older priest and as soon as Father Wesley sat down the monsignor slid it across to him.

The younger priest stared at it for a few seconds, not daring to touch it, as though it carried a mysterious plague as its contents. He turned his stare toward the monsignor before asking, "What's this about?"

"Why don't you open it," Monsignor Devine suggested, as he prepared to take another sip of coffee.

With what seemed a degree of caution, he did so. He carefully slipped a white engraved card out of the envelope. It had the official seal of the archdiocese on it. It was an appointment card. The cardinal wished to see him at four o'clock the following afternoon.

Again, Father Wesley raised his eyes to look at the monsignor. Once more he asked, "What's this about?"

"I'm not at liberty to say," the monsignor answered. "The cardinal will explain what it's about when you see him."

Father Wesley continued to stare at the monsignor only now his face sported a blank look. His mind was racing over the matter. *The cardinal wished to see him. Why?* Since his ordination he had been a simple parish priest at St. Ann's. He had done nothing to upset the applecart. He couldn't think of a reason as to why the cardinal would want to meet with him.

Then, out of the blue, it hit him. The cardinal must have had some questions about his unsavory past. It shouldn't matter since it was all behind him now. He had never hidden the fact that his life before the accident had been anything but righteous. But, perhaps, the cardinal needed to hear it himself. If that were the case he would gladly assure Cardinal Burke the archdiocese did not have to worry about Father Paul Wesley being in their ranks.

—◊—

Earlier in the day the lanky six foot Monsignor Devine joined his fellow priest, Monsignor Clarence Cunningham, a black roly-poly man, who was the pastor of the Blessed Sacrament Church in Jamaica Plain, for a meeting at the chancery with Cardinal Burke. Aside from their priestly duties the two men shared only one other thing in common. Both priests knew what made Father Paul Wesley the priest he had become. The two clerics had been brought together to give the cardinal the vital answers he needed.

The meeting took place at the chancery in the cardinal's lavish office, adorned in oak with shelves of theological books as a backdrop. In front of the desk were two high-back brown leather chairs. In the one to the cardinal's right sat the sixty-two-year-old Father Cunningham. On the cardinal's left sat Monsignor Devine. By the door, manning his post as if he were a sentry, stood Father Moore.

After the cordial introductions were exchanged, Cardinal Burke dove right into the matter at hand. He thumbed through a manila folder which documented the life of Father Paul Wesley. Neither priest had been informed as to why they had been summoned, but both men knew whatever was on the cardinal's mind was included in the folder in his hands.

"Father Devine," the cardinal began, "I see that since his ordination, Father Paul Wesley has been assigned to your church. Has he proved to be an asset?"

The two priests were stunned when the name of Father Wesley was mentioned. They, of course, knew of Father Wesley's hellacious past but it was history now, or so they thought. Surely it was not the reason the cardinal had petitioned them.

"Yes, Your Eminence, Father Wesley has been assigned to St. Ann's for the past three years. As far as being an asset...well...yes, you can say so."

"In what way?" the cardinal wanted to know.

Monsignor Devine had nothing to hide but in some strange way he did not want to offer any more information than was necessary. He had this eerie feeling as though he were on the witness stand in a court of law.

"Ah...Father Wesley has proven to be a favorite of all the children in the parish. He tries to spend as much time with them as possible, in the schoolyard during the recess breaks. They look up to him and I assure you, he is one priest you don't have to worry about when it comes to children. Just ask some of the parents in our parish."

"Father, don't for a minute think I believe there is a dark shadow hovering over Father Wesley. It's good to hear he has worked out so well in your parish." *Just what I was hoping to hear* was the thought the cardinal did not express.

"Father, I'm sure you are aware of Father Wesley's past before becoming a priest. Have there been any signs of a return to the belligerent nature which marked his younger days?" The cardinal seemed to be searching for something.

"None, Your Eminence. None whatsoever."

"That, too, is good to hear," the cardinal remarked. "Now, allow me to ask you this question. What do you see for Father Wesley in the future?"

"I'm sorry, Your Eminence, I don't understand."

"Well, Father, do you see any leadership qualities? Is he a take charge kind of guy?"

Monsignor Devine had no idea where this conversation was leading. But, by the nature of the cardinal's questions, he had something in mind for Father Wesley. He was curious to hear what the cardinal was intending to ask of this novice priest.

"If you're asking about theological matters then, yes, I think he'll mature as a priest and be everything the Church asks of him. He's already come a long way with his personal life, as I'm sure you well know."

"Yes, I do," the cardinal said as he leaned forward on his desk, his expression changing to show he was serious.

"Father, I am not interested in Father Wesley's capabilities ten or fifteen years from now. I am interested in what he is capable of doing today. I want you to tell me how you think he could handle an assignment of extreme importance, if I was to ask it of him. Can I count on him or is he apt to collapse like a house of cards under pressure?"

Monsignor Devine was becoming more mystified by the question. The cardinal had a complete dossier on the man in front of him. However, the manifest did not relate to the cardinal what kind of heart and soul Father Wesley possessed. If the cardinal could just give him a better idea of what he sought from the man, maybe he could give him a more direct answer.

"Your Eminence, Father Wesley is not one to back away from a challenge. The only difference between him now and what he used to be is that today he uses his head to sort through a problem. In the past, in his secular days, he used his fists. I hope that answers the question for you."

"It does, to a certain extent," the cardinal said through a satisfying smile. "Now, let me ask you this. How is he at taking orders? What I mean is: does he take them willingly or does he have a tendency to put up an argument if he feels the directive coming his way is wrong."

Monsignor Devine was becoming leery of the direction this conversation was headed. But, at last, he thought he might have something to make the cardinal pause and think about whatever it was he had planned for Father Wesley.

"Your Eminence, Father Wesley takes orders well but don't think, for a second, he is a docile little lamb. If he thinks you're wrong he'll give you an argument about it. Especially if he thinks you are out of touch with reality."

The monsignor did not get the response he was expecting. In fact, the cardinal seemed quite pleased with what Monsignor Devine had to say.

"Good," he replied. "I am certainly not looking for a *yes man*. Now, one final question, Monsignor. Is Father Wesley a manipulator? If he was asked to do something he didn't agree with, but thought it might serve to his advantage to go along with what was being asked of him, is he one to use it against the person or persons asking the so-called favor from him. I'm asking you: would Father Wesley try to take advantage of said situation and use it to his own benefit?"

Monsignor Devine gave the cardinal a cold and riveting glare before answering. The cardinal was looking for someone to go out on a cloak and dagger mission, and Father Wesley was the man he had in mind. He was going to have to be careful how he answered this question.

"He is not a snake, if that is what you are asking me. But, in all honesty, you have me feeling uncomfortable. I don't know if you have me selling Father Wesley up the river or what. I suggest if you want to know what Father Wesley is made of then you should question the man himself. I guarantee he'll give you a straight answer."

"I intend to do just that," the cardinal assured him. "That is, provided our meeting this afternoon goes as I hoped. So far it has. And, Father, I'm sorry if I have you feeling on edge. If Father Wesley proves to be the man I'm looking for then both you gentlemen will know of the assignment I intend to ask of him before you leave this room."

The cardinal then shifted his attention to Monsignor Cunningham. "Father, now it's your turn," he said.

Monsignor Cunningham was just as bewildered as Monsignor Devine as to what the cardinal sought from Father Wesley. As the discourse between the cardinal and Monsignor Devine went along, Father Cunningham tried to prep himself for the questions he might have to answer. He felt certain he had the responses necessary to bridge the gap between Father Wesley's days as a street punk to his decision to become a priest.

"Father, can you explain to me how you developed such a strong friendship with Father Wesley? I'd like to see if your version is as entertaining as some of the others I've heard."

Monsignor Cunningham smiled. Theirs was a unique friendship. He was sure some of the stories the cardinal had heard had been embellished somewhat.

"Where would you like me to begin?" he asked the cardinal.

"How about at the beginning," his superior replied.

"I met Father Wesley shortly after his accident while he was a patient at St. Elizabeth's Hospital. I do some chapel work for them on Sundays. Father Wesley had been there about a week when he was transferred to their rehabilitation center for the blind. His loss of sight occurred when he was involved in a horrific auto accident. An accident, which by the way, he admits causing."

Let's get that out of the way was Monsignor Cunningham's thinking. Unlike Monsignor Devine, he was not hesitant to discuss any aspects of Father Wesley's life. Monsignor Cunningham was proud to call his fellow priest a friend.

"The accident robbed him of his sight for three years. But on that fateful night Father Wesley lost something far more important than his sight. Lost in the accident was the life of his best friend, Billy Castleman. Billy's life came to an end because Father Wesley was behind the wheel and he was drunk. Father Wesley grieves his loss and will do so until the day he dies."

Monsignor Cunningham paused to collect his thoughts. As he did so it allowed the cardinal the opportunity to ask him: "This Billy Castleman. Was he also drunk?"

"No," Monsignor Cunningham answered in no uncertain terms.

"No!" the cardinal exclaimed, as if stunned to hear the news. "If that was the case why wasn't he behind the wheel? Didn't he know how to drive?"

"Your Eminence, the story goes a little deeper. On that night Father Wesley had broken up with his girlfriend. It was the girl who sent him packing and Father Wesley couldn't understand it. They had been girlfriend/boyfriend for a number of years. Their breakup, and no reason given for it, destroyed Father Wesley. With his life, seemingly in shambles, he did what so many other lovelorn males did in similar situations. He went out and got himself good and stinking drunk. He was in a foul and ugly mood because of his girlfriend's rejection. No one—and I mean no one—was going to tell him what to do that night. That included driving an automobile."

"I see," the cardinal said as he nodded his understanding. "However, one thing escapes me. If Father Wesley was so drunk on the night in question why did this Billy Castleman go with him? Why didn't he just let him go out on his own? He didn't have to go along and place himself in the dangerous position which ended up costing him his life."

"Your Eminence, Billy Castleman and Father Wesley were like brothers. It's why Billy Castleman went with him. In a way he was acting as his brother's keeper."

The cardinal shook his head in disbelief. It was an all too familiar story. Cardinal Burke didn't want to hear how one of the archdiocese's priests had been involved in such a stupid accident, even if it did happen in his temporal days.

At this time, Father Moore, standing at his post by the door, cleared his throat. He had a question of his own to ask.

"Monsignor," he called out, "isn't it true Father Wesley had quite a reputation with his fists during those days?"

Monsignor Cunningham did a slow burn. This question and answer session was turning into an inquisition. Now it was Father Cunningham's turn to develop a dislike for the direction Cardinal Burke's confab on Father Wesley was headed.

"Yes," he answered, not bothering to turn his head to acknowledge Father Moore's presence. "Father Wesley did have quite a reputation with his fists when he was younger. The way I hear it, he was so good he could have turned professional with the proper training."

"Really!" the cardinal said with a modicum of surprise.

"Your Eminence, these questions you have concerning Father Wesley leave me baffled, as I'm sure it does Monsignor Devine. If Father Wesley has done something wrong then we should at least know what it is. I mean no disrespect, but your way of handling whatever it is you need to know about Father Wesley should be—as Monsignor Devine mentioned earlier—put to the man himself. We have both come to know Father Wesley as a priest who has rediscovered life and made it better for himself and the people around him."

Cardinal Burke nodded his appreciation for what Monsignor Cunningham had to say. There was no doubt the men before him were in Father Wesley's corner. The cardinal liked the allegiance they had developed with the young priest.

"You are absolutely right," the cardinal began to explain. "I don't want either of you to think this is an attack on Father Wesley's character, for it is not. I need a special breed of priest. Someone who can be trusted and not use what I am asking of him for his own personal gain. I am beginning to believe Father Wesley is that priest. I need you two to convince me."

Monsignors Devine and Cunningham glanced at each other. It was a relief for both priests to know Father Wesley was free of some ill-gotten transgressions. Still, the question remained as to what the cardinal wanted from this priest of only three years. The cardinal had promised them an answer, should Father Wesley prove to be the man he wanted. It was obvious that question had been answered. Now their curiosity was piqued.

"Father," the cardinal continued with his questioning of Monsignor Cunningham. "The girl. Did she visit Father Wesley during his hospital stay or did she continue to keep him out of her life?"

"She never visited him."

The cardinal paused to think about what Monsignor Cunningham had said. *They had been involved for some time and she didn't have the decency to look in on him and see how he was recovering? There had to have been something very strange about their relationship.*

Father Wesley was proving to be an interesting study. Yet, there was something else in his life which disturbed the cardinal. "I understand Father Wesley's mother is alive. I also understand they do not keep in touch with each other. Any reason why?"

Again, Monsignor Cunningham was in the cardinal's vise and he wasn't feeling good about it. This talking about Father Wesley's former personal life was very unsettling. If Cardinal Burke needed to know everything there was to know about Father Wesley, then whatever he had planned for him was of an extremely important nature.

"Father Wesley's mother is an alcoholic. About all she can attest to is that she is his biological mother. She left the raising of him as a child

28

to others. She is another one who made no effort to see him while he was hospitalized."

Cardinal Burke had to shake his head in disbelief. "The poor guy had a tough go of it," he said. "No wonder he decided to become a priest. Which leads us to another line of questioning: why did he decide on a life in the clergy? After all, the man was sort of a rapscallion in his younger days. Monsignor Cunningham, you were there with him every step of the way during his transformation period. What can you tell us?"

"Well, it all started, I believe, with the death of Billy Castleman. Up until then he had been very angry with life. The death of his best friend made him angrier because he was responsible for it. The combination of the rejection of his girlfriend and mother, compounded by the fact he was being robbed of his sight, left him adrift in life. I witnessed what was happening and I felt sorry for him. But I was also concerned about his well-being. His doctors were certain the blindness was of a temporary nature. Given time, his optic nerves would heal, but until then he was going to have to rely on the aid and assistance of others to get him adjusted. I took it from there and allowed him to live out his recuperative period at the Blessed Sacrament. It was also part of a court decreed probationary period for his involvement in the accident. He lived in our rectory for three years. This was when he made his decision to become a priest."

"Very interesting," the cardinal was moved to say. "Now I have one last question to ask the both of you—"

Father Moore interrupted the cardinal by clearing his throat. He had a question of his own.

"Father, you have something else to say?" the cardinal inquired of his secretary, somewhat annoyed that Father Moore could not wait until he was finished with what he had to say.

"I do, Your Eminence," he replied as he stepped forward.

"What is it?" the cardinal said in a frustrated manner.

"Monsignor Cunningham, Father Wesley grew up on the streets of Paine. The beach to be more specific. Isn't it true that Paine has…shall I say…a rather salty cross section of life?"

Monsignor Cunningham had a feeling this question was going to be asked sooner or later. He was prepared for it.

29

"It is true, Father."

"So, Monsignor Cunningham, would it be safe to say Father Wesley came from a white trash background? A background where bigotry flourishes?"

"Yes, Father, it would be safe to say something like that." Monsignor Cunningham was developing an immediate dislike for Father Moore and his petty questions.

"So, I ask of you, what was Father Wesley's reaction when he found out you were black?"

A sly smile found its way to the monsignor's face and was followed by a sinister chuckle. "You want to know what he said, so I'll tell you what he said. He said 'beggars can't be choosers.' That's what he said."

Father Moore acted confused. "What exactly does it mean?" he asked.

"He made the statement when he moved into our rectory and I took it upon myself to ask him what it would be like to live under the same roof with a black man. We shared a laugh about it and it was then he said, 'beggars can't be choosers.' During his three years living at the Blessed Sacrament, Father Wesley did a lot of growing up. What he said to me on that day meant it was all right with him if it was all right with me. I assure you; I had no problem with the man, and as it turned out he didn't have one with me either. Father, he may have grown up in an atmosphere of bigotry and may have been a bigot himself. But by the time he arrived at the Blessed Sacrament the evil trait had been driven out of him."

Father Moore looked at the cardinal with his arms outstretched, palms up, as if he were delivering the Messiah. "Your Eminence, I believe we have found our man."

The cardinal drew a deep breath. "I believe you are correct, Father. I came to the same conclusion...about ten minutes ago."

The cardinal's cynical response brought a vindictive snarl from Father Moore. He didn't care for it when the cardinal attempted to make him look small and insignificant. The cardinal needed a little reminding as to who had found this man of the cloth to be Father Coniglio's soul mate in disguise.

Cardinal Burke returned his attention to the two priests sitting before him, as Father Moore remained at his post by the door. "Gentleman, now as for the reason I wished to speak to you about Father Wesley."

The cardinal had the attention of the two priests. The inquisition was over.

"I need a priest I can trust to handle a very unstable situation. You two have convinced me Father Wesley is the man I seek. Now, you might disagree with me as to the assignment I am going to ask him to carry out. But agree or disagree it's the way it is going to be."

The cardinal opened the top drawer in his desk and took out a white envelope. He motioned for Monsignor Devine to take it. "Father, please see to it Father Wesley receives this when you return to St. Ann's. It notifies him that I wish to speak with him tomorrow afternoon."

Now, how to go about the task of explaining to the two prelates before him the role Father Wesley was to play at St. Theresa's without revealing the covert aspect of the assignment. He drew another deep breath and went on.

"Fathers, as of June 1st, I am reassigning Father Wesley to St. Theresa's in Paine. Father Coniglio, who is the pastor of the church, is a dear friend of mine and he is in dire need of an assistant. Father Coniglio's health seems to be on the decline so he needs a little help in running his church. I've chosen Father Wesley to fill the role."

Both monsignors knew there was more to it than what the cardinal was telling them. *Why Father Wesley*, they wondered? Any priest could do what the cardinal was asking and serve as an associate. Both priests felt the cardinal wasn't leveling with them.

Monsignor Cunningham was the first to speak out. "Your Eminence, I strongly suggest you reconsider what you are doing. I'm sure you are aware St. Theresa's is the parish Father Wesley grew up in. The important thing to remember here is that parish and community hold nothing but bad memories for him. Think of Father Wesley. What you are prepared to ask of him is unfair."

The cardinal turned his attention to Monsignor Devine to get his reaction. "What do you think? Am I tossing Father Wesley into the deep end of the pool?"

"I'm sorry, Your Eminence, but I have to agree with Monsignor Cunningham. You're asking him to go back to a place which almost served as his ruination. The people of St. Theresa's are going to remember him for what he was, not what he's become."

"You both make solid arguments," the cardinal countered. "However, I'm going to have to disagree with the two of you. Father Wesley has proven to be not only an exceptional priest but an exceptional person as well. What I am going to ask of him is going to take a special kind of man. I believe Father Wesley is representative of that kind of man."

The cardinal's decision made, the meeting came to an end. The two monsignors left the chancery with their minds full of uncertainty. Cardinal Burke had never proven to be a bullheaded man. Yet, he had dismissed their opposition of Father Wesley's reassignment as if his mind had already been made up before they had arrived for the meeting. All he needed from them was the confirmation of Father Wesley's capabilities.

———

Father Wesley continued to stare at the appointment card, as if his death sentence was printed on it. This was serious business.

He raised his eyes so they met with Monsignor Devine's. "Father, this has something to do with my past, doesn't it?" he asked, waving the card in the air.

The monsignor tried to muster a smile. *This poor priest* was his thinking. Father Wesley had many strong qualities going for him but self-confidence was not one of them. His self-induced fear was making him an insecure man. Hopefully the cardinal would take notice of this characteristic and abandon the foolhardy plan he had for him.

Monsignor Devine raised himself from the table. "Father, the cardinal has great admiration of you for the transformation you have made in life. It is his intention to express to you, in person, just how much faith he has in you. Now, if you don't mind, I'm going to retire to my room for the night."

Father Wesley remained seated at the kitchen table, trying to put it all together. He was certain the cardinal wasn't going to give him a slap on the back for being a good boy, after so many years of being a bad one. Well, at least there was one thing he did know: he wasn't going to have to wait very long to find out what was on the cardinal's mind.

CHAPTER

FOUR

The new Toyota Camry motored its way along Commonwealth Avenue, headed towards the chancery for the archdiocese of Boston. Father Wesley had owned the car for a month and had put a scant 125 miles on it. Nonetheless, he was proud to own the vehicle. Prior to this automobile every car he had owned was just a few thousand miles away from the junkyard. Included in that lot was the old Ford Thunderbird which Billy Castleman had died in.

As he drove along his mind was still locked onto the thought as to why the cardinal wished to see him. He was probably doing a lot of needless worrying about the matter but he couldn't let go of it. The only thought floating around in his head was: the cardinal wished to see him because of his less than model life before joining the priesthood. But even if it was about those wasteful years, what was the cardinal going to do about it? Admonish him for sins he had already admitted committing? The cardinal certainly was not going to defrock him. Yes, there was something strange afoot and the only way he was going to find out was to have the cardinal explain it to him.

The Camry took a right on Lake Street and swung into the parking lot behind the chancery. It was 3:50 in the afternoon. Ten more minutes to find out what this was all about.

As he emerged from the car Father Wesley could feel his nerves and uncertainty getting the better of him. He was only ten minutes away from sitting down with the cardinal, face-to-face, and finding out what this meeting was all about. As he walked across the parking lot he was becoming more convinced he didn't want to hear what the cardinal had to say.

Once inside the chancery he showed his appointment card to the receptionist before being instructed to walk down a long hallway leading to the cardinal's office. Once there he saw two twin oak doors that rose nearly to the ceiling. Quite impressive but quite intimidating as well.

Just to the right of the doors sat a bespectacled, red haired priest who looked to be in his mid-forties and had the map of Ireland splashed across his face. The nameplate on the desk read: Father Patrick Walsh.

Father Wesley, after introducing himself, handed Father Walsh the appointment card. The priest examined the card and then looked at his wristwatch before glancing back at Father Wesley.

"Cutting it a little close to the wire, aren't we?" he asked in a slight Irish brogue. "His Eminence gets quite miffed at people who are tardy for their appointments."

Father Wesley took a glimpse at his own watch. It was three minutes to four. He wanted to remind Father Walsh of that basic fact, but then thought differently. Why get into a pissing match with the man. Just play the role of the contrite priest so he could get this whole fiasco over and done.

"I'm sorry, Father. I should have allowed myself more time." Father Wesley then flashed a wide grin which sent the message he had not meant a word of what he was saying.

Father Walsh picked up on Father Wesley's self-serving smirk, and with a frown of annoyance on his face, instructed his fellow priest to take a seat. He would let him know when the cardinal was ready to see him. Ten minutes later the large oak doors opened and Father Moore came out of the room.

Following the formal introductions and exchange of pleasantries the meeting got under way. Father Wesley remained antsy at what was taking place. Everything seemed quite civil at the moment. But the young priest refused to let his guard down. He was expecting the other shoe to drop at any given second.

Father Wesley sat in the chair that Monsignor Cunningham had occupied the previous day. Father Moore, for this meeting, had abandoned his post by the door and sat in the other chair in front of the cardinal's desk. Unlike the day before, he was going to be an integral player in this get together.

"Father, you've been a priest for three years. Has it been everything you hoped it would be?" the cardinal asked.

It appeared as though the cardinal was going to ease his way into the matter at hand, thought Father Wesley. Question by question he was going to become a little more serious while all along, he would be dissecting his life, trying to understand how a lowlife such as he had found God. Father Wesley had no choice than to play along.

"It has been what I hoped for and then some."

"So you have no qualms about your decision to become a priest. None at all?"

The cardinal's question gave Father Wesley a different thought. In recent years the Catholic Church had developed a public relations nightmare with the outrageous conduct of some of their priests. Pedophiles and fornicators had disgraced the ranks of the clergy. The cardinal could well be exercising some quality control to keep his diocese as devoid as possible from the perverts who, somehow, had slipped through the cracks.

As a result, when someone with a questionable background such as his came on the scene, the cardinal was going to make certain there was no fall from grace. It now seemed so clear to Father Wesley. He didn't particularly care for being lumped into that questionable category but he understood. All of a sudden his doubts and fears about being an unworthy priest had flown out the window. All was well with his world once again. His thinking was giving him a boost of confidence. He was going to need it.

"My three years as a priest have proven to be a very satisfying period in my life. I spent much of my youth wasting away what should have been productive years. I am grateful for the second chance."

"So you think God has smiled down on you?" It was Father Moore asking the question. He was just warming up.

"Yes," Father Wesley answered, with trepidation. There was something about Father Moore he did not like.

"So why don't you tell us what you have done as a priest that has made your life so fulfilling."

"I'm not sure what you mean," Father Wesley responded, warily.

"Well, I guess what I mean, Father, is how many souls have you saved from damnation? How many lives have you turned around because of your priestly insight?"

Now Father Wesley knew he definitely didn't care for Father Moore. The cardinal's secretary was leading up to something but in the process he was going to break his gonads.

"Father, if you're asking me have I talked someone down from jumping off a bridge, I haven't. If you're asking me if the sound of my voice and my belief in God has sent chills through the bodies of the disbelieving then, again, I have to say *no*.

"Now, if you're asking me have I performed my priestly duties on a daily basis? Have I offered spiritual guidance and educated those in need of a reminder of canon law then I say *yes*. I can't say I've always been successful but I can tell you it was not for a lack of trying. Does that answer your question...Father?"

The emphasis was on the word *Father* and the cardinal's secretary didn't miss it. It annoyed Father Moore, and disturbed him somewhat, to discover Father Wesley had a backbone. It was too early in the game to be establishing opinions of one another but Father Moore was finding Father Wesley to be an impertinent individual.

"Yes, Father, it does answer my question. But I must say I find you to be a tad on the arrogant side and out of line and disrespectful with your answers. Must I remind you who you are addressing here?" Father Moore was beginning to wonder if he was going to regret his selection of Father Wesley for this assignment.

As for Father Wesley, he was rapidly coming to the conclusion that Father Moore was one intolerable *son of a bitch*. He was also wondering what had become of the stomach churning fear which had punctuated his every thought leading up to this meeting. Father Moore was doing him a favor with his obnoxious attitude. He was bringing out the fire in him. Father Wesley was not going to allow Father Moore's antagonistic ways to get the better of him. He was not going to allow himself to be treated as some subservient moron.

"I'm sorry, Father, if I upset you. But you have to admit your initial line of questioning was a bit strong. In fact, I found it to be somewhat agitating."

"AGITATING! Why you—"

"All right," the cardinal finally interjected. "Enough. I think you are both acting out of character. We are here for another reason, other than going for one another's throat."

Father Wesley was feeling embarrassed. He now believed the tension that had been building had taken its toll and Father Moore had become an unintended victim. He surely wouldn't be having such antagonistic feelings towards a priest he had just met if it were not for the pressure he had placed himself under. This time his apology was to be a sincere one.

"I'm sorry, Your Eminence. I don't know what came over me. Perhaps it's just a bad case of nerves. Since being informed of this meeting I've been on edge."

The cardinal nodded his understanding before looking in the direction of Father Moore. "And you, Father?" he asked.

Father Moore, his eyes still locked on Father Wesley, answered in what was unmistakably an unsympathetic tone. "I, too, acted out of character."

"Good. Now that we have settled our differences, let's move to why we are here."

The cardinal shifted his attention back to Father Wesley. "Father, you grew up in the parish of St. Theresa's in Paine. Is that correct?"

"It is, Your Eminence."

"What do you remember about the place?"

Father Wesley was now completely baffled. He had made himself sick thinking this meeting was about his past. Well, in a way, it was. A past which saw him, as he moved into his teens, not content with the sedate ways St. Theresa's had to offer. He opted to move onto a more salacious and reckless lifestyle. He found what he was looking for and it nearly brought him to his end. In the process, some nightmarish memories had been created for him.

"Well, Your Eminence, it's a small church—it was often referred to as the *poor people's parish*. It was a one priest operation, even back in the days when most parishes had two or three priests assigned to a church."

"Do you remember the priest who ran the parish?"

"Certainly. Father Coniglio. Is he still there? He must be quite aged by now."

"Yes, Father, he is still there. Did you know Father Coniglio and I were classmates in the seminary?"

Father Wesley's face went flush. Here he was talking about an aging Father Coniglio so the cardinal had to be thinking he viewed him as some ancient relic as well. Father Wesley felt he was going to have to administer some damage control to save his own bacon from the sorry situation he had placed himself in.

"Ah...Your Eminence, I...I didn't mean to imply...well, you know... ah...it was not my intention..."

Father Wesley was tongue tied and the cardinal found the uncomfortable state the young cleric had placed himself in to be amusing. Father Moore also found it to be entertaining to watch the summoned priest struggle with the predicament he had created for himself. But there was a more important matter to be addressed here and the cardinal wanted to get right to it.

"There is no reason to apologize," the cardinal said, his right hand outstretched to indicate he wanted the priest to stop with his incoherent stammering that was meant to serve as an apology. The cardinal knew what Father Wesley meant by the word *aged*. The cardinal was the one feeling guilty. He had left Father Coniglio out there for too long without a lifeline.

"Father, I recently visited with Father Coniglio and I was disturbed by what I saw. The years have advanced on him and they have not been kind. I am partly to blame for it."

Okay, now where are we headed? Father Wesley wanted to know. If he had been asked here to discuss St. Theresa's and Father Coniglio then the best he could give them was what he recalled from his youth, and much of that was sketchy. His tie to St. Theresa's ended when he was twelve.

"Your Eminence, you have me completely baffled. I came here today with all kinds of disturbing thoughts on my mind as to why you wished to see me. Now you ask me about a church and a priest I have had no association with in the last twenty-five years."

"I understand all of what you say," the cardinal countered. "Yet, I would still like to know what your memories of St. Theresa's are?"

Father Wesley shrugged. If that's what the cardinal wanted to hear then that's what he would tell him.

"It's always been the same story at St. Theresa's, as I remember it. Father Coniglio had to run the place on a wing and a prayer while the church up the street was strong-arming its parishioners to make donations."

"Strong-arming?" Father Moore queried. "Are you talking about St. Matthew's?" an air of irritability in his voice.

"I am, Father. You don't get married or have a baby baptized in that church without opening your wallet and making a sizeable contribution to the St. Matthew's coffers," an unsuspecting Father Wesley answered.

Father Moore began to do a slow burn as Father Wesley was expressing his disdain for St. Matthew's. He hadn't anticipated him being sympathetic to St. Theresa's cause and hostile to St. Matthew's money making capabilities. This situation could prove to be a problem.

"Father, if I may. Am I to understand that you find it improper for a church such as St. Matthew's to show a profit? You would rather see an apocryphal type of church that for every dollar it earns it puts it back out on the street before the day is done?"

"No, Father, I'm not a bleeding heart idiot. What I do have a problem with is a church which shakes down its parishioners."

"Fathers, please, not again," the cardinal could see the two of them were headed for another verbal joust. The petty differences the two priests were exhibiting for each other had to cease. They were going to have to work with one another once Father Wesley was reassigned. It was time for them to learn to coexist even if they disliked each other.

Cardinal Burke decided to forgo any further preliminaries and get right to the matter at hand. He was beginning to feel a little better about himself now that he was sure Father Wesley was the man he wanted for the assignment. He was just a few minutes away from seeing that his old pal and classmate received some much needed assistance.

"Father, St. Theresa's is not an affluent parish, never has been. The archdiocese is currently in a phase of downsizing. It is our goal to close ten churches which no longer show a profit and can be absorbed by other parishes. Included on that list is St. Theresa's. Does it sadden you to hear this news?"

Father Wesley had to pause for a few seconds to allow the information the cardinal was giving him to settle in. Ever since he could remember there had been talk of St. Theresa's closing. But it had been nothing more than that—talk. Now it was about to become a reality. Father Wesley thought it was probably an unavoidable business decision on the cardinal's part but he still found it somewhat unsettling to accept. He certainly understood the economics involved but he also felt bad for the parishioners. He knew a good number of those people would give up going to church, especially if St. Matthew's was the alternative.

"What becomes of the parish once you close its doors?" Father Wesley had to ask.

"Eighty percent of the parish will become part of St. Matthew's. The other twenty percent will be taken over by Our Lady of Lourdes. But this will not happen until Father Coniglio either retires or passes on."

A quizzical look came over Father Wesley's face. Something wasn't adding up. He had to ask but he wondered if he should.

"Your Eminence, you just mentioned you had recently seen Father Coniglio and you were disturbed by what you saw. If what you told me is correct then I think it might be in the best interests of Father Coniglio to ask him to retire and proceed with your plans to close St. Theresa's."

"My sentiments, exactly," Father Moore was quick to quip.

Father Wesley shot a quick glance at Father Moore before returning his glare back the cardinal's way. Something stunk about this situation and Father Wesley couldn't help but feel he was up to his ears in whatever it was.

"Your Eminence," Father Wesley went on, his eyes seemed to be pleading for mercy. "The reason I was requested to be here today. May I ask why?"

Cardinal Burke smiled. The time was now at hand.

"Father, your life story is one of tremendous resolution to overcome some mighty obstacles. You have taken the devil's directive and told him to shove it. God was good to you and you didn't disappoint him. We can never begin to fully understand His ways. I believe He had something planned for you and despite your attempts to defy Him you were able to right yourself before it was too late. Your life reads like a biblical character of renown. With that storybook history in mind I am assigning you, as of the first of June, to serve as Father Coniglio's assistant at St. Theresa's."

He couldn't have possibly heard that correctly. In a fleeting second the images of Father Coniglio, his mother, Anne Marie Wells, Ruth Ann and Billy Castleman flashed before his eyes. This couldn't possibly be happening to him. *No, don't do this to me,* he wanted to cry out. This was a mistake—a very big mistake! He was going to have to enlighten the cardinal on his serious error in judgment.

"Your Eminence, I know this is out of line, but I think you are making a dreadful mistake. I am not the person to be picking up the pieces for Father Coniglio. You want a more experienced priest, someone capable of running a parish without anyone knowing it. I don't think I'm the man."

"Father, you do not surprise me with your humble attitude. However, I think your lack of experience works to our benefit. I believe your association with St. Theresa's works to an even greater advantage."

WRONG! Father Wesley wanted to shout out. But now he believed he might have the cardinal to his advantage. A little enlightenment to the cardinal as to the life and times of Paul Wesley along Paine Beach should do the trick

"Your Eminence, if you think the parishioners of St. Theresa's are going to welcome me—"

"Save your breath," Father Moore butted in. "The cardinal knows all about your past."

Father Wesley, now with a sad puppy dog look about him, asked, "You do?"

"Yes, I do."

"And you don't think my past serves as a disadvantage?"

"On the contrary, Father. I think your past and how you have resurrected yourself will serve as an inspiration for the parishioners of St. Theresa's. You will give them hope for a better tomorrow, a hope that will replace oppression and a lack of inner faith that permeates so many of their lives."

In the blink of an eye Father Wesley knew what was going on and he wasn't happy about it. He decided to talk to the cardinal as a man and not as some dutiful subordinate.

"Very eloquently put, Your Eminence, but let's be truthful with one another. What you are looking for is a caretaker, but a very special kind of caretaker. You need someone from the old neighborhood who can slip into town and not arouse any suspicion. It matters not that he was once the scourge of his surroundings for he has now found the light. He then lulls the parishioners and the old priest—who happens to be the flock's inspiration—into accepting and trusting this Johnny-come-lately. How am I doing?"

A conspiratorial frown found its way to the cardinal's face. Nevertheless, with a lackluster wave of his right hand, he motioned for Father Wesley to continue.

"But our hero is not who they think he is. No, their so-called new hope and inspiration, the prodigal son, has not changed his ways. He's just become a little more sophisticated at it. He is a fraud. He is there for only one reason. He is there to watch over the demise of the unassuming priest while readying his faithful congregation for the yawning jaws of St. Matthew's. He has been asked to be a traitor to his old parish because he plays the role so well. In the end the parishioners will be forced to say: *we should have known.*"

The cardinal's face developed a troubled look. The young priest had struck a nerve. He looked to Father Moore and said in a cold and factual manner, "Inform Father Wesley of his duties."

Over the course of the next fifteen minutes Father Moore laid down the policy Father Wesley was to adhere by, once he began his assignment at St. Theresa's. It was quite simple. He was to report to Father Moore on a weekly basis, by phone, on the day-to-day activity of the parish and the condition concerning Father Coniglio. If some policy making was necessary, in regard to the church or the parish, then Father Moore would make it.

As their meeting came to its sorry conclusion Cardinal Burke had one final thing to say to Father Wesley. This time it was he who was seeking penance.

"Father, try not to judge me unfairly. What I ask of you I do with the most noble of intentions. Father Coniglio has been like a brother to me and I have done him a grave injustice. I want to do some right by him before his time comes."

Father Wesley did not respond, merely giving the cardinal a not-so-convincing nod of understanding. It wasn't good enough for Cardinal Burke. He wanted the young prelate to be aware of the anguish within him.

"Father, I want you to prove me wrong. Go back to St. Theresa's and make it flourish. You're a special person, Father Wesley. I can feel it. Like your namesake, Saint Paul, you will do what is asked of you and you will do it well."

"Right," Father Wesley muttered to himself. "Saint Paul you say. Let's try Judas Iscariot."

CHAPTER
FIVE

Alfredo and Salvi were a couple of old-timers who spent the gentle days of spring, the sultry days of summers, and the comforting days of autumn on a park bench along the parkway ogling the young girls as they paraded along Paine Beach. Both men were in their mid-seventies and had been, supposedly, retired for several years. The two men had also shared the same occupation. Alfredo wasn't one to say much about what had been their line of work, but Salvi was not one to shy away from the subject. They had dealt in the world of financial affairs as bookkeepers, at least according to Salvi. More precisely put: they had been *bookies*. Even during their working days many of their transactions had taken place on this bench when a beautiful day came upon the area. The bench came to be known as their *Office*.

The two men differed greatly in appearance. Alfredo had aged gracefully. A handsome man in his earlier years, Alfredo still had a debonair look about him with a full head of neatly coiffured silver-gray hair. He had also been a quiet man who had developed a reputation in his day for charming the ladies. Over the years he had earned the nickname of *Cesar Romero* from his jealous male counterparts.

Salvi was the character of the pair. His appearance was a little hard on the eyes. He had an emaciated frame with liver spots dotting his arms, neck and head to go along with a network of varicose veins which gave his body the look of a road map. Many of the young girls who flaunted themselves along the beach were annoyed by Salvi and his sexist catcalls and whistles as they walked by. It had been said that Salvi couldn't score in a whorehouse with a fistful of hundreds.

Grimaldi often rode his battered and old *Schwinn* bike along the beach in the morning hours when the weather suited him. On this picture perfect day in May he was looking forward to joining Alfredo and Salvi in a little gabfest. He had something of substance to pass along to them.

"Hey, guys," Grimaldi called out as he pedaled his old bicycle in their direction. "Have you heard the good news concerning St. Theresa's?"

"What good news? Nothing good has ever happened at St. Theresa's," Salvi fired back.

"It has now," Grimaldi continued as he braked the bike before the pair. The caretaker was spending the morning telling anyone who would listen how Dame Fortune had smiled down on the little church. "We're getting another priest at St. Theresa's to help Father Coniglio. What do you think of that?"

"I thought the archdiocese was looking to close that place down?" Alfredo asked.

"That's what everybody thought but I guess the cardinal had a change of heart after visiting St. Theresa's a couple of months ago. You'll never guess who the new priest is."

"Grimaldi, spare us the guessing game. Just tell us the name of the new priest," Alfredo said, smartly.

"Paul Wesley. Father Paul Wesley," Grimaldi answered.

"Paul Wesley? We don't know any Paul Wesley. Is that name supposed to mean something to us?" Salvi didn't pick up on the name but Alfredo did.

"Honestly, Salvi, sometimes I think your brain has turned to mush," Alfredo chimed in. "You saw him fight a number of times. He used to beat the crap out of that gay kid, Red Foley, every Friday night here on the beach. Now do you remember him?"

"I think I do. Good looking kid with fast hands and a chip on his shoulder. Got seriously hurt in a car accident, didn't he? You're telling me that mean bastard became a priest? You've got to be kidding me."

"He had every right to be mean, considering that mother of his," Alfredo added.

"That's right." Suddenly Salvi's mind had been jogged sufficiently. "Foley used to give the kid a lot of crap about his mother being a whore and a drunk."

"Just a minute," Grimaldi interrupted. "We're talking about a priest's mother. Let's show a little respect."

"Like what are we supposed to do?" Salvi wanted to know. "Are we supposed to deny she was a girl out looking for a good time? I remember one night when she must've taken on seven or eight guys in the backseat of a car. Hey, Alfredo, you were always good with the ladies. You ever give her a shot?"

"Are you crazy," he answered, without hesitation. "Get involved with someone like that and you don't know what you're taking home to your old lady."

"Hey, guys, you're pissing me off with this kind of talk. Knock it off about his mother." Grimaldi was becoming incensed.

Neither Alfredo nor Salvi seemed to be listening to Grimaldi as they went on. "If I remember correctly, another reason the kid was so tough was because he didn't know who his father is." Salvi was really getting into it now.

"Take it easy, Salvi," Alfredo said, trying to calm him down. "I don't think his mother is whoring anymore."

"Who would want to be with her? Have you seen her lately? The booze has made her look like she's eighty-years-old and I know she's a lot younger than that."

"Can you two knock it off. I don't think it is right to be talking about a priest's mother like that. It has to be sacrilegious or something." Grimaldi was now regretting having told them about Father Wesley's assignment to St. Theresa's.

"Grimaldi, will you get your head out of the clouds," Salvi countered. "He's going to have to face the snickering once he gets back. It's not like the old hag is dead. He'll probably bump into her one day, rummaging through the trash barrels, looking for some bottles or cans so she can buy another bottle of hooch."

"All right, Salvi, that's enough." This time it was Alfredo trying to get him to stop with the unflattering remarks about the priest's mother.

"Hey, what about the girl?" Salvi blurted out.

"What girl?" both Alfredo and Grimaldi asked at the same time.

"The Wesley kid—"

"Father Wesley," Grimaldi insisted.

"Father Wesley," Salvi corrected himself with a sneer. "He had a girlfriend. Little thing with brown hair and an impressive rack."

"You know, you're right, Salvi. I guess your brain is not as lame as I thought," Alfredo said with a simpering expression on his face. "She was about five or six years younger than him if I remember correctly. Her name was Ruth Ann. I don't think I ever knew her last name."

"I don't even remember her first name but I do remember that rack." Salvi had only one thing on his mind.

"It seems to me she vanished about the same time the Wesley kid did. Excuse me, I meant to say Father Wesley." Alfredo was quick to pick up on his slip of the tongue in front of Grimaldi.

"That auto accident he was involved in; didn't a kid get killed? Grimaldi, you know all about that stuff. What happened?"

"Yes, Salvi, there was an accident. It was the Castlemans' kid, Billy, who ended up losing his life."

"Don't remember him either. Let's get back to the girl. Grimaldi, you know everyone's business. What was the girl's last name?"

"There was a Travers family living over in the Pines back then. They had a daughter by the name of Ruth Ann. Maybe that was her."

"Name doesn't ring a bell with me," Salvi remarked. "Could have been her name, then again maybe it wasn't."

"So, Grimaldi, when does this priest officially arrive at St. Theresa's to swell the ranks of their official staff from one to two?" Alfredo asked with a touch of sarcasm in his voice.

"The first of June."

"Now, why do you suppose the archdiocese is sending a priest to a church they've been talking about closing for years?" Alfredo continued.

"I don't know," Grimaldi answered. He had to admit the same question crossed his mind when he first heard the news.

"There has to be a reason. Think of it, Grimaldi. What does Father Coniglio think about all this?"

"He thinks the cardinal is up to something."

"I tend to agree."

Grimaldi had now come to regret this whole conversation with Alfredo and Salvi. They were ruining his day. He had to get out of here before he locked horns with them and found himself regretting something he might say. "I have things to do so I'd better get going," Grimaldi lied as he rode away.

Alfredo kept his eyes locked on the caretaker as he pedaled down the parkway. He found whatever was taking place at St. Theresa's to be of a very suspicious nature. He had his reasons.

"So Salvi, what's your take on this Father Wesley joining Father Coniglio at St. Theresa's?"

"I don't know and I don't care. Why are you so concerned about St. Theresa's getting a new priest?"

"Because there's something about it that stinks."

"Well, I wouldn't let myself get so bent out of shape over it. Now it'd be a different story if the priest and the girl hooked up again after all these years. That'd be something. Do you think the priest ever did the nasty with her?"

"Salvi, you've got a sick thought process."

"Yeah, right. Like the thought never crossed your mind."

Alfredo said nothing. The two men sat on the bench in silence for the next minute with different thoughts on their minds. Then, once again, it was Salvi who reflected on the situation.

"Alfredo, do you think the priest can still use his fists if he had to?"

Alfredo shot him an incredulous look before answering. "Salvi, you are a complete idiot."

CHAPTER
SIX

It was the night before the parish of St. Theresa reentered the life of Father Paul Wesley. He had spent a good portion of the day traveling through the streets of St. Ann's saying obligatory good-byes to the parishioners he had come to know on a personal basis.

The day of reassignment is a difficult one for all priests but in the case of Father Wesley it was particularly excruciating. Most priests had the luxury of joining the staff of a church where they were not known. Those clergymen went forward with a clean slate, to be judged solely on their efforts to come. Father Wesley did not have such good fortune. He expected the parishioners of St. Theresa's to be fair in their assessment of him as a priest. But he was not dealing with a highly educated community to serve as his jury. His past was somehow going to play a part in that assessment. He was certain an impartial verdict could not be rendered in his case.

Father Wesley leaned back against the headboard of his bed. His last night at St. Ann's promised to be one of sheer, emotional agony. His thoughts of the past were of a harsh nature. His days of joy as a Roman Catholic priest were about to be altered. Until now he had been a new foot soldier in God's army. But things had changed. He was now on special assignment, a foray into the unexpected where he was deemed sacrificial as long as the job was done. He needed something to buoy his spirits. Something to dismiss the culpability he was feeling for an act he was being ordered to do. Did he have it within his conscience to pardon himself for the act of treason he believed he was committing?

His head was becoming a torture chamber and it pounded to an unmerciful rhythm. He slithered his body forward until he was prostrate on the bed, his head resting against the pillow. He closed his eyes and allowed his mind to go back.

The childhood of Paul Wesley had been one of pure anguish, as if he were doing penance for being born. His mother had little time for him; she had her cousin Anne Marie Wells look after her son's needs. If it were not for Anne Marie he might not have survived his early years. She instilled in him a purpose to his life, showing Paul the way to love and compassion while his mother shared what she had to give with others. Anne Marie did what she could to keep a little boy happy. But his mother's disregard for her young son left a yawning chasm of despair. At the time, it seemed incapable of being rectified and was reflected in his deportment in the streets as he made the transformation from a prepubescent boy to that of a reckless young man.

Much of Paul Wesley's childhood was spent growing up in a lounge on Paine Beach called Maxine's. Anne Marie had worked there as a waitress while his mother hung out in the place. Night after night Paul's mother would sit in a booth and socialize with the male customers. She was not a prostitute. Joan Wesley was, simply put, a girl out looking for a good time on a steady basis. Hers was a life of ceaseless partying. Joan Wesley may not have been a girl for hire but she was a whore.

Joan Wesley's very existence depended on her cousin. It was Anne Marie who provided lodging and kept her from starving to death. It was Anne Marie, a devout Catholic, who insisted Joan have her baby and not go through with any thoughts of an abortion. It was Anne Marie who took it upon herself to see that Paul Wesley was raised properly. It was because of Anne Marie that Paul Wesley had a chance to make it. It was also because of Anne Marie that Paul Wesley hit a speed bump in life.

It sickened Father Wesley to recall growing up in that seedy environment. It saddened him to remember how his mother made herself available for the human scum who frequented Maxine's. It hurt him to know he was going back to St. Theresa's and his mother didn't give a damn. His was a heritage of the begotten forgotten. He wondered if even as a priest, he had it within his heart to forgive a mother who loved to be loved but was incapable of giving love to the one to whom it meant the most.

The memories were dark and grim but he had to deal with them. It was necessary if he hoped to develop a meaning for going back. It was necessary if he hoped to give a meaning to his life.

Father Wesley's mind focused on his seventh year. It was a particularly troublesome time in his life which was somehow saved because there were those who cared and reached out. It was a period he would like to forget but it demanded to be remembered.

Paul Wesley had been in the second grade of the Lincoln Public School which was in the parish of St. Matthew. As a result he ended up being enrolled in the St. Matthew's First Communion class. What followed was the first truly traumatic episode in his life which sowed the seeds of contempt for his uncaring mother.

After attending his final communion class the young Paul Wesley was taken aside by one of the priests and informed that it had been brought to the attention of the clergymen of St. Matthew's that he had never been baptized and thus he would be unable to make his First Communion. The news crushed and embarrassed the child. This didn't happen when you had parents who cared.

Ashamed, the young Paul Wesley ran from the church and did not stop running until he reached Maxine's. There he found his mother sitting in a booth with a couple of guys, each of whom he had never seen before and would never see again. She was lost in the moment as she always was, drinking and mugging it up with her newfound boyfriends. It was always disgusting when Paul found his mother in such a compromising situation. But on this day all he was feeling was shame and humiliation. His mother had made his life an abomination but more so on this day. He was a bastard but so was she.

His tears and visibly shaken state had no effect on Joan Wesley. Her kid was disrupting her good time and she barked at him to go away. Her son was hurting but she didn't care.

The young Paul Wesley was fortunate Anne Marie was working that day. As she had done so often in the past, she came to his assistance. Whatever was troubling the child was going to be resolved by Anne Marie and he trusted in her. It was at this point in his life that Paul Wesley decided Anne Marie was going to be his surrogate mother. His own mother could be swallowed up by the earth for all he cared. If she didn't have any love for him then he had none for her.

With tear-drenched cheeks he explained to Anne Marie what had happened. As he told her the story his mother's cousin became incensed. She had badgered Joan about having Paul baptized and Joan had assured her that she had taken care of the matter. Anne Marie felt a sudden fury come over her. But she also had to share part of the blame. She knew she could not believe a word her cousin had to say yet she had. Now young Paul was paying the price for it.

The next day Anne Marie took Paul by the hand to St. Matthew's. She was going to make a case for the boy and see to it that the problem was resolved. But her efforts were in vain—no baptism meant no First Communion! It was a cut and dry issue as far as the prelates of St. Matthew's were concerned. She pleaded with the priests to reconsider and baptize him so he could move on and receive the sacrament of Holy Communion. But her pleas were falling on deaf ears. A certain protocol had to be followed and the priests of St. Matthew's were not about to tamper with it. Have the boy baptized in the proper manner and he would be able to receive his First Communion next year, she was told. It was the best they had to offer. Anne Marie, with Paul in tow, left St. Matthew's feeling exasperated.

Despite the frustration Anne Marie refused to admit defeat. She had a thought. There was a new priest in charge of St. Theresa's, a Father Coniglio. Maybe there was a chance he could help with Paul's problem. It sure didn't hurt to try.

A young Father Coniglio was very attentive to what Anne Marie had to say. He agreed young Paul had a problem on his hands that was not of his own making. However, he did not consider it insurmountable.

The priest proposed that Anne Marie return to St. Matthew's and secure from them, in writing, that Paul Wesley was prepared to receive his First Communion, except for the fact he had not been baptized. Father Coniglio was going to dare to be different, but before doing so he wanted to make sure he had the proper documentation in his hands.

Anne Marie did the leg work and returned the next day with the papers Father Coniglio desired. Once he had them in hand he let Anne Marie in on what he intended to do to amend the situation. Anne Marie listened ardently, convinced young Paul's problem had been solved.

Father Coniglio's remedy to cure a somewhat troublesome situation was to have Anne Marie and a male friend stand up for Paul as sponsors or as his godmother and godfather. That would take care of the baptism end of the dilemma.

"Will the priests of St. Matthew's then allow him to make his First Communion?" she asked Father Coniglio.

"Who knows and who cares," the priest informed her. "He doesn't have to make his First Communion there."

"Huh?" Anne Marie was confused.

Father Coniglio then proceeded to tell her the rest of his maverick plan and a smile quickly graced Anne Marie's face.

On the following Friday night, with Anne Marie and Joe Bartalato, a bartender at Maxine's, serving as his godparents, Paul Wesley was officially baptized into the Catholic Church. The next day a class of seven from the St. Coletta's School for special need students was to receive their First Communion at St. Theresa's. However, on that day, eight children partook in the Eucharist for the first time. Paul Wesley had joined their small but special group.

—⁂—

Father Wesley shot upright from his recumbent position. He was perspiring freely and his heart was racing. There was, indeed, a debt of gratitude to be paid. Father Coniglio had done him a favor and it was his turn to provide the now old priest with a favor of his own.

He shook his head in dismay. Both Father Coniglio and Anne Marie had been there for him in his time of need. Both had shown that special trait it takes to be a good Christian and they ended up with nothing to show for it—especially Anne Marie.

His mother's cousin continued to raise him as if he were her own son. Then, five years later, there was a fight at Maxine's which turned ugly. In the aftermath of darting insults and flying fists, guns were drawn and shots exchanged. The outcome saw Anne Marie, at the age of thirty-five, lying dead on the grimy floor, an innocent victim caught in the crossfire. It was the day Paul Wesley became bitter and started raising himself.

Father Wesley swung his legs over the side of the bed and sat there with his thoughts intact. He owed Father Coniglio and Anne Marie a great deal for the compassion and caring they had shown him. On the spot he made his decision. He was going to go back and aid Father Coniglio in his time of need. But he was not going back as the cardinal's answer to a guilty conscience. He was now going back to St. Theresa's to be a beacon of hope. Now all he had to do was figure out a way to save the place.

CHAPTER
SEVEN

Since turning his life around, Father Wesley had developed into an early riser. During his days of debauchery and unruliness, it was common for him to rise around noon with a pulsating headache and hangover to match. But no more. As he arose on this day his mind was unsure of what to expect but within himself he carried a certain zeal that was worthy of a Holy War crusader.

After saying his good-byes to Monsignor Devine and Father Bryant—a fellow curate in residence at St. Ann's—Father Wesley hit the road on what was a picturesque late spring day, and started back to where it began. In doing so he was also going to have to revisit the last night of Billy Castleman's life.

It was late on a Saturday afternoon at the seawall on Paine Beach. That was the designated spot where he always met Ruth Ann. Her family looked down on him so she insisted their rendezvous be done this way. Until this particular Saturday he had never thought of their relationship as being binding. But when she told him, on that day, they were through as a couple her rejection cut straight through to his heart.

She was moving away, she informed him, and they were never to see each other again.

When Ruth Ann made her decree she seemed to do so with a heavy guilt. She was biting her lower lip, as if trying to stave off the impending tears. Her actions confused Paul and when he tried to plead with her to give him a second chance she let him know, in no uncertain terms, that it was not going to happen.

"Get out of my life and stay out of it," she screamed in what was meant to be a fit of anger. He couldn't understand what was happening between the two of them and she was in no mood to explain. It had to be her parents' decision, he tried to convince himself but, then again, she had never listened to what they had to say in the past regarding their relationship. Then, settling into his mindset came the unthinkable. She was dumping him for someone else.

Oh no, he postured, while his rage reached a fever pitch. If he ever managed to get his hands on the bastard he'd kill whoever it was. He now realized how deep his feelings were for Ruth Ann. If it meant eliminating the competition then he was prepared to do so.

Paul Wesley found himself heading down a road so many other men had traveled. And like so many other men who found themselves in this state, he took his grief to the nearest watering hole, a place called the Seafarer Lounge which was located on the beach. On that day he was willing to fight anyone just to release the anger building inside him. Even Billy Castleman—Paul Wesley's best friend—was in danger of being pummeled by his savage fists. Ruth Ann had done him wrong and someone was going to pay for her leaving him with such an unwanted feeling.

Billy Castleman was willing to take the chance with his good friend. Paul had been drinking boilermakers for an hour when Billy found him. He was aware of what had happened between his best friend and Ruth Ann. He had to talk to Paul because he knew him and he was convinced he could get through to him. He had to talk to him before he took his wrath out on the wrong people. He had to talk to him because it was necessary.

It was a noble effort on Billy Castleman's part. The only problem was Paul Wesley wasn't listening. An irate Paul Wesley was a dangerous

Paul Wesley, and there was no way of talking any sense into him while he was in his inebriated state. Billy decided to ride it out, hoping to keep himself in a reasonable state of sobriety while his friend danced with the devilish genies in a bottle.

Billy sat in the Seafarer Lounge and listened to Paul as he anguished about the rotten hand life had dealt him. Paul Wesley was showing Billy, through the tears in his beer, a side of him his best friend never knew existed. In his drunken stupor Paul professed his love for Ruth Ann and how her sudden rejection was killing him. What Billy witnessed pained him as much. On that night he couldn't find the words he wanted to say to relieve the anguish his friend was experiencing. But he did know he had the strength to stand by him and help him make it through this ordeal.

Then a problem developed. The more Paul drank the more self-pity he seemed to wallow in. Billy knew a Paul Wesley feeling sorry for himself was a Paul Wesley to fear. He was a cause for concern and Billy intended to be there for him, hopefully to stop the damage he might inflict on others if this feeling of abandonment was to get the better of him. A gallant gesture by a true friend but a gesture that proved to be costly for Billy Castleman.

After spending half the night at the Seafarer Lounge, Paul Wesley decided he wanted to take his binge to the city. "You're going with me," he told Billy. "We'll pick up some bimbos who know how to treat a man right, if you know what I mean," he added for emphasis. "I'll show Ruth Ann that I can get along without her just fine."

Billy Castleman wasn't interested in any tawdry behavior on this night but he was concerned about his friend. He was willing to go into Boston with him but there was one condition. Billy insisted on driving.

"No way," Paul told him. "Paul Wesley doesn't get chauffeured around by anyone, and that includes you. You're going to Boston with me and if you don't, I'll break your goddamn head."

This was the Paul Wesley everyone feared. Billy knew, despite the fact they were the best of friends, Paul would inflict harm on his being because of his intoxicated state. Sure, he'd hate himself in the morning because of it, but that was guilt to be dealt with on another day. On that night, sanity and reason had been left twisting in Ruth Ann's rejection.

Reluctantly, Billy agreed to join Paul. The two of them piled into Paul's old Thunderbird and headed for the bright lights of Boston. Less than ten minutes later Paul Wesley's world was in for a drastic change while Billy's ended.

—⚏—

Father Wesley had to shake himself out of his mini-trance as he crossed over the town line and drove into the city of Paine. After thirteen years he had returned. As he drove his Camry down Paine Beach Boulevard and then onto Everton Street, he noticed how there had been little change. Everything about the neighborhood looked eerily familiar. The same could also be said as he pulled his car in and parked on the side street next to the church. St. Theresa's, as well, hadn't changed. Paul Wesley was back.

As he emerged from the car, Grimaldi came running around the corner. Mildred had him doing guard duty again but this time he was enjoying it. He was anxiously awaiting Father Wesley's arrival.

"Father, can I give you a hand?" he asked as Father Wesley was opening the trunk of his car. "My name is Grimaldi. I'm the caretaker here at St. Theresa's."

Father Wesley looked at the man. He couldn't place the face, so obviously this was someone he had never come to know. "It's nice to meet you," the priest replied. "Your name is Grimaldi what?"

"Antonio Grimaldi," the small man replied. "But most people just call me Grimaldi. Like Cher or Rasputin. Who knows that Rasputin's first name was Grigori."

"You can include me on that list," Father Wesley replied as he chuckled at the caretaker's attempt to impress him with his knowledge about a maniacal dead Russian monk.

"So, can I give you a hand?" Grimaldi asked a second time.

"Yes, Antonio you can. I have a couple of cases of books in the backseat. Could you please see that they are placed in my office. That is, if I have an office."

"Oh, you do, Father. Mildred has seen to that. I'll take care of the books and your luggage. I'm sure you'd like to take the time to reacquaint yourself with the place."

That didn't take long, Father Wesley noticed. "So, Antonio, you know that I'm originally from around here."

"Yes, Father, and so does most of the neighborhood. We've all been looking forward to your arrival. Oh, by the way, you can call me Grimaldi. Don't feel funny about it. Nobody else does. I only answer to the name of Antonio at home."

"Well, if that's the only way to grab your attention then that's the way it will be. Let me ask you Grimaldi: how is Father Coniglio doing? I've been hearing some troubling stories about him."

"Don't believe everything you hear, Father. Sure, he's not as sharp as he used to be but that's because he's been trying to run this place by himself. Now that you're here, I'm sure we'll see a change in him. You're going to be good for this church. I can feel it."

"Well, thank you, Grimaldi. Speaking of the church, I hear it hasn't been doing too well of late."

"She's a good church, Father, but a poor church. If something breaks in the place it's never replaced. It's pretty rundown. The archdiocese doesn't seem to care because she doesn't generate a bundle of cash. We've all heard stories that the place will be shut down because of that reason. St. Theresa's has a solid core of supporters. They just don't have a lot of dollars to be throwing around. My daughter, Anna, is going to be married in St. Theresa's in a few weeks. I wouldn't think of having her get married anywhere else. She was christened here. Received her First Communion here. Was confirmed here and now she's going to get married here. Father…" Grimaldi stopped and turned his head as if he were looking up the street in the direction of St. Matthew's.

"Grimaldi, what is it?" Father Wesley had to ask.

The caretaker slowly returned his gaze back at the new curate and asked: "Father, tell me if you can. Does a church have to show a profit to prove that it's prosperous?"

Father Wesley answered with a smile before saying, "Point well taken. Now who is this Mildred? And where can I find her?"

After exchanging welcomes with Mildred—who was waiting for the new prelate at the front door to the rectory—she gave Father Wesley a quick tour of the place. His room was on the second floor while his office was just off the living room. Both rooms were adjacent to Father Coniglio's sleeping and working quarters. The guided tour ended in the kitchen. Father Wesley appreciated the warm reception both Grimaldi and Mildred extended to him, but someone was notably missing to greet him. That someone, of course, was Father Coniglio.

"Mildred, thank you so much for your help. Both you and Grimaldi have made me feel quite welcome. But I guess the same cannot be said for Father Coniglio. Where is he?"

"Oh, he's out in his garden. He's been expecting you but can I make you aware of something, Father?"

"Sure."

"Father, you have to understand that Father Coniglio has been running St. Theresa's by himself for the past thirty years. It's…it's… just going to take some time for him to get used to sharing the priestly duties around here. Do you understand what I'm saying?"

"Absolutely. You say he has a garden. What does he grow? Does he have a green thumb by chance?"

"He's tried his hand at growing a number of things—tomatoes, zucchini, and cucumbers. This year he's trying eggplant. But, to be honest with you, the only things edible seem to be the tomatoes."

"I'll keep that in mind should he try to convince me to try something other than the tomatoes. Well, I guess I should go out to the garden and introduce myself."

Father Coniglio had his back to his new associate and was on his knees doing some garden work as Father Wesley made his approach. "Good morning, Father Coniglio. I'm Father Wesley," he said as he extended his hand should the older priest need it to regain his footing.

Father Coniglio rose to his feet on his own and did a slow turn of his old and aching body. "So you're the one the cardinal sent to look over me and my church," he said, cynically.

Quite perceptive for someone supposedly tottering on the edge of dementia. "Yes, I've been assigned here. But I don't know anything about looking after you."

"Please, Father, spare me the altered truth. I know the cardinal and I know what he's up to. I've been told you grew up in this parish. I don't remember you."

"I did, Father, but that was a long time ago. I wasn't much of a churchgoer back then. I had a very checkered past. It's safe to say I was no altar boy. Speaking of altar boys, or should I say altar servers, how many do you have here?" Altar boys was sort of an antiquated term now. Altar servers was the correct terminology since young ladies were now invited to participate in church services.

"It's altar boys here and we have four: Frankie Napoli, Jake DeSimones, Michael Marino and a Vietnamese kid by the name of Phu Luong. You tell me if you want to meet them and I'll instruct them to come around."

"Sure. I'll leave it up to them as to when we can meet. I've got time. I don't have any pressing matters at the moment."

"Except for babysitting St. Theresa's until she is ready for the slaughterhouse."

"Father, I wish you would stop talking like that."

"All right, have it your way. Let me give you a tour of the church, although it hasn't changed much in the past thirty years."

"I'm in your servitude," Father Wesley said, jauntily.

"Yeah. Okay," was all Father Coniglio could drum up as a reply.

—m—

That evening, following dinner, Father Wesley decided to take a walk down to the beach. He wore his priestly garb so the people in the neighborhood could see that the new priest was in town.

It was as pleasant a night as one could hope to enjoy. Once reaching the end of Everton Street the Atlantic Ocean stared him right in the face. Paine Beach was a beach he knew well—a beach that held many memories for him, most of which he had tried to flush away.

Since it was such a serene and warm evening, the beach had attracted a busy gathering. Standing at the seawall Father Wesley glanced to his left. Somewhere down that road lived his mother. He wondered if she knew that he was back. He also wondered if she cared. Someday he was going to have to look her up and try and help her with life. However, today was not that day. Father Wesley turned to his right and began walking.

He had strolled about a hundred yards when a State Police car pulled up alongside him. The priest found the scene to be somewhat amusing. Considering his outlandish past he had to wonder if there were some outstanding default warrants out for him. Wouldn't that be a bummer: new priest arrives in town and ends up getting jailed.

A stocky cop climbed out of the car and, while leaning over the top of the vehicle, said: "Are you Father Wesley?"

"I am," the priest answered.

"I thought so. My name is Officer Richard Kilcullen," the policeman said as he walked around the squad car. "I heard that you'd be arriving today. I'd like to be one of the first to welcome you back," he went on as he extended his meaty right hand.

"If you're welcoming me back then I assume you know about my past," Father Wesley responded as he took the police officer's hand and shook it.

"Sure do, Father. You're the talk of the beach. The story goes that once upon a time you were pretty good with your fists."

"I think the myth is greater than the fact."

"I don't know about that," Officer Kilcullen went on. "One thing I do know is that it's nice to know you'll be around."

"How so?"

"Although me and the missus attend St. Matthew's, I have a soft spot in my heart for Father Coniglio. He's a dedicated priest and I imagine running that parish of his is no picnic. Now that he's getting older some of these street punks have tried their hand at making his life miserable. They have zero respect for the man. But I think now that they know you're around, they'll think twice."

"What kind of disrespect are we talking about?"

"Humiliating stuff. A few weeks ago these cuties made a public disgrace of themselves by urinating on the shrubs at St. Theresa's. One of them even defecated on the church steps."

"Were they arrested?"

"No."

"Why not?" What Officer Kilcullen was telling him was disturbing news.

"Can't get anybody to say they witnessed it. These people around here are petrified of those bikers. We can't do a thing until somebody is willing to speak out against them."

"I can't imagine Father Coniglio being intimidated."

"They never do anything in front of him. Just in front of the parishioners. They usually do their deed at night. I guess the old priest goes to bed early. But, like I said, I don't think we'll be seeing any of that nonsense now that you're here."

"Officer, I'm now a man of God. I don't go around beating up people the way I once did. But it wouldn't surprise me if these punks you speak of tried to test me as well. I grew up on this beach. I know the thinking that thrives down here and how the law of the jungle sort of applies. But, my friend, rest easy. I assure you I'll be ready for them should they come calling." Father Wesley closed his remarks with a sly wink of his right eye.

Officer Kilcullen smiled. "If you have any trouble, be sure to call me."

"Thanks for alerting me to the situation."

"My pleasure," Kilcullen answered as he prepared to reenter his squad car.

"Another thing, Officer, before you go."

"What's that, Father?"

"Why don't you and your wife give St. Theresa's a try. We could use all the support we can get."

"I think we may do that," Kilcullen answered.

As the police cruiser drove away, Father Wesley stood at the seawall with one thought in mind: *yes, I am back!*

CHAPTER
EIGHT

It was Sunday, June 14th, an overcast and warm day. On this day Grimaldi's daughter, Anna, was to marry Arthur Gregorio. The wedding was scheduled for two o'clock in the afternoon. Even the threat of rain wasn't going to deter the moment at hand. This was a day of celebration for the Grimaldi family.

Father Wesley stood by the front window of the rectory and watched as the friends and family members of the Grimaldies filed into the church. The procession seemed never ending. A few of the faces he had come to know. Watching the parade outside the window had the young priest believing his dream was not out of reach. If you can summon this many people for a wedding, why not for Sunday devotion? Something was lacking and he had to come up with the answer. He was determined to find it.

His daily jaunt along the beach had allowed him to come to know Alfredo and Salvi. As he watched the pair enter the church, Alfredo was dressed as dapper as one might expect. Salvi, however, looked out of place, dressed in his Sunday finery. Father Wesley had come to think of the pair as two disconsolate souls who liked to sit on a bench down by the beach and gawk at the young girls, perhaps commiserating about their own lost youth, especially Salvi.

Out of the corner of his eye he caught a glimpse of Maria Castleman as she approached the church. The sixtyish Maria was a tall woman but she looked tired, at least to Father Wesley. She walked along with her husband, Frank, and their daughter, Heather. Frank was a short man with a weather-beaten look about him. He had always seemed angry to Father Wesley, and he looked that way today. The disruptive thought of confronting Maria and Frank bothered the priest so he shifted his thought to Heather. What he recalled of her was of a much more pleasant nature.

The last time he had seen Heather she was a young girl of twelve. She was attractive, intelligent, gifted and seemed to excel in whatever task she took on. Father Wesley remembered Billy's dream of his little sister being the first Castleman to amount to something. If she was still here had she somehow become stagnant in her life? Father Wesley had to think if that were the case then, Billy's living would have made a difference; that's how much faith he had in Heather. It saddened the priest to think he was the one responsible for taking Billy's dream away.

Most of the guests were in the church when the limousine arrived with the bridal party. Father Wesley broke into a hearty laugh as he watched Grimaldi emerge from the vehicle. He was not the same man Father Wesley had grown accustomed to seeing in the past two weeks. On this occasion he beamed and looked elegant in his tuxedo and ruffled shirt. This was not the man in overalls with dirt, grass stains and whatever else he tinkered with soiling his clothes and body. Father Wesley was feeling good for Grimaldi. At least someone associated with St. Theresa's was in a pleasant mood on this day.

The young priest continued to watch as the limo door was opened for Grimaldi's daughter, as her father took her arm. Anna was no beauty; her head seemed a little too big for her body and her nose was long. But on a day such as this, all brides radiated with a dignified magnificence of their own despite the imperfections they might have inherited. As he watched father and daughter enter the church, an envious feeling overcame Father Wesley. He would have loved to have been a part of this joyous occasion but this was Father Coniglio's show, as well it should be. All Father Wesley could do was stand by the wayside and observe.

The young priest felt a tap on his shoulder. It was Mildred. She was dressed in pink. St. Theresa's Girl Friday had been invited to the wedding but she still insisted on performing her duties in the rectory until it was time to meet her husband in the church.

"What is it?" he asked as if angered at being disturbed.

"I have a message for you," she answered, sheepishly, not expecting Father Wesley to snap at her. "You are to call Father Moore when you have a chance."

A jolt came to the priest. It was those damn reports. He could feel his anger building to a boiling point.

"I'll call him back when I have the chance," he informed her. "Now, Mildred, forget about the housekeeping chores and get into that church and enjoy the moment."

"Thank you, Father," she said in an almost obligatory manner. Mildred then made a mad dash out of the rectory and rushed into the church. She was the last one in and Father Wesley watched every step she took.

Once she was out of sight he turned, went to his office, and looked at the phone on his desk. Now that he was alone it was the ideal time to call Father Moore. Yet he could not bring himself to do it. Father Moore was going to have to wait.

About fifteen minutes later Father Wesley made his way over to the church. The tiny building was nearly filled to capacity. He walked through the vestibule and sat in the last pew. He watched as Father Coniglio performed the sacrament with the assistance of Phu Luong, the older priest's favorite altar boy. It still saddened him to know there were more people in the church for Anna Grimaldi's wedding than had been present for the three Masses celebrated that morning. He shook his head in disappointment.

At the conclusion of the matrimonial service Father Wesley returned to the vestibule and watched as the bridal party and guests filed out. As they walked by him the people smiled and Father Wesley smiled back. However, when Maria Castleman strolled by there was a sad look on her face as the two made eye contact for the first time in years. He could only imagine the pain which had to have been resurrected in her heart as she looked at the man who was responsible for the death of her son, her first born. Neither of them said a word. Their hearts were still heavy with sorrow.

Once the church emptied out, Father Wesley watched the conglomeration of people standing in front of the place. There had to be over 200 in attendance. As he continued to gaze at the guests, and the mutual exchange of hands and picture taking, a voice called out to him. "Father, Father," the voice beseeched. It was Grimaldi. He knifed his way through the crowd and made his way to the parish's new priest.

"Grimaldi, your daughter looks very beautiful. You must be a proud and happy man on this day."

"I am Father, but my wife and I want to invite you to the reception. It will be at the V.F.W. Post. Please, tell me you'll come. My Nanette will be very disappointed if you don't."

"I'd love to, Grimaldi, but I can't. Tell your wife I appreciate the invitation but someone has to stay behind and mind the store."

"Are you sure, Father?"

"Yes, I am. Also, I have some things that have to be taken care of." The thought of making the phone call to Father Moore pained him.

"Well, if you should change your mind please come and join us."

"Thank you, Grimaldi. Now stop worrying about me and go and enjoy this special day in your life."

Grimaldi left his side and Father Wesley watched as the crowd dispersed. He waited until the last person was gone before making his retreat to the rectory. His pace was a slow one; he was in no rush to make this dreaded phone call. There was little to pass onto Father Moore since he had only been stationed at St. Theresa's for two weeks. Still, the thought of talking to the man turned his stomach.

Upon walking into the rectory he turned the television on and tried to settle into watching a baseball game. But he couldn't get his mind into it. He kept thinking about the phone call that had to be made.

After about an hour and a half he turned off the television and went upstairs to change his clothes. He removed his black priestly attire and replaced it with a blue shirt and black slacks. He returned downstairs and went to his office where he reluctantly picked up the telephone on his desk. He couldn't put it off forever. He punched in Father Moore's private number. It rang twice.

"Hello. Father Moore speaking."

Damn, he was hoping to get the answering machine. "Father, this is Father Wesley returning your call."

"Isn't this a pleasant surprise. Where have you been?"

"I beg your pardon."

"Father, you've been at St. Theresa's for two weeks. You are to report to me on a weekly basis. I don't care for the fact that I had to call and track you down. If that continues someone is going to figure out that something is up."

Father Wesley would have enjoyed telling him that Father Coniglio already sensed a conspiracy at hand. But he decided against it; fearing the repercussions Father Moore might try and implement. The only information he was going to offer was the obvious.

"I'm sorry, Father. I thought you might allow me some leeway to adjust to the surroundings."

"I don't remember that being mentioned at our meeting."

"Again, Father, I'm sorry. I never should have assumed such a thing."

"What do you have to report?"

"Nothing. I've only been here for two weeks. Were you expecting something to transpire in such a short period of time?"

"How about Father Coniglio? How is he doing?"

"He's fine. He doesn't seem to be the dimwitted individual who was described to me. I have yet to see any signs of diminished capacity."

"You will. Now, tell me, what did St. Theresa's take in collections today?"

This was Father Moore at his best, Father Wesley thought to himself. It was his chance to twist the knife that was already in the back of St. Theresa's.

"I believe it was just shy of $200," Father Wesley told him.

Father Moore broke into a robust laugh. "You wonder why I want to close that broken-down church. I just put a call into St. Matthew's. Do you know what they've taken in today?"

"No, I don't. But I'll bet you're going to tell me."

"You've got that right. Monsignor Cosgrove estimates that they took in more than $3,000. What do you think of that, Father?"

"Impressive numbers."

"Impressive is right. Father, I think you should make a trip up to St. Matthew's and get to know Monsignor Cosgrove. It'll make the transition all the more smoother and put us all on the same page when the day comes for St. Theresa's to become part of St. Matthew's."

"Forget it," Father Wesley replied, tersely. "It's bad enough that I'm doing what has been ordered of me. I'll be damned if I am going to start cavorting with the enemy who has St. Theresa's in their crosshairs."

"Have it your way," Father Moore answered. "Just make sure you make those weekly reports, and do it by phone. I don't want any e-mails or text messages. I want our correspondence to be of a more personal nature. I expect you to come to me; not me to you."

"I understand, Father."

"Good. Enjoy what's left of the day."

"You too, Father."

Father Wesley hung up the phone and a feeling of relief rushed over him. He wouldn't have to talk to Father Moore for a week. He looked at his watch. It was just after 4:30. He usually took his daily walk along the beach just after dinner but today he decided to do it earlier. It was only a difference of a few hours but it was a few hours that would make a difference in the life of Father Paul Wesley and the Church of St. Theresa.

It was still overcast and a stiff breeze was blowing in off the ocean. The flimsy blue windbreaker Father Wesley was wearing provided little protection against the prevailing wind. A fog was developing and it was rolling in off the ocean cover. He stopped at the Banana Boat, a roadside eatery, and bought a cup of coffee. He then walked across the parkway and sat on the seawall. Cradling the paper cup, allowing the hot brew to warm his hands, he heard sirens off to his left. Turning, he saw it: billowing clouds of black smoke being buffeted by the gusty ocean breeze.

Father Wesley dropped the cup and began running in the direction of the fire. A large congregation of people had already gathered to watch a bar called the Beachhead burn. As Father Wesley reached the area so did the fire department. He stood with the onlookers for about three minutes when he stepped forward and alerted one of the firefighters that he was a priest and should he be needed, he would be here.

The firefighter instructed Father Wesley to talk to a man standing next to a red Bronco that was the Fire Chief's vehicle. The man he was told to speak to was Bob Quinn, the Paine Fire Chief.

Father Wesley walked over the outstretched water hoses in the direction of Chief Quinn. Once he did reach him he explained he was a priest and if needed, he was here to help.

The Chief, between barking out commands, explained that the fire chaplain should be on the scene shortly, but he would appreciate it if Father Wesley did decide to hang around for a while. You never knew what kind of casualties you were dealing with, especially when it was a bar that was burning.

Father Wesley remained by the red Bronco and watched as the Beachhead was reduced to cinders. It concerned him to see the flames stretch skyward and bond with the wind and drift off in the direction of the neighborhood behind the burning bar. He feared the ramifications if the inferno was not brought under control and brought under control quickly. He could hear crackling sounds emanating from the building, and he feared those sounds may have been that of bodies snapping and popping due to the intense heat. Right now Father Wesley felt totally helpless.

There was a tap on his right shoulder and he turned to see who it was. Facing him was a short but stout man dressed in jeans, a baseball jacket with a fire helmet adorning his head. He was Father Emilio Torrez, the Fire Chaplain of the Paine Fire Department. "You never get used to these things," he said after introducing himself.

"I think I know what you mean. My name is Father Paul Wesley. I'm assigned to St. Theresa's. If I can be of any help, I'll be right here."

"Yes, I know. One of the firefighters informed me that you offered your assistance. Thank you. I hope I won't need it, but it's comforting to know you'll be around."

The fire chaplain did not say another word as he moved past Father Wesley to get closer to the burning building. Meanwhile, Father Wesley remained stationary, a helpless feeling still engulfing him. The firefighter he had originally spoken to came running from the building caressing something against his chest. He rushed over to the frustrated priest and said, "Can you hold this for the time being?"

"What is it?" Father Wesley asked.

"It's a puppy. Found it in the rear of the building. It was the only one we could save. The mother and the other three pups burned to death. This one had enough sense to crawl behind some trash cans to avoid the flames. I'll be back to take it off your hands when I get the chance."

Father Wesley took the pup from the firefighter's grasp. The tiny thing was soaked with the water from the fire hoses. The puppy was black with brown paws and a brown snoot. He held the animal above his head to determine its sex. It was a male. The priest placed him inside his windbreaker to keep the small thing warm. He could feel his teeny heartbeat against his chest.

The fire was finally extinguished about an hour later. The young dog's wet coat rapidly dried against Father Wesley's upper body. They maintained a needed watch by what was once the Beachhead Lounge. He snuggled the pup a little tighter and felt his short tail wagging against his stomach. Father Wesley could feel himself becoming attached to the small animal.

Father Torrez returned and said, "We were busy with this one. There were no casualties, however. Thank God for that."

"Yeah, except for a dog and three of her pups," Father Wesley had to say.

"It's too bad but they're only animals, let's be thankful there are no human bodies around for us to tend to. There are more important issues to life than dogs and cats. You'd understand what I'm saying if you witnessed a few of these fires that turn out to be truly tragic."

As Father Torrez spoke the little mutt stuck his head out from underneath Father Wesley's jacket. "But it looks as if you've found a friend," Father Torrez remarked upon seeing the puppy.

"Yeah, he's the only one to survive."

"Father, don't try and be a hero. There is very little you can do with him."

"I'm not trying to be a hero," Father Wesley answered.

"Good," the fire chaplain replied.

Father Wesley wasn't an animal worshipper but it didn't seem right for any form of life, be it human or animal, to be denied the right of life no matter how trying the circumstances. The priest had a feeling he and this dog had a lot in common.

The building had been reduced to a smoldering pile of ashes when the firefighter who had asked Father Wesley to watch over the pup returned. "Father, I'll take care of the dog for you," he said as he approached.

"What becomes of him?" Father Wesley demanded to know.

"I'm not sure. I'll turn the poor thing over to the dog officer and he, in turn, will pass it along to the Animal Rescue League. In all probability it will be destroyed."

"Why?" Father Wesley insisted on knowing.

"Father, I'd say the thing is about two or three days old. There is no way it is going to survive on its own. Even if we could find another dog that has given birth and lactating, I doubt if she would ever allow a pup which is not hers to suckle. I know you have the best of intentions in mind, but don't be cruel to the animal."

"I'll let what you're suggesting happen over my dead body."

"Father, it won't survive the night without its mother. I guarantee it."

"Then, I guess, that's my problem. At least he'll go as God intended."

"It's up to you, but I know tomorrow you'll regret the decision you're making today."

"Perhaps, but allow me to say this: I've known heartache and I've known death. If this dog should die in the ensuing hours at least I'll know I gave him a chance. Your way might be the right way or at least the most convenient way. But it is not a Godlike way. I'll take my chances."

"That's rather noble of you, Father. But, as I told you, in the morning you'll find yourself bearing the grief that awaits you now."

"We'll see," was Father Wesley's snappish reply.

"Well, good luck," the firefighter said as he turned and walked away.

"Wait a minute," Father Wesley called out.

The firefighter turned. "Yeah," he said

"What kind of dog was the mother? He's so young I can't determine what breed he is."

"She was a German shepherd," the firefighter answered, smiling as he did so.

"Thanks," Father Wesley said as he turned and walked away, the puppy secure under his jacket. It seemed as if with every step he took the young dog was nibbling at his chest, trying to find the nipple that would sustain his life, while the words of the firefighter echoed through the priest's head: *Father, he won't survive without his mother.*

Was he doing the right thing or was he fooling himself? Be it right or wrong Father Wesley was willing to live with the decision he had made on this cool and damp evening.

———〰———

It was after seven when Father Wesley returned to the rectory. His newfound friend was now warm and dry but the same could not be said for the priest. Between the sweat of having to go through the ordeal of the fire and the dog's damp body, his shirt was like a sponge. In addition, his little cohort had found time to urinate twice on the trip. The telltale signs were on Father Wesley's pants.

"We're home," Father Wesley announced as he entered the rectory.

Father Coniglio and Mildred had returned from the wedding reception an hour earlier. Mildred was in the kitchen when she heard Father Wesley come through the front door.

"Father," she called out. "I'm in the kitchen. I have a nice plate of prime rib, potatoes and carrots for you. Grimaldi insisted I bring it home to you. I'll heat it up."

As she placed the plate in the microwave oven Father Wesley entered the kitchen. He had a disheveled look about him and Mildred could see that he was carrying something underneath his jacket. His appearance disturbed and confused her. But her apprehension was quickly dispelled when he unzipped his jacket and exposed the puppy.

"My God!" she exclaimed. "Where did you find him?"

Father Wesley cleared his parched throat and in a hoarse voice told her, "There was a fire down at the beach and this little thing ended up being a victim of it so I sort of adopted him. Where is Father Coniglio?"

"I think he's in the bathroom," Mildred said as she moved a little closer to get a better look at the puppy.

"What do you think of him?" Father Wesley asked.

"He's a cute little thing," Mildred answered as she petted his small head. "What's his name?"

"Haven't had the time to name him yet. What do you think we should call him?"

Mildred looked, sternly, into Father Wesley's eyes. "He's never going to let you keep him. You know that, don't you?"

"You mean Father Coniglio?"

Mildred nodded. She loved the thought of having the pup around but she knew Father Coniglio would disapprove.

"Leave Father Coniglio to me," Father Wesley assured her. At that moment they heard the faint sound of the toilet being flushed.

Less than a minute later Father Coniglio came slowly walking into the kitchen. He was going to inform Mildred that the day's activities had made him weary and he planned to retire early. But before he could say a word he spotted Father Wesley. His new assistant looked like hell and smelled like smoke. Then he noticed the puppy and he looked straight into the eyes of Father Wesley. "What in heaven's name are you holding?" he said in a voice that demanded an answer.

"It's a dog, Father. A puppy to be exact."

"Looks more like a rat. Where did you find him?"

"There was a fire at a bar on the beach. His mother and the three other pups in the litter burned to death. I think his mother may have been a watchdog for the place."

"I see. Now let me ask how you managed to become its foster parent?"

"The fire department intended to have him destroyed. He's young, very young, maybe three days old, and they didn't think he was going to survive. I couldn't, in good conscience, allow that to happen. If he is destined not to live then he will go gracefully."

"What if he does survive? Do you intend to keep him?"

"I haven't thought that far ahead, Father."

"Let me do the thinking for you. I have never known a priest who has owned a dog. I'm not sure if it's permitted. However, I'll allow you to keep him until he's old enough and we can decide what to do with him, although I tend to agree that he will not survive the night." Father Coniglio shook his head in disgust. "Where is St. Theresa's headed? Now I guess we have to find time for a shaggy mutt."

Father Coniglio waved his hand in an indifferent manner and left the kitchen. As he did so Father Wesley developed a satisfied look on his face. In the meantime, Mildred, who was standing next to the younger priest said, "I never thought he'd let you keep him."

"He's not as tough as he would like us to believe. I think he also gave us a name for our new friend."

"And that would be?"

"Well, let's see, he mentioned we now have to find time for a *shaggy mutt*. As far as I'm concerned this shaggy mutt's time has come. So we'll call him Shagtyme, only we'll spell the *time* portion of his name with a 'y' just to be different."

"I kinda like it."

"I'm glad you do. Also, let me tell you something else, Mildred. He'll never let go of Shagtyme."

"What leads you to that conclusion?"

"I can see it in his eyes. I think he relates to this dog. Like him, Shagtyme is a symbol of the unwanted; the unwanted capable of surviving despite the steepest of odds."

"Sounds nice," Mildred uttered, "but now we have to find a way to make him survive."

"It'll be a challenge but I think we can do it," Father Wesley replied, half believing what he said and half praying Shagtyme's future was secure in their hands.

CHAPTER
NINE

Shagtyme did survive the night and the nights which followed, as Mildred and Father Wesley went about the task of bringing the young puppy through a very unstable and unpredictable time in his young life. Mildred put together a small bed in Father Wesley's bedroom for Shagtyme to sleep in. She found a small hand wound clock in the basement and instructed the priest to place it in the dog bed, hoping to fool Shagtyme into believing that the ticking of the clock was his mother's heartbeat. But the ploy didn't work, so Shagtyme spent the first three weeks of his life sleeping with Father Wesley. The pup cuddled against his chest and felt his heartbeat. It was a heartbeat which was real and it was a heartbeat he'd come to know and trust.

Nourishing Shagtyme also proved to be a Herculean task. Mildred tried feeding him through a baby bottle but the small dog shied away from it. It was Grimaldi who provided the assistance for this problem.

Grimaldi lived his personal life as though he were a peasant from the old country. He had a large garden in his backyard and also raised two pigs and two goats. One of the goats he had raised himself so he was no stranger to the situation involving Shagtyme.

He had a device which he gerrymandered by using a hot water bottle. It had a thin, two foot long hose attached to it with Grimaldi's custom designed nipple, which was meant to serve as the dog's mother's nipple.

He set up a hanger in the priest's room to hold the hot water bottle in place, and he ran the hose through a stuffed animal so Shagtyme could lie on the floor and feed from his pseudo mother. This time Shagtyme was fooled.

—m—

Three months passed. It was mid-September and Shagtyme was growing rapidly. It was obvious to all who observed him that the dog was going to be an extremely large German shepherd. During the day Father Wesley chained Shagtyme to the railing of the steps leading to the rectory's front door. It was a long leash of twenty feet and gave the animal enough leeway to play with the younger children in the neighborhood, who came by to spend time with the canine on a daily basis. The dog was now St. Theresa's main attraction. He was also proving to be the children's best friend.

Father Coniglio claimed to be perturbed by the growing number of children now congregating on the grounds of St. Theresa's but he never did anything about it. Father Wesley, however, saw something different. If there was a way of bringing St. Theresa's back to respectability, it was through the children. Thanks to Shagtyme, Father Wesley could see an avenue being opened for him. It was going to take some hard work but that was the reason he was here. Father Moore could be damned. Shagtyme was doing his part and Father Wesley intended to do his as well. St. Theresa's was far from dead and Father Wesley intended to prove it.

Father Coniglio did have one steadfast rule: Shagtyme was not to be allowed in the church. Prior to the dog's arrival the older priest took his afternoon nap between two and three. But once the school season began the sounds of the children, returning from their day at school and had gathered to play with Shagtyme, disrupted his afternoon siestas. Because of the dog, Father Coniglio was now forced to take his afternoon snoozes from one to two. Life was, indeed, changing around St. Theresa's.

Father Wesley took advantage of the opportunity bestowed upon him. While Father Coniglio napped, and the children were busy with their day in school, he would allow Shagtyme to enter the church with him. It was his way of keeping Shagtyme occupied, and it afforded him some time to spend with his dog. Shagtyme adapted well to the church. He seemed to enjoy his time in this tired old building. Then came the afternoon of September 17th.

Father Wesley and Grimaldi were in the church, with Shagtyme at the priest's side. There was a problem in the church, an ongoing problem that could turn into a catastrophe, if it were not addressed. Grimaldi felt more comfortable discussing it with the younger priest. He had tried with Father Coniglio and nothing came of it. Maybe Father Wesley could find a way of resolving it.

There was a small leak in the roof. Father Wesley looked up and saw a drip of water fall aimlessly on one of the confessionals. As he stared at the problem the priest knew the archdiocese probably wouldn't fund what was needed to repair the roof. Father Moore would see to that. Why put money into a church he was just waiting to close. If he could get through to the cardinal he might have some success, but that meant going through Father Moore. The cardinal's secretary would block him and drag it out until the damn roof collapsed.

"You can't fix it?" Father Wesley asked Grimaldi, knowing what the man's answer would be.

"Sure. I can do some patchwork but the leak we see today is going to reappear someplace else. Before you know it the roof will begin to sag and then…BOOM…it will collapse. I can only do so much patchwork before the problem becomes serious. Father, we have to address this matter before the winter is upon us. I worry about the first major snowstorm we have. I'm not sure if this section of the roof can withstand another season of snow unless we locate the leak and fix it. It won't be necessary for the archdiocese to close St. Theresa's. St. Theresa's will do it for them."

Those were words he did not need to hear. "How much will it cost to repair the roof?"

"About $15,000 right now," Grimaldi told him. "The longer we wait the more expensive it becomes. I know some people so maybe I can get it for a little cheaper price."

"I assume Father Coniglio knows about this problem?"

"Oh, he does," Grimaldi informed him. "I brought it to his attention when I first noticed it. He claimed he'd get the money from the archdiocese but we have yet to see a red cent. That's why I brought it to your attention. I thought maybe you could get them to move on it."

Father Wesley's face winced with pain. In order to secure that kind of money he definitely was going to have to go through Father Moore. *Damn that Father Moore!*

Father Wesley sat in a pew and buried his face into his hands, trying to solve this dilemma on his own. A minute later he looked up at Grimaldi and said, "Go ahead and hire the people it's going to take to get the job done. I assume the structure is not going to collapse once the roof is fixed. There aren't any other problems I need to know about, are there?"

"The structure is fine. This church is on solid footing. But, Father, the money. Are you going to be able to get it from the archdiocese? I can't ask people to work on a promise."

"Forget the archdiocese. I'll sell my car. That should cover whatever expenses are involved. It's less than a year old and I paid cash for it so there is no problem in that area."

"But, Father, without a car how do you plan to get around?"

"I have two feet. What more do I need."

"If you really plan to sell the car then maybe I can get my Anna to buy it. She's been looking for another vehicle. She'll pay you top dollar for it."

"If Anna's interested then consider it a done deal. I want this roof work completed before the winter sets in. As you said, we don't need a layer of ice and snow coming through it and sending us to Kingdom come some Sunday morning."

"What do I tell Father Coniglio when he starts asking questions?"

"Tell him Anna decided to make a generous contribution to the church."

Grimaldi smiled. "Father, I'm beginning to like your style."

"Yeah, yeah," he replied helplessly.

"Well, let me get going," Grimaldi said. "I want to get this project started as quickly as possible." The caretaker then made a hasty exit through one of the side doors to the church.

Father Wesley stood up, stepped out of the pew and began to walk out of the church with Shagtyme at his side when he spotted a woman sitting in the last pew. As he neared her she waved, indicating she knew him. Father Wesley thought the face looked familiar but her name was escaping him. When he was within ten feet of her she spoke.

"That's a good-looking dog you have there, Father."

Father Wesley looked down at Shagtyme and then back at the woman. "He is," he answered.

"You don't seem to remember me."

Father Wesley sat down, sideways, in the pew in front of the woman while Shagtyme rested in the center aisle of the church. "I'm sorry," the priest shrugged, "your name has somehow slipped my mind."

The woman leaned forward, her face about four inches from his. "I'm Sharon Beasley," she whispered.

Father Wesley sat in silence. Sharon was the first of the old gang from the beach he had encountered since his return. She had changed her hairstyle and had colored it from brown to auburn. She was still somewhat shapely, although her face seemed puffier than he remembered. Sharon Beasley was—or had been—Ruth Ann's best friend.

"Sharon, of course, how have you been? I'm so ashamed I forgot your name." He was leery of bringing up Ruth Ann's name.

"I'm doing fine, Father. I'm married now and have two lovely boys, David and Daniel. They're seven and six."

"That's nice. I'll bet they're a handful. Your husband, is he someone I know?"

"No, you don't. I met him ten years ago. His name is Ray Presley. He's a good man. He's put together a good life for me and the boys."

"That's good to hear. What does he do for a living?"

"He runs his own sporting goods store in North Paine."

"That's great, Sharon. Do you attend St. Theresa's?"

"No. We live in St. Mary's parish."

At least it wasn't St. Matthew's, Father Wesley thought. It seemed as though everyone he came across had some affiliation to St. Matthew's.

"How are our old cronies doing? I haven't seen any of them since I've been here at St. Theresa's."

Oh, they have scattered in all different directions. Some of them—if you can believe it—have become quite successful. Johnny Rogers now owns Rose's. Willie Pomona went into radio sales. Nicole Sintro is a schoolteacher. I'm surprised you haven't run into her. She teaches the fourth grade right up the street at the Lincoln School."

"It's nice to hear that some of them turned out so well. I also assume some of them never got out of that rut which could have ruined all of us."

"That's true, especially Bryan Fogarty. He never seemed to grow up. He still calls the beach his home. You usually see him around at night cruising the parkway on his big motorcycle. He's sort of the kingpin of the group that now hang out there."

Father Wesley decided it was time to get away from the small talk and on to the crux of the matter. She was here for a reason. He and Sharon had their share of disagreements in the past. She had always been a very opinionated individual. He had tolerated her because of Ruth Ann. Sharon was not here to welcome him back to the neighborhood.

"So, Sharon, what brings you here?"

Sharon wrestled with the question for a few seconds. She wondered if she were overstepping her bounds. "When you say you haven't spoken to any of the old gang I assume that includes Ruth Ann."

Father Wesley felt as though he should terminate this conversation, immediately. Ruth Ann was a part of his past and that is where he wanted to keep her. She had made a decision to walk out of his life and it had cost him dearly. He now respected her decision but it didn't mean he agreed with it. But being a priest he had to exhibit some form of tolerance. "No. I haven't seen or talked to her in thirteen years. I don't even know where she lives."

"She lives locally, over in Peachtree. Her life is a mess. She claims to have been married but now she's divorced. She has a daughter, Rachel, who she has been having a problem with. I think it might do her a world of good if you looked her up."

Father Wesley had to drop the priestly routine. This was a personal matter so he was going to have to talk to Sharon from the heart, regardless of the spite it carried.

"I can't do that, Sharon. I don't think seeing her would do either of us any good."

"You're still angry at her for what she did to you," Sharon accused him.

"I like to think the two of us took separate routes in life because that was the way it was meant to be. If the path she chose has been rocky then I feel bad for her. But there is too much between us and it cannot be dismissed. There is little I can do for her as a priest or as a man."

"Sounds to me as if you are bitter," Sharon remarked.

"There was a time when I was bitter. But, ironically, her leaving me led to a better life. A life I am proud to lead."

"So what you are saying is you have found your safe and secure haven and any contact with Ruth Ann threatens that life. Let me put it another way: you are running scared when it comes to Ruth Ann!"

This conversation was becoming quite tiring and humbling for Father Wesley. "I know it sounds that way," he said. "But, believe me, seeing her would do us more harm than good."

"I wish you could see it differently. Father, when I say this I mean it: what Ruth Ann did to you hurt her as much as it hurt you. I only wish you knew the truth."

"And what is the truth?" Father Wesley asked.

"That's for Ruth Ann to tell you, not me. But, apparently, you are not willing to let that happen. I feel sorry for you because you are being so narrow-minded."

Sharon got up to leave, stepping out of the pew and genuflecting. She was about to turn when Father Wesley said, "Sharon, hold on a second."

"What is it?" she asked.

Father Wesley stood up and took a deep breath before continuing. "I assume Ruth Ann knows I'm here."

"She does."

"If she wants to see me then she knows where to find me."

"Oh, I see where you're coming from," Sharon reasoned. "You'd like her to come back, on her hands and knees, begging your forgiveness. Well, if that were the case I wouldn't be here begging for her. You see, she's just as stubborn as you are, although for a different reason. You do it for the pain you incurred. She does it because of the shame. Someday the two of you will confront one another again. I can only pray by that time it will not have been too late."

Father Wesley, his mind in a quandary, watched as Sharon made an about face and stormed out of the church. Shagtyme, sensing his master's discomfort, sat up to reassure him he still had a friend. He heard the side door of the church open but his mind was still locked on the words Sharon had left with him. He didn't bother to turn and see who it was. He was feeling emotional pain again and he didn't know why.

"Father Wesley," the voice bellowed. "What have I told you about that dog." It was Father Coniglio.

Father Wesley looked at Shagtyme. "Oh boy," he said to his canine companion. "We're in trouble now."

CHAPTER
TEN

It was Thanksgiving. Shagtyme was on his leash in the front yard. The children were not around, except for one. The lone child was a six-year-old girl by the name of Jenna Napoli. She was usually in the company of her nine-year-old brother, Frankie. But such was not the case on this day.

Jenna was a tiny thing. She wore hand-me-down clothes, her hair always seemed unkempt and her face always seemed in need of a washing. But one thing could not be denied. She had an angelic face that captured hearts at a glance. She was also Shagtyme's favorite playmate.

When the children first came around to play with Shagtyme, Jenna was petrified of the rapidly growing puppy. Shagtyme would rear up on his hind legs and knock her to the ground. The dog would then proceed to stand over her and lick her pretty face as if he were cleaning it for her. Jenna would run and hide behind her brother, seeking safety from the large dog.

But that was in September. It was now November and the relationship between Jenna and Shagtyme had changed. She no longer feared the big dog and loved him as much as Shagtyme seemed to care for her.

It was ten o'clock in the morning when Father Wesley heard her giggling. He went to the window and watched as Jenna and Shagtyme played. She was on her knees, trying to teach him something. But Jenna seemed to be having a difficult time doing so because Shagtyme could not resist the chance to lick her face. Little Jenna turned her face away from the dog and tried to scold him. "Shagtyme, how are you ever going to learn if you keep trying to kiss me?"

Shagtyme seemed to heed her admonishment and the dog sat erect as if in obedience school, his tail wagging. A heartwarming smile came over Father Wesley's face as he watched this innocent scene play out.

Jenna held up her right forefinger. "One," she said. Shagtyme, in turn, barked several times. "No," she said, wearily. "You're supposed to bark only once." Shagtyme answered with several more barks.

"Let's try it this way," Jenna told him. "One, woof."

Shagtyme seemed confused so he barked twice. "No, that's two," Jenna corrected the dog. "Let's try it again. One, woof."

This time Shagtyme barked only once. "That's right," she exclaimed. "You're so smart. Now let's try two."

Mildred came up behind Father Wesley. "What's going on out there?" she asked.

"Little Jenna Napoli is trying to teach Shagtyme how to count."

"Is she having any luck?"

"So far so good. They've gotten past one."

"That's so sweet," Mildred observed. "These kids have really taken a liking to your dog."

"They have. By the way, what is the temperature outside?"

"It's about forty degrees. Why?"

"That little Jenna has no coat on. She's apt to catch her death out there. What, in heaven's name, is wrong with her parents sending her out like that?"

"She has just her father and brother. Chances are she dressed herself and simply forgot her coat," Mildred let the priest know.

The painful thought of his own childhood came flooding back to Father Wesley. In a way he could relate to Jenna. Painful memories were not something he wished to dwell on, especially on a day such as this. He changed the subject quickly. "What time do we eat?" he asked.

"Two o'clock," she told him.

"What about your own family? I hope we're not putting you out?"

"Not at all, Father. My husband and I are going to my sister's place. She said they'll be eating sometime after three. Her house is only five minutes away."

"That's a relief. I didn't want to think Father Coniglio and I were a hindrance. Although, I must admit, it disturbs me to know you have to labor over a turkey and then go some other place else to eat."

"Father Coniglio never complained, why should you?"

"I don't think it should be part of your job description."

"If I left it up to you two then you'd be having a couple of bowls of Cheerios for Thanksgiving."

"Point taken," Father Wesley had to admit.

At 1:30 Mildred entered the living room, ladle in hand, and announced that dinner would be ready in thirty minutes. She cautioned the two priests that they had a twelve-pound turkey so—unless they were a couple of gluttons—they had better be prepared to eat turkey for a few more days.

Father Coniglio was sitting in the easy chair reading the archdiocesan newsletter while Father Wesley was sitting on the sofa watching a football game between the Detroit Lions and Kansas City Chiefs. It bothered the younger priest that there was so little conversation between him and Father Coniglio, except for the everyday vernacular that was necessary. He wanted to reach out to him but the venerable old priest seemed determined to keep him at a distance.

As Father Wesley continued to watch the football game a strong wind could be felt lashing against the rectory. The draft it created rattled the windows and it reminded Father Wesley that the dreary days of winter were not far away. It also reminded him of Shagtyme and how the dog had been out since eight that morning. It was time to bring him in and feed him before he did his usual stunt of begging for table scraps.

Father Wesley grabbed his jacket out of the closet and proceeded to the front yard to bring the dog in. As he left the rectory he could hear Shagtyme barking. Jenna was still with him. They were up to three.

As Father Wesley approached the front yard, he removed his jacket and placed it around Jenna's shoulders. As he was doing so he asked her, "Jenna, do you expect to play with Shagtyme all day?"

She looked up at the priest and through deep but sorrowful blue eyes asked, "Would it be all right?"

"Jenna, it's Thanksgiving. You should be at home ready to eat some turkey with your father and brother."

The young girl reached into the pocket of her worn jeans and produced a piece of paper which she handed to Father Wesley. It was a note and Father Wesley unfolded it and began to read:

Dear Fathers,
I would appreciate it if you could
watch my little girl. I have to work
today but I'll be home around 6:30.
Her brother has been invited to a
school friend's house for the day and
because of the holiday I can't find anyone
for her to spend the day with. She's not
much trouble. You don't have to feed her.
Once I get home I'll see that she has her supper

George Napoli

Father Wesley took the note and placed it in the right hand pocket of his trousers. *Poor thing*, was his thinking. "Jenna, why didn't you give this note to me earlier? It's freezing out here. You could get sick."

"I'm sorry. I started playing with Shagtyme and I forgot about it."

"Weren't you cold?"

"No."

"Then why are you shivering?"

"Maybe just a little," Jenna corrected herself.

"Well, Shagtyme's getting cold. It's time for him to go inside and get warm and the same goes for you." The priest then unchained the dog and taking Jenna by the hand the three of them went into the rectory.

"I'll bet you're hungry?" he asked as they made their way up the stairs to the front door.

"Just a little."

"I think you're going to like what we have to eat. We have a big turkey for Thanksgiving. How would you like to join us?"

"I don't think I've ever had turkey before."

"Guess what?"

"What?"

"You're going to have it today."

Shagtyme was the first one through the door with Father Wesley and Jenna right in his wake. Father Coniglio dropped the newsletter he was reading and peered over his eyeglasses when he saw the young lady. "Who's this?" he asked.

"This is Jenna Napoli," Father Wesley told him as he reached into his pocket and produced the note. "I've invited her to have Thanksgiving dinner with us," he went on as he handed the note to Father Coniglio.

The older priest scanned the note and didn't say a word. Then again he didn't have to. The nodding of his head was enough to assure Father Wesley that he understood. As he was reading George Napoli's note, Jenna clutched Father Wesley's left leg as though she were going to strangle it. "What's the problem?" Father Wesley had to ask.

"He's the scary priest," she answered.

Father Wesley laughed aloud and patted her on the top of the head to convince her she had nothing to fear. "He might be old but he's not scary," he told her.

"He scares me and the other kids. He's always yelling at us."

Father Coniglio raised his eyeglasses so they rested on the top of his head. "Young lady, come over here," he said as he patted his lap. The rasping, deep timbre of his voice suggested displeasure. Father Wesley could understand why the children feared him.

"Go ahead," Father Wesley told her. "He's not going to bite you. Even if he does you have Shagtyme to bite him back."

"That's right," Jenna said, her fear repressed. "If I sit on his leg can Shagtyme be with me?"

"I don't see why not," Father Wesley told her.

As Jenna settled onto Father Coniglio's lap Shagtyme laid down and rested his head against the old priest's feet. Father Coniglio then began to explain the meaning of Thanksgiving to the young girl.

Mildred reentered the living room to announce that it was ten minutes until dinner. Upon spotting Jenna she said, "May I ask what's going on here?"

"You can," Father Wesley answered. "Set another plate. We have a guest."

Mildred developed a beaming smile on her face as she watched the child bobbing on Father Coniglio's leg. "I'll do it with pleasure," and she meant what she said.

Dinner was served promptly at two. There was the turkey and stuffing in addition to squash, green peas, potatoes, turnips and cranberry sauce. Father Coniglio carved the turkey and carefully prepared Jenna's plate. In a matter of minutes they had become fast friends. Jenna's eyes were agog with the amount of food before her; she had never seen anything like it at home. But before she ate— and she was famished—little Jenna insisted Shagtyme have a plate of his own. The dog was her best friend and she wanted him treated as fairly as she was being treated.

Father Coniglio tried to explain to her that Shagtyme was not fed real people's food. Jenna looked at Shagtyme's panting face, his tongue dangling from the side of his mouth, and replied, "Why not? He's real."

Father Coniglio shrugged his shoulders and looked over at Father Wesley. He was going to allow his younger associate to make the call. "Father, you're a big proponent of bending the rules. Do you mind if we give Shagtyme a treat?"

"I don't have a problem with it," Father Wesley responded.

"Then it's a done deal," Father Coniglio said, excitedly, in the direction of Jenna. "What shall we feed him?"

"The same as me," Jenna insisted.

"Okay," Father Coniglio said. "But I don't think he's going to eat it all."

"He will," Jenna tried to guarantee.

It turned out to be an enjoyable Thanksgiving dinner. Jenna ate frantically and soon became stuffed. Father Coniglio and Father Wesley also ate to their content and they both developed a laggard feeling.

Shagtyme did not disappoint Jenna. The German shepherd ate all which was placed before him, except for the cranberry sauce. Once the group was finished they had no room for dessert, at least for the time being. The apple pie with the vanilla ice cream topping was going to have to wait.

"Jenna, you look tired. Would you like to take a nap on the couch?" Father Wesley asked as he arose from the kitchen table.

"Would it be all right? I am tired."

"Then let's adjourn to the other room. The dishes can wait," he told her. "Jenna, you go stretch out on the couch and relax. I'll get a pillow and a blanket to make you more comfortable." Father Wesley then turned to speak to Father Coniglio. "I'll watch over her. Why don't you take a nap? You look as though the meal tired you out as well."

"You're not going to get an argument there," Father Coniglio let him know as he made with a large yawn to illustrate the point.

It didn't take long for the young girl and veteran priest to slip off into dreamland, and Shagtyme had joined them, sleeping in his usual spot on the living room carpet. In the meantime, Father Wesley took care of some of the cleanup work that otherwise was going to fall Mildred's way, who was returning at 8:30 that night.

Everything considered, it took the younger priest just over thirty minutes to tend to the housekeeping chores. Once he was finished he retired to the living room and dropped himself onto the easy chair. He, too, was tired but he felt compelled to stay awake. However, it was a futile attempt. He dozed off in about five minutes.

When he awakened he thought he had been asleep for about twenty minutes. But a quick glance at his watch told him differently. It was 5:30. He had slept for two hours.

He looked to the couch and saw that Jenna was gone and so was Shagtyme. Then he heard her giggling coming from the kitchen. She was there with Father Coniglio and they seemed to be having a grand time together. *So much for the scary priest theory.*

He was about to join them in the kitchen but then thought better of it. Jenna was bringing Father Coniglio out of his shell-like prison and Father Wesley did not want to tamper with the good she was bringing to St. Theresa's on this day. Little Jenna, in a single afternoon, had accomplished what the young curate had come to believe was impossible

—◊—

An hour later, as he promised in his note, George Napoli showed up at the rectory. Father Coniglio answered the door and when he saw Jenna's father his expression changed. It was back to the stern and distant grimace which had, somehow, become his trademark. But this was no act. The plight of Jenna had touched him. He asked George Napoli if he could see him alone in his office. There was a matter of importance they needed to discuss.

They spent twenty minutes together, behind a closed door, and in that short time span Father Coniglio found out everything he needed to know about George Napoli and his family. The old priest heard a somewhat familiar but, nonetheless, disturbing story that could be applied to many of St. Theresa's parishioners. Money was tight for George Napoli. Burgeoning medical and funeral costs surrounding his wife's illness and death had plunged him into a bottomless financial pit. He was a picture of a sad and broken man. He was lonely, with two kids to raise, and he was financially strapped. Life seemed to be running out of options for him. The mere fact he had to dispatch his daughter to spend a family holiday with the priests of St. Theresa's, while he worked, seemed to make his despair even greater. It was humiliating and George Napoli had once been a proud man. No longer did that seem to be the case.

Father Coniglio sympathized with what George Napoli had to say. But there was one thing that demanded an explanation. The priest needed to know why he had sent his daughter out without a proper coat to wear on such a chilly day. It was a matter which could not be overlooked because of a hard luck story.

George looked as though he were on the verge of tears. He disliked revealing the facts of his sad sack life to the priest but he had run out of hiding places to conceal his bad luck. He had no choice but to recognize the scorn of the priest who had to be thinking of him as an uncaring and unworthy parent. But it was not the case. It sickened him to tell the old priest this story but what choice did he have? The St. Theresa's pastor was demanding an explanation. George was going to give it to him no matter how humiliating it seemed.

George Napoli explained that Jenna had one winter coat and he didn't want her wearing it until the weather became truly cold. She had a tendency to wear out or rip her clothing before its time had come. Right now their situation was tougher than usual and he simply couldn't afford a play coat for her. He had instructed her to go straight to the rectory with the note he had given her. George Napoli had no idea his daughter was going to spend a good portion of the morning and afternoon playing in the front yard with the dog.

Father Coniglio nodded the fact he understood but it brought him to another question. Why hadn't he brought Jenna to the rectory himself, instead of sending her on her own?

Father Coniglio's litany of questions was beginning to put George on edge. He never thought his confab with the old priest was going to turn into an inquest. Talking about his inadequacies was not easy. In fact, it was downright embarrassing. But he had to give it a try. He didn't want the priest to be judging him unfairly.

It was pride, nothing more than stubborn male pride, he explained. It was belittling enough that he had to come here now and get her. Having to make two trips to the rectory in the same day would have been insufferable.

As he sat before him Father Coniglio noticed a beige, see through, plastic bag on George's lap. In the bag were two items, a quart of milk and a can of a generic brand of beef stew. The old priest figured the can of stew was meant to be Jenna's Thanksgiving dinner or supper. Thank God, he and Father Wesley had the chance to rectify what could have been a miscarriage of human dignity.

Father Coniglio opened the top drawer of his desk and took out an envelope. In it was cash. He counted its contents, which was seventy-one dollars, before sliding the envelope across his desk. It wasn't much but he wanted George to have it. He wanted George to buy some kind of coat for Jenna to play in.

"Please," he urged him. "Take it."

LEO F. WHITE

George Napoli placed his left hand on the envelope and slid it back towards Father Coniglio. George considered Father Coniglio's gesture an insult. It was bad enough that the old priest had forced him to spill his guts about his sorry plight in life but charity he could not accept. He would find a way to get Jenna a play coat. George Napoli admitted he didn't have much but he had not sunk to the depths of accepting handouts. He appreciated what the priests had done to see to it that his daughter had a decent Thanksgiving meal. But that was to be the extent of their generosity.

George Napoli stood and extended his right hand. He again thanked Father Coniglio for being so kind to his daughter. Father Coniglio shook his hand but as he did so he implored him to reconsider taking the money. But it wasn't going to happen. The man's pride had been severely bruised and he was not going to allow it to take any more of a battering.

Once George and Jenna left the rectory, Father Coniglio returned to the living room and sat on the sofa before burying his face in his hands. There was now no doubt in his mind that St. Theresa's was the poor people's parish but there was little he or Father Wesley could do to help their flock, since they had no money of their own. Despair was haunting Father Coniglio's tired old body.

Father Wesley entered the living room and sat in the easy chair and watched as the old priest wrestled with his despondency. After a minute he finally said, "Sad, isn't it?"

Father Coniglio raised his head and looked at his associate, his lower lip quivering as he spoke. "It's more than sad. It's downright pitiful. The people of this parish need our help and we have little to give. Then, again, I wonder how many of them would accept our help. I offered that man seventy-one dollars to buy his daughter a play coat but he refused to take it. His pride wouldn't allow it. I hate to admit it but maybe the cardinal should close down this parish and let St. Matthew's deal with them. Lord knows St. Matthew's could do a lot more for those people than St. Theresa's can."

"Don't talk like that," Father Wesley said, in a riled mood. "The people of this parish cannot afford St. Matthew's. I never thought I'd see the day when you'd talk in such abominable terms. You have fought for years to keep the doors of St. Theresa's open. Now, because of one

94

sad case, you are ready to pack it in. It's kind of late in life for you to start feeling sorry for yourself."

"Then what do you suggest?" Father Coniglio asked.

"Maybe George Napoli and some of the others will not accept the meager charity we can offer but there is someone they cannot turn their back on; lest they alienate their own children."

"And who, pray tell, is that?" Father Coniglio asked with a certain air of curiosity.

"Santa Claus!" Father Wesley stated, emphatically.

"Santa Claus?" Father Coniglio replied. "What in heaven's name are you talking about? Must I remind you that even Santa Claus needs a few bucks to get the job done? Money we don't have."

"I have an idea," Father Wesley went on. "Maybe it will work or maybe it won't but I'm willing to explore it."

"Just where do you expect to get this money? Not to mention should this idea of yours ever see the light of day we would inherit every child in Paine looking for a present. It's not practical. Then, again, what am I worried about. It'll never get off the ground."

"You never know unless you try," Father Wesley responded with a wry smile on his face. He was convinced he could bring it to fruition. "Now, if you'll excuse me, I have to take Shagtyme for his constitutional," he told the elder priest.

"Father, would you mind if I took Shagtyme for his walk? I think it's time your dog and I got to know one another. Also, I need to get out and stroll the streets of my parish." Father Coniglio seemed to be pleading.

"It's okay by me," Father Wesley answered.

As soon as Father Coniglio and Shagtyme left for their walk, Father Wesley rushed to his office and picked up the phone. This time he was going to enjoy making the phone call. He was going to weasel the cash out of the archdiocese. The phone rang three times before someone at the other end picked up.

"Father Moore's office. Father Cardillo speaking."

"Good evening, Father. This is Father Wesley. I'd like to speak to Father Moore."

"I'm sorry, Father, but both Father Moore and Cardinal Burke spent a good portion of the day traveling throughout the archdiocese tending to the needy. They are now having a late Thanksgiving dinner. Could I have him call you back?"

What a crock, Father Wesley thought. *Tending to the needy. I'll give them some needy.* "You tell Father Moore that Father Wesley of St. Theresa's in Paine is calling. Tell him it is urgent. I'm sure once he receives the message he'll make the time to take the call."

Father Cardillo put Father Wesley on hold and two minutes passed before Father Wesley heard the voice he detested.

"Father Wesley. This is Father Moore. Is there a problem? You're not going to tell me Father Coniglio choked on a drumstick, are you?"

"Very funny," Father Wesley answered, quite agitated by Father Moore's crude remark.

"So what's the problem that couldn't wait? Why the urgency?"

"St. Theresa's needs some help from the archdiocese."

"In what way?" Father Moore asked, leery of what he was going to hear.

"We need about $7,000."

"What?" Father Moore exclaimed.

"You heard me. St. Theresa's needs the cash and I expect the archdiocese to provide it."

"For what?" Father Moore couldn't believe what he was hearing.

"Father Coniglio and I would like to have a Christmas party for the children of the parish."

"Huh?"

"Are you hard of hearing or something? I said Father Coniglio and I—"

"I heard what you said. Let's make this perfectly clear. If you want to stage a little party then you go out and raise the money like any other church. We have avoided putting money into that losing proposition of a parish for years. We are not about to start by financing your little lark of goodwill."

"You would if this were St. Matthew's calling."

"But we are not talking about St. Matthew's, at least I'd know they'd be good for the money."

"I thought we were in the business of saving souls, not profiting from them."

"Father, you are testing my patience. Why can't you just raise the money? You certainly had the wherewithal to find the cash to fix the roof on that dump."

Father Moore had a way of saying something that could set Father Wesley off and he had just done so. "Father, I have some late breaking news for you. The money for the roof came from me. We just camouflaged it to look like a contribution so as to not upset Father Coniglio. By the way, don't ever call St. Theresa's a dump again."

"It was your money? That was kind of stupid of you."

"I knew I couldn't count on you for any help."

"And you can't count on any now, either. I'm not going to secure the funds for your holiday bash. That's it! Case closed!"

"Okay, Father, have it your way. But, let me ask you this: what do you think would happen if I were to have a slip of the tongue and revealed the deceitful act you and Cardinal Burke have devised for this impoverished parish? You have led the good parishioners of St. Theresa's down the primrose path, leading them to believe their little church is safe from the grim reaper the modern day Church has become. I've come to know the people of St. Theresa's and they'd be an angry lot if made aware of your intentions. I also think the archdiocese would get a rude awakening from the ugly publicity that might be generated. It's bad enough we have priests going around trying to plug little boys in the behind. Shall we also have them thinking that the Church also practices deceit on the people who trust and believe in it?"

"Father, you're part of that devious scheme you refer to, or have you forgotten? You'd be cutting your own throat."

"Father, I cut my throat when I was forced to take on this assignment. I just haven't started bleeding yet."

"Father, this is blackmail!"

"It is. But it's a lesser offense than the treason you and the cardinal are perpetrating on the good people of St. Theresa's."

Father Moore paused for what seemed like an eternity. Father Wesley had his fingers crossed hoping he had boxed him in. Finally, Father Moore was back on the line.

"Okay, Father, I'll see to it you get the money you need. However, I'm warning you, this is a one-time deal. I don't want you calling me back in a few months with some grandiose plan about an Easter egg hunt. Do we see eye-to-eye on it?"

"Gee, I never thought of an Easter egg hunt."

"Father, now it is you who is being funny. Do we have an agreement?"

"We do, Father. I don't mean to be pushy but when can we expect the money. I hope it will be sometime before Christmas Eve."

"You'll have it by next Wednesday. Happy Thanksgiving, Father, and I won't bother to wish you a Merry Christmas since you have taken it upon yourself to make sure you have one."

The conversation complete, Father Wesley sat back in his chair and folded his hands behind his head. "Boy, that felt good," he said to himself.

CHAPTER
ELEVEN

The two priests had a month to give the parishioners of St. Theresa's a Christmas to remember. Father Coniglio was ecstatic that Father Wesley had secured the funds needed to stage a Christmas party for the children but was mystified as to how his fellow priest managed to get the chancery to go along with it. He had been fighting with that body of the archdiocese for years over monetary matters with zero results. Now, along comes a priest, with just three years under his belt, who accomplishes what he had failed to do in the blink of an eye. It was confusing to Father Coniglio and if he were fifteen years younger, he might have delved into the matter to see what was going on. But the times were now different. No longer did he need to fight with the chancery. He knew his clock was running down and his days of battling were behind him. He now had Father Wesley to do his fighting for him.

What did matter to Father Coniglio was the newfound relationship he had developed with the children of the parish. He decided whatever time he had left would be devoted to them. Also, his contempt for the new curate the cardinal had sent his way no longer existed. He was adjusting to the fact that he could live out his remaining days in peace. Father Wesley was proving to be a very capable administrator for the day-to-day operation of the parish. He now appreciated the younger priest's help and realized the timing of his arrival at St. Theresa's could not have been better.

Father Wesley concocted a plan as to how the children's Christmas party should be conducted. He wanted each child in the parish to be registered to assure they received a gift. The party would be open to all but the gifts would be restricted to the children under the age of twelve. Five thousand dollars was set aside for the presents while the rest of the money went to feeding this brood. The party was to be held on the afternoon of December 24th between the hours of two and five. Since they had a limited budget, and expected a large delegation of people to participate, the church was going to be used as the site for the party. Had this been a month earlier Father Coniglio would never have allowed such an event to take place in his sacred church. But he was now a changed man. What now concerned him the most was that the children enjoyed their day.

Father Wesley also managed to raise some additional cash and gift donations from some of the merchants in the parish. He accomplished the task by pounding the pavement and knocking on doors. He was returning from one of these money raising efforts when he spotted what he thought could turn out to be a problem. It happened on the afternoon of December 21st.

Father Coniglio was in the front yard with twelve of the children and Shagtyme. The older priest had instructed Grimaldi to go to the rectory basement and bring out the Nativity scene. It had once been a traditional sight on the lawn of St. Theresa's during the Christmas season. But for the past five years Father Coniglio had chosen not to put the manger scene on display. He had lost his Christmas spirit but it had returned this year. The vivacity which now seemed to permeate St. Theresa's was proving to be contagious in this season of seasons. Father Coniglio was informing Grimaldi as to how he wanted the Holy Family setting to look. The children seemed to follow the old priest's cue and were bellowing demands of their own while Shagtyme barked incessantly.

It was an unusually warm afternoon for late December, the temperature nudging sixty. Father Wesley was walking along Everton Street when he saw Father Coniglio and the children. But he also saw something else, something which bothered him if the stories he had heard were to be believed. Across from the rectory sat two bikers resting on their motorcycles watching Father Coniglio and the children. They were a grisly looking pair. Their mere presence gave Father Wesley the impression they were looking for trouble.

The young priest opened the walkway gate and joined in the frivolity that abounded on the lawn. Yet, as he did so, he kept a careful eye on the troublesome looking duo watching from across the street. He had a strange feeling they were plotting to test his mettle. The warning Officer Kilcullen had given him on the beach was rattling around in his head. Since his return to St. Theresa's he had hoped the unruly bunch from the beach would not try to challenge him. But now he was fairly certain that they were preparing to do so.

As Father Wesley approached the group on the lawn, Shagtyme separated himself from the others and rushed to his master. The dog's eyes followed Father Wesley's as he kept an eye on the roguish pair across the street. Shagtyme seemed to sense his master's distress and raced over to the wrought iron fence. The dog was on his haunches, his front legs braced against the fence, barking at the nefarious looking twosome.

The pair seemed to share in a good laugh at Shagtyme's expense. The growing dog didn't scare them. In unison the duo turned the ignitions of the motorcycles and, after gunning the bikes and producing two large clouds of black exhaust, they rode away, continuing to laugh, defiantly. Father Wesley expected them to return and when they did he was going to be prepared for them.

Grimaldi came up from the rear and joined Father Wesley. "There's something I have to tell you," he said.

"If it's about the urinating on the shrubs I already know about it."

"You do? How did you find out?"

"I have my ways."

"They're up to something," Grimaldi said in a very concerned manner.

"Don't worry about them. If they return here with the intention of doing some damage then they'll have to answer to me," Father Wesley promised, his voice not lacking for conviction.

Grimaldi wondered if the priest meant he was going to use his fists to make his point. He couldn't imagine it happening but if it did he felt these punks from the beach deserved it.

—m—

Once the sun set, word spread rapidly throughout the neighborhood—thanks to Grimaldi—that those hellions from the beach were planning another act of defamation against the grounds of St. Theresa's. However, the news, this time, wasn't as unsettling as in the past. If they tried to deface the sacred property again they were going to have to deal with Father Wesley. The man who once ruled the beach with his fists was prepared to use them again, this time against those brutes who had replaced him on the shores of Paine Beach. Or so the rumor went.

Once dinner was complete Father Wesley excused himself from the table and went to the basement of the rectory. It was the first time he had been in the cellar, so finding what he was looking for was going to take some time.

In a corner of the basement was a work area which Grimaldi kept. Once the prelate spotted this location he knew his search was nearly complete. Hanging from the wall, and leaning against it, was an assortment of shovels, rakes and garden hoes. On the floor was what he wanted. It was the garden hose. Grimaldi had placed it neatly on the basement floor. All Father Wesley had to do was pick it up and sling it over his shoulder.

He ran his hands along a pipe and it brought him to a valve. Grimaldi had closed it for the winter. Father Wesley opened it. Now he was ready to do battle.

The priest exited the basement and walked around to the front of the rectory. Fumbling through the shrubs he found the spigot he needed and attached the hose. Then he opened the outside valve. Now it was a waiting game.

Father Coniglio went to bed at nine. Fifteen minutes later Father Wesley shut off all the lights in the rectory. He wanted to give the appearance that the two priests had retired for the night. In the dark he sat, in the living room, and bided his time.

The hours seemed to drag on and Father Wesley began to wonder if he had been wrong in anticipating trouble on this night. He prayed it was the case. But there was one thing he was not going to do. He was not going to abandon his watch. Considering the warm weather, and the forecast for much colder temperatures, then this had to be the night they would strike.

It was just after two in the morning. Father Wesley had dozed off in the easy chair, while Shagtyme was sleeping on the rug in the center of the living room. At the moment it was a peaceful setting, one of nocturnal bliss. Then came the roar of howling engines to interrupt the early morning calm. Motorcycle engines!

Shagtyme was the first to detect their coming. His head jerked up and his ears became erect. A growl soon followed and it awakened the curate. As he raised himself and walked over to the window Shagtyme sat up. The dog sensed trouble.

Father Wesley stood in the shadows and peeked through the window curtains. Four motorcycles came to a halt in front of the rectory. On each bike rode a male with a female companion clutching to him. Father Wesley remained by the window and watched as one of the bikers dismounted and walked over and kicked open the walkway gate. The leather clad misfit made his way to the Nativity scene. It was the prelate's cue. Father Wesley patted Shagtyme on the head and said, "You're staying here," as he rushed to the kitchen and went out the back door.

As the rogue from the beach approached the Nativity setting, Father Wesley was making his way to the corner of the building, still out of sight. He stood in the dark, waiting for the sacrilegious moment to occur. He didn't have to wait long.

The other three bikers dismounted their motorcycles and hurdled the fence to join their friend. It was obvious to Father Wesley they were all inebriated. As if it were staged they all unzipped their flies in unison and began urinating on the Nativity scene.

"Hey," one of them shouted, "it's raining over Bethlehem."

It was then the foursome received a wet welcome. Father Wesley turned the hose on and let the surly group have it. The jetting water hit the unsuspecting miscreants in the face and then the priest turned the garden hose on their exposed genitals. "You're right," he shouted, "and now it's turned into a monsoon."

As the priest was hosing down the four heathens from hell a fifth motorcycle came cruising up the street from the direction of the beach. Its rumbling sounds escaped Father Wesley and the four soggy conspirators. The combatants on the front lawn had just one thing on their mind, and that was to even the score with this foolhardy priest. Father Wesley, on the other hand, was taking great delight in the humbling lesson he was imparting on these four reprobates.

"You son of a bitch," one of them yelled. "Priest or no priest, I'm going to give you a beatin' you'll never forget."

"Oh yeah," Father Wesley shouted back. "Let's see about that. You wanted to test me and you did. You know I'm not going to back down so why don't you just get the hell out of here while you can."

One of them grunted and rushed the priest. He threw a right and Father Wesley caught it with his left forearm and then slammed his knee into the man's testicles. A pained expression came to the biker's face and he grabbed hold of his groin and fell to his knees. As he was going down Father Wesley caught him by the throat and pushed him so he landed on his back, writhing in pain.

"Who's next?" Father Wesley demanded to know.

"No one," a raspy voice lashed out.

Father Wesley turned to his left to see who was about to join the fray. The face he knew but the rest of the anatomy didn't match what he remembered. The man's hair was a mussed and tangled knot of gray. The unsavory individual also sported a rather prodigious belly, obviously the end result of many years of pounding down the beers.

"Hello, Father," he said. "Do you remember me? I warned these clowns what would happen if they crossed you. They didn't want to listen so I decided to let them find out for themselves." He looked at the four drenched victims of Father Wesley's wrath. "And I can see they have."

"Bryan?" Father Wesley asked, as if unsure as to who was speaking to him.

"That's right. You've changed, Father."

"And so have you," Father Wesley observed as he took note of the heavy paunch and the long hair.

As they were awkwardly renewing their acquaintances a squad car came racing down the street from the direction of the beach and came to a screeching halt in front of the rectory. Officer Kilcullen, who was working the overnight shift, emerged from it with a rewarding smile on his face. He never thought these rogues would test Father Wesley but they had and he was glad to be here to apprehend them.

He walked slowly to the group, intending to enjoy the moment. "Well, guys," he began, "it looks like you bit off a little too much this time. How do you want to handle the situation?" he asked the priest.

"You don't have to get involved in this, Kilcullen," Bryan Fogarty said.

"I wasn't talking to you, Fogarty. I'm talking to the Father. So keep your mouth shut."

"You get your rocks off on something like this, don't you?" Fogarty replied.

"I told you to keep your mouth shut."

"Gentlemen, gentlemen," Father Wesley had to intervene. "Let's allow our better judgment to prevail here."

"Okay, Father, why don't you tell me what these creeps did, as if I didn't know."

"Hey, what about us?" one of the bikers protested. "We have rights too."

"That's right," one of the female companions called out. "The priest nailed Scottie right in the nads."

"I want you all to shut up! I'm talking to the priest," Kilcullen uttered again.

"Officer, these gentlemen here mistook our Nativity scene for a restroom. I don't think it's necessary to press charges against them. I think they learned their lesson."

"You've got to be kiddin' me." Officer Kilcullen was disappointed to hear what the priest had to say. "Father, I urge you to reconsider. Let them get their just due." The police officer seemed to be making a plea.

"Wait a minute," one of the bikers said. "If you want us to get our just due, then what about him? He kneed me right in the family jewels, and he's a priest!"

"Shut up, Scottie. I think the Father is trying to do you a favor," Fogarty told his fellow biker.

"So you think repentance is in order?" Father Wesley asked Officer Kilcullen.

"I do, Father."

"Then, maybe, there is something I can ask of them." Father Wesley then looked at Fogarty. "Bryan, can I talk to you for a moment?"

"Certainly."

The priest and burly biker separated themselves from the others. "Bryan, I saw Sharon Beasley recently and she led me to believe that you are sort of the leader of that undisciplined bunch down on the beach. If that's true maybe you can help me out."

"How?"

"We're having a Christmas party for the children of the parish on Christmas Eve. We could use some help with the cleanup work that's going to be necessary once it's over."

"And you want this motley crew here to do the job?"

"Yes. Let's call it community service."

"It also beats going to court on an indecent exposure or urinating in public charge, Kilcullen is ready to pitch their way. Sure, why not. Father, consider it done. They should count their lucky stars that you are being so understanding."

"That's good. Now, while I have your attention, I have something to ask of you."

"What's that?"

Father Wesley placed his hands on Fogarty's large belly. "Bryan, I need a Santa Claus. I think you'd be perfect."

"Oh, come on, you don't need me. Can't you find someone else? I'd scare those kids."

"I disagree. I think you'd be a natural. You'd be doing me a tremendous favor if you did agree to do it. You know, one friend doing a favor for another."

"You're not going to let me go until I agree to do it, are you?"

"I'm doing my damn best, right now."

Bryan took a deep breath and then let out an exasperated sigh. "All right. I have to wonder, though, what this will do to my image."

"It might get you into heaven."

Fogarty smiled. "That would mean canceling my standing reservation in hell."

Bryan's remark brought a laugh from Father Wesley. Grateful, he slapped his old friend on the back and hailed Officer Kilcullen to join them. "Officer, we have come to a compromise," he said as the policeman was approaching.

"Oh, I bet you have," Kilcullen said.

Father Wesley put his arm around Fogarty. "Bryan and the boys are going to help us out at the children's Christmas party."

Officer Kilcullen rolled his eyes skyward in disbelief. "I don't think they'll show," he said.

"They'll show and so will I," Fogarty promised.

"I'll believe it when I see it," Kilcullen replied, still convinced they would be no shows.

While the three men conversed the front door of the rectory opened and a sleepy eyed Father Coniglio poked his head out. "What's going on out here?" he asked in a weary voice. "You're making enough of a ruckus to wake the dead."

"It's nothing, Father. You can go back to bed," Father Wesley assured the older priest.

"Yeah, he's just gaining some new recruits for your church," Kilcullen added.

"Yeah, sure," Father Coniglio answered before closing the door and returning to his room. He wasn't going to worry about whatever had taken place on the lawn of St. Theresa's. He didn't have to; he now had Father Wesley to handle such matters. He went back to bed with a satisfied feeling about the future of his little church and its parish.

CHAPTER
TWELVE

On the afternoon of Christmas Eve, 152 children between the ages of seven and twelve. accompanied by either a parent or guardian, filled the church. The tiny house of worship hadn't seen this kind of numbers in years.

In the vestibule, tables had been set up to accommodate the food and there was an abundance of it. Thirty boxes of pizzas plus ham, turkey, roast beef, cheeses and three different kinds of salads adorned the tables. There was coffee and hot cider for the adults and ice cream, hot chocolate and fruit drinks for the children. Mildred and three other women from the parish were handling the serving of the food. One of those women was Maria Castleman.

Scottie, Eric, Tony and Mike—the bikers who had confronted Father Wesley and lost—were doing their act of contrition by helping out the women and removing the trash which was accumulating, at a rapid pace, from the premises. On this day they did not display the evil traits that was a part of their daily regimen.

Bryan Fogarty would prove to be a big hit as Santa Claus. He didn't want to admit it but he was enjoying himself, as were the children. He, too, for a change, felt as though he were doing something good with his life. He played the role of Santa Claus to perfection and the children reveled in his presence.

Grimaldi had taken the big black chair from Father Coniglio's bedroom and placed it at the front of the center aisle. Behind it was a large twelve foot high Christmas tree which was decorated to the fullest. The tree had been a gift from Fogarty and the boys and Father Wesley was not about to ask where it had come from, since it was delivered in the darkness of the night a day earlier. If it had been attained the way he thought, then it was one indiscretion Father Wesley was willing to let slide.

The registration cards proved to be a prudent decision, guaranteeing each child a gift. Each gift had a number on it which corresponded with the number that had been issued to each child. The presents were not ostentatious matter. The gifts were small articles such as stuffed animals, games or clothing and each present was wrapped so every child could experience the element of surprise. Bryan Fogarty was to reach into a bag and pull out the corresponding card and call out the child's name. One by one the children were to come forward and Fogarty would pass the numbered card to Father Coniglio, who was serving as Santa Claus's assistant, and he would hand the child his or her present. It seemed foolproof. So foolproof that Father Wesley had placed an additional twenty gifts in the church sacristy should some stragglers, who had failed to register, showed up. The priests of St. Theresa's were going to make certain that none of the youngsters from their forlorn parish were overlooked on this day.

As the gift giving segment of the party was about to begin Father Wesley gave Fogarty a card. He informed him this was to be the final gift handed out. Bryan took the card and placed it inside the big black glove on his left hand.

Father Coniglio was serving as Santa Claus's warm up act and he seemed to be enjoying himself. He was very animated as he told the parish children Christmas stories. As he was doing his act Father Wesley slipped in the side door and made his way to the back of the church.

Father Coniglio was in the middle of a story when he cupped his right ear. "Do you hear what I hear?" he asked.

"No," the children screamed out in unison.

"Well, listen a little more closely," he told his young audience. "I think he's here."

That was Fogarty's cue to come through the side door and as he did so he was bellowing out a mighty, "Ho, ho, ho," to the children's delight. The sad and sorrowful times which St. Theresa's had known was now officially over. The place was alive with vitality.

Father Wesley was watching as the name of each child was being called when he felt a tap on his shoulder. He turned and looked straight into the eyes of Maria Castleman. "This is really something special you have put together for these children," she said.

"Thank you," he responded. He couldn't think of any other words to say.

"You know there was a time when I was very bitter towards you and…I guess…God." Maria was getting right to it.

"I think I understand," Father Wesley said in a struggling manner.

"No, you don't. Sure, I was angry at you because of Billy's death. But what really made me bitter was that you were allowed to survive. It didn't seem fair."

The painful reminder as to why they made that fateful excursion into Boston came back to haunt him. *Damn that Ruth Ann.*

"Over the years the bitterness I had built up began to fade and when I heard you had become a priest I knew I couldn't carry that grudge any longer. But when you were transferred here I felt as though God were testing me. You were to be that everyday reminder that Billy had died and you had lived. Now I look around and see what you have done. I think I now know why you were spared. You're good for this parish and I am so ashamed of the ill feelings I harbored towards you."

Maria began to sob and Father Wesley put his arm around her, hoping to provide some comfort. Then another thought entered his head: *Damn that Father Moore and the cardinal.*

The children's roll call reached 111 when Frankie Napoli's name was called. The boy was sitting in the next to last pew with his sister and their father. He rushed up the aisle and took his gift from Father Coniglio. He then hurried back to the pew, eager to see what it was. He tore the wrapping paper off and seemed disappointed when he discovered it was a pair of gloves. "Be grateful," his father told him.

Jenna did not say a word as she watched her brother unwrap his gift. She was beginning to worry. She tugged on her father's arm and he leaned over to hear what she had to say. "I think they might have forgotten me," she whispered in his ear.

"Don't be ridiculous," he informed her, hoping he was right in what he said. "Santa Claus doesn't forget anyone."

There was one gift left when Santa Claus stood and roared out another, "Ho, ho, ho. One present to go and it's a big one."

Jenna, sitting in the pew, had her fingers and short legs crossed, hoping and praying this gift was hers. "Please, God, please. Let it be me," she mumbled.

"This present belongs to Jenna Napoli," Santa Fogarty shouted out.

"Yes!" Jenna cried out, her arms upright in the air. She sprinted down the center aisle of the church and took the present from Father Coniglio and made another mad dash back to the pew where her brother and father were sitting, cradling the big box as tight as she was able. She sat at the end of the pew and tore off the wrapping paper. As she hurriedly opened the box she said, "What do you think it is, Daddy?"

"I don't know," George Napoli answered.

"Daddy, it's a coat. It's pretty and it looks warm."

"It certainly does," he replied as he glared over at Father Wesley who was standing a mere thirty feet away.

The coat was an expensive red and white ski parka. George Napoli wasn't sure if he should be angry or grateful to Father Wesley and Father Coniglio for their largesse. He looked down on charity but he also knew he could not afford this coat which his daughter needed. He considered what had taken place to be well-disguised charity on the part of the two priests but a gesture of goodwill. He was going to have to accept it. This was, after all, a gift from Santa Claus. He could live with it.

CHAPTER

THIRTEEN

Spring was about and it was moving into mid-May. It was proving to be an extraordinary season, each day seeming to be more elegant and picturesque than the day before. In New England it was unusual for spring to make such an orderly march towards summer.

At St. Theresa's a progression of a different nature was taking place. Shagtyme was nearly a year old and he had grown into a stout dog, weighing nearly 100 pounds. The children still stopped by on their way to and from school to spend some time with the animal. Father Wesley had only one rule: they were not to feed him. Shagtyme was still a growing dog and Father Wesley did not want him turning into an obese one. It was thanks to the children's involvement with Shagtyme that Father Wesley was able to spot a problem and address it.

The group of children that usually stopped to play with the dog were Frankie and Jenna Napoli, Billy Molinaro, Gerry McDonald and Phu Luong. Father Wesley watched them every morning and afternoon from the rectory window.

Phu Luong, Father Coniglio's favorite altar boy, was Vietnamese and was now at an age that could prove to be difficult. As he turned eleven he had grown quite tall at five-foot-ten. He was also a very intelligent young man with the kind of mind that was always seeking answers and trying to learn as much as he could about life. He had an endearing personality and was difficult to dislike; unless you were prejudicial. Unfortunately, racial umbrage still thrived on the streets surrounding St. Theresa's.

It was a Wednesday afternoon when Father Wesley noticed Phu Luong's left eye was swollen, as if he had been in a fight. On Thursday Phu Luong had a large gauze bandage on his right cheek. On Friday morning Father Wesley did not see Phu Luong with the other children as they made their way to school. Yet in the afternoon he was in their group as they returned from school and his trousers were ripped on the left leg by the kneecap. Father Wesley had to get to the bottom of this matter before it was too late. He knew there was a problem concerning the young boy.

The door to Father Coniglio's office was open and Father Wesley charged in. The older priest was sitting at his desk frantically searching through the drawers for something. Father Wesley sat in a chair and said, "Father, can we talk?" His voice sounded distressed.

"Sure. Damn! Why is it I can never find anything when I need it?"

"What are you looking for?"

"Some paper clips."

"I have a box in my office. You can have them."

"Thanks," Father Coniglio responded. He stopped his frantic search and settled down to have his talk with Father Wesley. "Now, what is bothering you?" he asked.

Father Wesley leaned forward and placed his elbows on his knees. "It's Phu Luong. I think he's in some sort of trouble."

"Trouble? That kid? You've got to be kidding me. He's like an angel. Keeps telling me he wants to be a priest when he's older."

Father Wesley edged forward so that he was sitting on the edge of the chair. "I don't mean he is starting trouble. I think someone is providing trouble for him. I think he is being bullied."

"I see," Father Coniglio uttered as he leaned back in his chair. "Always feared this day might come. What brings you to the conclusion he is being intimidated?"

"Father, I'm not talking about intimidation. I'm talking about physical abuse."

"What?"

"Father, twice this week I've seen him battered and bruised. This morning he did not go to school with the other children yet he returned with them this afternoon, his pants torn."

"Let's don't be rash about this. Perhaps he was running late this morning," Father Coniglio tried to rationalize.

Father Wesley stood up. "Father, I'm not looking for easy answers. If there is a problem I want to get to the core of it. You know the kid better than I do. How's his home life? Maybe that's where the problem is?"

Father Coniglio shook his head. "You can forget that one. He lives with his mother. The father disappeared years ago, a real deadbeat. She gets aid from the state but also cleans houses whenever she can to earn some extra cash. She lives for that kid and makes sure his education comes first."

"So it leads me to believe that there are some brutes out there laying the muscle on him," Father Wesley explained in a frustrated manner.

"Father, relax for a minute. This is a very multi-ethnic laden community and with strong ethnic cultures comes prejudice. Paine has been forced to open its doors to an outside way of life and, unfortunately, a segment of the population has not responded favorably to it. Until now Phu Luong has been insulated from discrimination. But now that he's getting older he becomes easy prey. I'll talk to him and his mother to see what's going on."

"And I'll talk to Kilcullen," Father Wesley was quick to say. "Maybe if the cops were aware of what was happening they'd help."

Father Coniglio waved his right hand in a negative fashion. "I wouldn't look for much help from them. Unless the child is taking a savage beating they'll look the other way."

"What about the teachers? I'll talk to them," Father Wesley said, somewhat exasperated.

"Don't count on much help there either. Those teachers do what they have to do. If it happens on school grounds then they'll try to tend to the matter. If not…then what can I tell you."

"This is insane. What does it take?" Father Wesley demanded to know.

"Do you want an aphorism or reality?" Father Coniglio asked him.

"I'll settle for reality," Father Wesley responded.

"It's the weekend so allow me to talk to Phu Luong and his mother. Come Monday we'll know how to address the situation." Father Coniglio seemed confident he could resolve this issue on his own.

"Do what you want, Father. But come Monday morning those teachers are going to hear what I have to say. I am not going to stand by, idly, as Phu Luong becomes just another forgotten mishap in another forgotten story because he happens to be Vietnamese. Pretty soon his own kind will take up his cause without even knowing him. He'll give them a reason to organize. That's how gangs are started. That is how dissension can rip a community apart."

Father Coniglio now seemed quite alert and curious. "You seem to know what you are talking about?"

"I do. I've seen it and I don't want to see it again." It wasn't necessary for Father Wesley to expound upon the fact that he had once been part of the problem.

"Then you do what you think is right and I'll do what I think is right." The older priest knew his young assistant still had some purging to do.

—⁓—

An hour or so later Father Wesley went outside. He was trying to put the Phu Luong problem aside until Monday. Right now he intended to take Shagtyme for a walk but Jenna was in the front yard playing with the dog so his walk was going to have to wait.

He sat down on the front steps of the rectory, his mind in a twisted web, when he heard a voice. It was Frankie Napoli calling out for his sister to come home. He was standing in front of the church. "C'mon, Jenna, don't make me come and get you."

"I'm coming, I'm coming," she shouted back in her brother's direction. She returned her attention to the dog and said, "Now, Shagtyme, you be a good dog. I'll see you later."

The sight of Frankie gave Father Wesley a thought. "Jenna, why don't you continue playing with Shagtyme a little longer. I want to talk to your brother for a minute."

"Okay," Jenna let the priest know.

Father Wesley strolled over to the front gate. Maybe the answers he was looking for were closer at hand than he realized. He motioned with his right hand for Frankie to come over by the gate. "Frankie, can you come over here? I need to talk to you about something."

"Sure, Father," Frankie called out as he came sprinting towards him. "What is it, Father?"

Father Wesley put his right arm around the boy. "Frankie, do you know what it means to be a friend?" he asked the youngster.

"I think so. Why are you asking me that?"

"I have a question to ask you and it concerns one of your friends."

A crestfallen look came over Frankie's face and he seemed to stiffen up. "Are you talking about Phu Luong?" the boy asked.

"I am. You don't have a problem with that, do you?"

"Father, Phu Luong told us not to say anything about it. He says he can handle it."

"Handle what?" Father Wesley asked.

"I shouldn't say."

"Frankie, I understand. Phu Luong is proving to be a courageous and honorable young man. But sometimes such strong virtues as courage and honor can prove to be a person's undoing. I don't want you thinking you'd be betraying Phu Luong's trust. Friends help friends. They don't stand idly by and do nothing. Do you understand what I'm saying?"

"I think so."

"Do you want to help Phu Luong?"

"I do. I don't like what's happening to him."

"So why don't you tell me what is happening to him so I can try and do something about it."

"Ah…Father," he began with a trace of hesitation. "They beat him up and call him names."

"They?"

"Yeah, a couple of kids that go to high school. I think their names are Freddy and Danny."

"Is it just Phu Luong they bother?"

"Yeah, they want his money."

"What money?"

"His lunch money."

"Okay, let's go back to the beginning. When did this all start?"

"On Monday."

"What happened on Monday?"

"They stopped Phu Luong and told him to give them his money. He said 'No,' so one of them held him while the other one took the money out of his pocket."

"What happened on Tuesday?"

"The same thing."

"Wednesday?"

"On Wednesday he didn't take any money with him. He took a lunch. These kids got real mad when he didn't have any money so they beat him up and took his lunch and threw it in the street."

That explains the swollen eye, Father Wesley deduced. "All right. What happened yesterday?"

"He didn't bring a lunch or money so those guys took a lit cigarette and put it out in his face."

Father Wesley winced with displeasure at Frankie's account. "What about today? He didn't go to school with the rest of you but he did come home with your group and his pants were torn."

"That's because he went to school through the backyards and across the railroad tracks. That way they wouldn't see him. He tore his pants climbing a fence."

Father Wesley was now burning with anger. A good kid like Phu Luong was being tortured by these punks because of nothing more than his culture. Also the fact he had been forced to cross the railroad tracks disturbed the priest. There was a commuter train which roared under Everton Street every morning around eight and you couldn't hear it until it was just about on top of you. Phu Luong could have been killed.

"Okay, Frankie, just a few more questions. When they burned his face with the cigarette who bandaged it?"

"The school nurse."

"So the teachers were aware that Phu Luong was being harassed?"

117

"I guess so."

"And have they tried to do anything about it?"

"I don't think so."

Wasn't that interesting, Father Wesley mused. He intended to be at the school bright and early Monday morning and settle this matter with the teachers. Then he was going to take care of the two bullies who were making Phu Luong's life pure misery.

"Frankie, one more thing. You said this Freddy and Danny called Phu Luong some names. What kind of names?"

"They call him a *gook* and *zipper eyes*."

"Okay, you've told me all I need to know. You and Jenna can go home now."

"Father, will you be able to help Phu Luong?"

"My little friend, you can count on it."

———※———

Father Coniglio extracted the same story from Phu Luong and his mother. The young man was embarrassed to tell his tale of woe but in a way he was thankful and felt safe thanks to the concern of the priests. There was not going to be any more trouble, Father Coniglio assured him. Father Wesley was going to meet with the teachers on Monday and see to it that he was not harassed any longer. It was safe for Phu Luong to go to school with the other children.

———※———

The Lincoln School was located on Everton Street, about a quarter of a mile from St. Theresa's to the west and a quarter of a mile from St. Matthew's to the east. It was an old two-story brick building. In front of the aging edifice was a schoolyard which abutted the street. Father Wesley was familiar with the building since he attended the school as a child. He was also familiar with the layout of the principal's office, which was where he was headed on this morning.

The office was on the ground level and had an excellent view of the schoolyard. On the opposite side of the street was the bus stop where

Phu Luong had been antagonized the previous week. It was a clear view from the principal's office. It led Father Wesley to believe he was going to be asked to swallow a lot of fluff because of the teachers' myopia.

The principal was a tall, pencil thin, gentleman of about fifty by the name of Henry Coleman. He had been on the job for three years. He greeted Father Wesley enthusiastically, seemingly anxious to find out what was on the priest's mind. The principal's demeanor had Father Wesley thinking this was nothing more than a façade. The teaching staff at the Lincoln School knew what was going on; they just didn't have what it took to take care of the matter. Right then, Father Wesley knew this experience was going to be difficult.

The priest skipped the small talk and moved on to the reason he was here. He wanted to know why the teachers did not come to Phu Luong's aid when he was being physically assaulted. What the young man was going through defied human civility.

Henry Coleman tried to play a somewhat dumb role, claiming the teachers were not aware of the problem involving Phu Luong and his being assaulted. The man's verbal tap dance around the issue at hand irritated Father Wesley. He had no intention of sitting in this room and listening to his excuses for his staff's lack of awareness to what was happening to Phu Luong..

Phu Luong had been accosted four days in a row in front of his window and the principal had seen nothing? This was just a little too much for Father Wesley to accept. Phu Luong would do his best to hide the truth but he would never lie. Each word Henry Coleman uttered led Father Wesley to believe there was an underlying reason for the teachers looking the other way.

The priest started with a very sensitive question: did the staff's lack of involvement have anything to do with the young man's nationality?

Father Wesley made a direct hit on the nerve he was looking to attack. Henry Coleman became visibly upset with the priest's question. Who was he to march into his school and accuse his staff of bigotry? If Father Wesley wanted to hear the truth of the matter then he had better be ready to accept what the principal had to say, whether he liked it or not.

Henry Coleman claimed his teachers were restricted in what they could do. The students had to be on school grounds for them to intercede. Their hands were tied by the teachers' association which demanded they adhere to such policy. He then educated Father Wesley on some recent history concerning the Lincoln School. Sixteen months earlier one of the teachers had been stabbed in the street attempting to break up an altercation which took place outside the school. The children of today were trying to grow up fast and a certain segment of them showed their so-called independence through violent behavior. Most teachers were now leery of doing anything to break up a fight. They would make the necessary call to the police and let them handle the matter, but they were reluctant to do anything that might put their own lives in jeopardy.

Father Wesley stood up and walked over to the window and stared out at the street. What the Lincoln School principal was telling him was not sitting well. He could understand the teachers' reluctance to interfere if they felt in danger of being harmed. The balance of order had been disrupted. It had come to the point where the inmates were running the asylum.

As he continued to stare out the window he noticed two teenagers standing at the bus stop. They had that *wiseass* look about them. Father Wesley was willing to bet those two were the agitators wreaking havoc in Phu Luong's life.

Father Coniglio was exiting the church when he took notice of the group of children passing by on their way to school. It was good to see Phu Luong in their ranks. He knew the young man was ready to stand up to the discrimination being flaunted in his direction. It was also comforting to the old priest to know that the young man would reach his destination without incident since Father Wesley was waiting at the other end.

As the group moved on, Father Coniglio went into the front yard and unleashed Shagtyme. There were threatening clouds in the sky and the forecast had been for rain. It was his intention to take Shagtyme inside. It was Shagtyme's intention to stay outside. The dog broke loose from Father Coniglio and went chasing after the children.

———◆———

Father Wesley continued to watch the two teens. He was waiting for them to make a move—any move—that would allow him to take matters into his own hands. These two kids did not scare him. However, the priest had to be precise in his thinking. He was not going to allow them to have a second of an advantage.

One of them glanced to the left and as he did so, he took a cigarette from his shirt pocket and lit it. Father Wesley turned to see what the boy was looking at. It was Phu Luong and the other children, heading right in the direction of trouble. They were about 150 feet from the two teenagers when Father Wesley turned to make a hasty exit. Before doing so he told Henry Coleman, "Why don't you stay here and watch. I'm going to do what you don't have the guts to do."

As Father Wesley ran from the office the school principal moved over to the window. "Oh my God," he stammered as he peered out at the street. He quickly turned, picked up the phone on his desk and dialed 911.

———◆———

Father Wesley rushed through the front door of the school. He was not going to do anything until the pair initiated their act of street terror. He then noticed he might not get the chance to manhandle the two thugs. He now saw Shagtyme coming up behind the children.

"Hey, egg foo young, we missed you last Friday," the one with the lit cigarette said when he noticed Shagtyme nudge himself between Phu Luong and Billy Molinaro. The kid with the cigarette backed up two steps, fearful of the large dog.

The other one stepped forward. "What's wrong with you?" he admonished his cohort. He pulled an object from his back pocket and pressed his thumb against it and a blade appeared. He waved the switchblade in a defiant manner. "It's only a dog. I can silence that mutt in a heartbeat."

"Don't you hurt Shagtyme," Jenna said as she stepped forward, willing to defend the dog with her life.

The cocky teen leaned over and pointed the knife at Jenna. "Then, little girl, tell your doggy friend to—." He didn't have a chance to finish what he was saying. You didn't point a knife in front of Jenna without antagonizing the dog.

Shagtyme rushed the knife wielder and knocked him backwards, into a chain link fence. The teen careened off the fence and fell, still clutching the knife. He tried to bring his hand up to stab the dog but Shagtyme was too quick. In a fraction of a second, Shagtyme had the assailant's wrist in his mouth, ready to dig his teeth into it.

"Enough, Shagtyme," the voice ordered. Hearing the command, the dog released the young man's wrist. As he did so Father Wesley's foot replaced the dog's mouth and he pressed the punk's wrist and hand against the sidewalk. "Let go of the knife," the priest demanded.

The teenager, stunned by what had occurred, did as he was told. "Now, get up," Father Wesley ordered. He was hot under the collar. He looked at the other kid and said, "Get rid of the cigarette or maybe you'd like me to put it out in your face." The kid's hand was shaking as he took the butt from his mouth and dropped it on the ground. This priest sure wasn't acting like a man of the cloth. The clergyman scared him.

Father Wesley grabbed the kid who had drawn the knife by the collar and asked, "What's your name?"

"Danny, Danny Corrigan. Did you see what the dog did to me? I'm going to see to it that the little girl's dog is gassed."

Father Wesley squeezed the kid's collar tighter. "Is that right? The dog happens to be mine. Now let's forget about the dog for a minute. What do you think is going to happen to you for pulling a knife on defenseless children?"

A squad car pulled up in front of the school and two of Paine's finest emerged from the vehicle. The two cops sprinted across the street and the older looking one called out, "What's going on here, Father?"

Father Wesley did not bother to look at the inquisitive approaching police officer. Instead, he smiled at Corrigan's obstinate face. "It seems these two gentlemen have been terrorizing these children for a week. Today they went too far and pulled a knife on them."

"That's a lie," Corrigan screamed. "The dog attacked me. I pulled the knife to protect myself."

"Oh, I see," the officer replied. "So you're trying to tell me the priest is lying."

"That's right."

"What's your name?" the cop asked.

"Danny Corrigan."

"And what's your name?" he asked the other teen.

"Freddy Brandt."

"Are you related to the attorney, Jerry Brandt?"

"He's my father."

"Then you'll have good legal counsel."

"That's right."

"Let me ask you this, Freddy. Do you agree with what your buddy here has to say?"

"Ah…yeah."

The officer looked wearily at Father Wesley. "Father, let's hear what you have to offer."

"Gladly." He took Phu Luong by the hand and separated him from the other children. "This young man, Phu Luong, has been the subject of both physical and verbal abuse from this pair for the last week. They have robbed him, beat him, and snuffed out a cigarette on his cheek. He has been forced to endure racist slurs such as *gook* and *zipper eyes*."

The officer looked at Phu Luong. "Son, is this true?"

Phu Luong looked at Father Wesley, unsure if he should answer the question, fearing some future reprisals. "Go ahead," Father Wesley told him. "Don't be afraid."

Phu Luong looked back at the police officer. "Yes, it is," he answered.

The officer returned his line of questioning to Father Wesley. "What about the dog? Did he attack him the way Corrigan says he did?"

"No," Father Wesley answered, sternly. "He pulled the knife out when he saw the dog. The dog attacked when he pointed the knife at the little girl." Father Wesley placed his right arm around Jenna as he backed away from the two teens.

"Does she own the dog?"

"No, I do. But she and the dog are very close. If your intention is to hurt her then you'll have to deal with the dog first."

"I see. Father, I'm going to leave this up to you. Do you want to press charges against these two?"

"No. I'm going to show some compassion this one-time. Let this serve as a warning. But if they continue to harass these children then I'm going to come down on them like a hammer on a nail."

"Well, I'm not going to be so soft," Corrigan shouted so all could hear. "That dog attacked me and I want him put down."

"You do," the officer replied. "Father, you can always reconsider. You know, I'd like to go through their pockets. God only knows what I might find," The officer turned his head back towards Corrigan, a sly grin gracing his face.

"All right, all right. Skip the charges against the dog."

"Good thinking, Corrigan," the cop said. "Now let me tell you something. If I hear of another complaint like this or of any kind of wrongdoing against Phu Luong I'm coming after you. Are you receiving my message? By the way, give me the knife."

"Yeah, yeah," Corrigan answered, still trying to act surly.

"Okay. Murph, let's get out of here," he said to his fellow officer.

The younger string bean of a cop, who had not spoken a word, came up to Father Wesley and handed him a piece of paper. "What's this?" the priest asked.

"A citation," the young cop said.

"A citation for what?"

"I'm sorry, Father. We were sent here on a call that there was a large dog on the loose in the neighborhood and the animal was chasing children. We didn't realize the consequence involved but we do have a leash law in this city. Once the complaint is brought to our attention, and we find it to be accurate, we have to issue the citation. It's only fifteen bucks."

"Who filed the complaint?"

"I shouldn't tell you but you'll find out anyway. It was the school principal."

"Spineless bastard," Father Wesley muttered.

In a matter of seconds all the participants went their separate ways, leaving just Father Wesley and Shagtyme standing on the sidewalk. He looked at his dog and said, "Come on, you felon, let's head home."

FOURTEEN

The doors to the cardinal's chambers opened and Father Moore entered. He had a disgruntled look on his face. He walked to the cadence similar to that of a military officer. In his right hand he carried a manila folder. The cardinal looked up from his desk. On most days Cardinal Burke could tell how his secretary's day was going by the expression on his face. His disposition was usually one of discontent or satisfaction. However, on this day, his look was one of aggravation. Whatever was bothering him was inside that manila folder.

"Why the sour puss?" the cardinal asked.

Father Moore dropped the folder on the cardinal's desk. "It's in here," he said before taking a seat opposite the cardinal, crossing his legs and bridging his hands in front of his face, as if mired in deep thought. The cardinal could now truly sense his aggravation.

"What's in here?" Cardinal Burke asked as he picked up the folder.

"It's a report on St. Theresa's, that little parish in Paine that your friend runs. The parish, you insisted, could use the help of a new curate to help Father Coniglio through his final days."

A look of concern came over the cardinal's face. "Is there something wrong with Ronny? I mean Father Coniglio."

"No. Your friend, Father Coniglio—or Ronny, as you prefer to call him— is doing just fine. In fact, he seems to have attained his second wind in life."

"That's marvelous news, unless you find discouragement in the fact that Father Coniglio's health seems to have taken a turn for the better."

Father Moore was careful in what he said next. He did not want to sound as though he had Father Coniglio's grave dug and he was anxious to toss him in it. "It's not Father Coniglio. It's the damn parish and that Father Wesley we sent to help him out. Your Eminence, it's not going according to our plan."

The cardinal opened the folder and began flipping through the pages, not studying any one page in particular. "Father, are you going to explain to me what the problem is, or do I have to read each word of this report?"

Father Moore stood up and leaned against the front of the cardinal's desk, his arms outstretched as though they were about to get into a heated discussion. There was a menacing scowl on his face, as though he were going to give the cardinal a lecture on what it takes to run an archdiocese.

"It's not in black and white," he began. "We have encountered a stumbling block. We dispatched Father Wesley to St. Theresa's to act as a caretaker. He was to simply watch over the day-to-day operation of St. Theresa's and look out for Father Coniglio. But it seems he has taken it upon himself to turn the parish around."

"Father, get to the point. Has Father Wesley done something wrong?"

Father Moore slumped back into the chair. "No, he hasn't done anything wrong but he hasn't done what was asked of him, either."

"And what was that?"

Father Moore leaned forward in the chair. "Your Eminence, a year ago St. Theresa's was averaging around $100 in collections on Sunday. Now, after Father Wesley's been there for a year, it's five times that amount. I don't know what he did but it has me disturbed. We sent him to a parish that was like an old car with a worn out engine and four flat tires. Now it's running like a brand new model, right off the assembly line, roaring up the highway."

"Interesting analogy, Father. Now, why does this disturb you?"

"Your Eminence, if this keeps up we'll never be able to close St. Theresa's. He's turned the place into a living and breathing shrine for Father Coniglio."

"Oh, it slipped my mind about your grand plan to have St. Theresa's gobbled up by St. Matthew's. Well, Father, even $500 of weekly collections is not going to do it. He'd have to get it up to a thousand dollars before I'd even consider keeping St. Theresa's doors open. I applaud Father Wesley for what he has done but I think he has tapped that parish out. He's reached the limit. Let's don't worry about something that's not going to happen."

"I wish I was as sure as you are," Father Moore replied. "You once called him a modern day Saint Paul and he's proving to be just that. He makes me nervous. Father Coniglio may pass on but Father Wesley will still be there and standing just as tall. We are compounding the problem by keeping him there."

"Are you suggesting we reassign Father Wesley?"

"Exactly! Let's get someone in there who will listen to what he is told."

"Father, this is beginning to sound like a personal vendetta between you and Father Wesley. I don't think your concern is so much with St. Theresa's as it is with him. It sounds to me as if you are out to get him."

"I've had it up to my eyeballs with Father Wesley," Father Moore said as he took the side of his hand and ran it horizontally in front of his eyes. "His insolence makes me do a slow burn."

"Insolence? This is the first I've heard of any insolence."

"I never told you this but last year Father Wesley held us up for $7,000 to stage a Christmas party for the children of the parish. He threatened to blow the whistle on us and what we were trying to do with St. Theresa's and Father Coniglio."

What Father Moore had to say had the cardinal concerned. "I don't like what I'm hearing. I won't stand for any priest working in my archdiocese using bullying tactics to get what they want. Now, Father, this is very important. Did Father Wesley ask for the money before having to resort to an act of extortion to get it?"

"Well…"

"Now, come on Father. I know you. Sometimes you can conveniently hide or forget certain aspects of the truth to get your point across. Now, I ask you again: did Father Wesley ask for the money before holding you up for it?"

"All right, he did."

"Do you happen, by chance, remember what you said to him?"

"I think I said, *no.*"

The cardinal began to look at the report on St. Theresa's more closely. He came to an item and looked Father Moore squarely in the eyes. "It says here that he raised $15,000 to fix the roof on St. Theresa's. If he could do that then why couldn't he raise the money for his Christmas party?"

"There's a little discrepancy in that fact. It seems he didn't raise the money at all." Father Moore wanted to leave it at that but he knew the cardinal was going to want more. He looked away from his superior and mumbled what he had left to say. "The money was his. He said it was a contribution so he wouldn't upset Father Coniglio."

The cardinal didn't miss a word. "Why didn't he ask the chancery for the money? Did he think we'd turn him down, and take a chance that the roof might not cave in on some innocent parishioners?"

"He claimed he didn't think he could get the money from us so he acted on his own. He sold his car."

The cardinal sat back and allowed the thought process to take over. He was impressed by Father Wesley's style. He didn't even mind the insolent part. The cardinal was aware how Father Moore liked to intimidate. Father Moore enjoyed making his fellow priests shake in their boots when he confronted them, but not Father Wesley. The priest was not afraid to lock horns with his controlling secretary.

The satisfied expression on the cardinal's face agitated his personal secretary. "There is something else you should know," he informed the cardinal, still hoping to tear down Father Wesley's credibility.

"And what would that be?" the cardinal asked.

"He owns a dog. A large German shepherd, weighing over a hundred pounds."

"So."

"Your Eminence, I've never heard of a priest owning a dog. I tell you Father Wesley is a maverick and has to be brought under control."

The cardinal stood and walked around to the front of his desk. His mind was made up. "Father, I have no problem with Father Wesley owning a dog. I imagine Saint Francis of Assisi had one or two of his own, so I don't think Father Wesley is committing any great sin. In fact, I kind of envy him. I wish I had a dog of my own. I also have no intention of transferring him. Let's don't forget that you were the one who handpicked him for the assignment. Let's also don't forget that we dispatched him to St. Theresa's because we thought he was the only priest the parishioners would trust, lest the truth be told. It seems to have worked and obviously he has proven to be a blessing for Father Coniglio. I don't want to disrupt the good he has done. You two can continue to wage your little war against each other. I don't care about that. What I do care about is that my good friend is enjoying life for the first time in a long time. I refuse to tamper with the good which has come his way."

Father Moore raised himself out of the chair. "Have it your way, Your Eminence. But I'll tell you this: I'm going to watch Father Wesley like a hawk, and if he again steps out of line I'm going to be there and come down on him like the walls of Jericho."

The cardinal smiled. "You do that, Father, but beware. Don't be surprised if it is he who is the one looking to land the knockout punch."

CHAPTER
FIFTEEN

The Dog Days of Summer dawned on a sultry note. But for one person, the toasty early morning hours in August were somewhat comforting. As the sun rose in the east, Father Coniglio took advantage of the long days to tend to his garden before the day's heat became unbearable. He moved about silently, trying not to awaken Father Wesley. He didn't have to worry about Mildred since she didn't arrive until 8:30. The only one to join Father Coniglio in his early morning routine was Shagtyme. Once the old priest was up, so was the young dog.

Father Coniglio and Shagtyme began to develop a mutual bond and dependency for one another. The priest was enjoying his renewed lease on life, and he allowed Shagtyme to share these pleasant times with him. Each morning as he did his tilling, Shagtyme joined him. If Father Coniglio had to journey into the church he allowed the German shepherd to come with him. His rule about the dog not being permitted in the church had gone by the boards. Since he was up so early, he made the daily 7:00 AM Mass his responsibility. Those Masses were distinguished by the fact that Shagtyme was in attendance, off to the side of the altar. The old priest and the dog had developed a unique friendship.

Mildred was standing at the kitchen door, smiling. Father Wesley came down the stairs and entered the kitchen. "What's for breakfast?" were his first words of the day.

Mildred turned, as if startled. "I'm sorry, Father. I was just standing here watching Father Coniglio and your dog in the yard. They seem to be having the time of their lives."

"My dog?" Father Wesley had to ask as he sat down at the kitchen table. "That's a joke. The dog is closer to Father Coniglio and the children than me."

"You might think that way, Father," Mildred answered as she moved towards the kitchen counter to pour Father Wesley a cup of coffee. "But it's your voice he responds to when you're around."

"That's because he thinks I'm his mother," he was quick to point out.

"Then you've been a good mother, and then some," Mildred added as she placed the cup in front of him. "All you have to do is look out that door and see the good you've accomplished."

Father Wesley took a sip of coffee before getting up and moving towards the door. As he looked out he could see Father Coniglio raking some dirt. At the edge of the garden, his tail wagging while his tongue hung from the right side of his mouth, sat Shagtyme. It was then that Grimaldi entered the scene. After saying something to the pastor the two men exchanged handshakes. Father Coniglio then pointed at the back door of the rectory and Grimaldi started ambling towards it.

Father Wesley retreated to his seat at the table as Grimaldi knocked on the kitchen door and opened it in the same motion. "Good morning, all," he said as he entered. The St. Theresa's caretaker was beaming.

"Antonio, now don't you be tracking dirt all over my kitchen floor," Mildred warned him.

Grimaldi wiped his feet on the mat and with a smile on his face that stretched from ear to ear said: "Mildred, even you and your iron maiden ways cannot upset me on this beautiful day."

"Grimaldi, you seem to be the picture of life. What gives?" Father Wesley asked.

"It is my Anna. After all these months of trying she is finally pregnant. Yes, yours truly is going to be a grandfather."

Mildred covered her mouth in utter surprise before walking over and planting a massive hug around Grimaldi. "Antonio, what wonderful news. They were having so much trouble. It's good to know God has finally smiled down on them."

"They were having problems?" Father Wesley asked.

"Yes, Father," Grimaldi answered. "They were having a lot of problems. They took tests and had some counseling but nothing seemed to work. The tests showed there was nothing wrong with either one of them. The doctors said it had to be stressed related. I guess they finally got over that hurdle."

"That is good news. Patience can be rewarding," Father Wesley told him.

"When is the baby due?" Mildred wanted to know.

"March 2nd," Grimaldi informed her, his voice ringing with pride.

Father Wesley stood up, walked over to Grimaldi and placed his right hand on his shoulder. "Congratulations, Grimaldi. Give Anna our best and let's hope there are no complications from this point on."

"Thank you, Father. I'm with you on that one." Grimaldi replied.

Father Wesley walked back to the kitchen door. He placed his hands behind his back and looked out at a now vacant backyard. Father Coniglio and Shagtyme were no longer there. "I wonder where they have gone?" he muttered to no one in particular.

"Father Coniglio told me he was going to take Shagtyme for a walk," Grimaldi told him.

"I hope he remembered to put his leash on him. I don't need any more citations."

—⁂—

Father Coniglio and Shagtyme strolled down Everton Street towards the beach. As they walked along people came out of their homes to greet the prelate and give the dog a pat on the head. Most of the people who extended their greetings were parishioners who were thrilled to see the aging priest up and about in the neighborhood once again. It had been years since he walked these streets.

Shagtyme knew the route the old priest was taking since he walked the same way every night with Father Wesley. However, once they reached the rotary at the parkway, where Father Wesley went right, Father Coniglio went left. The dog followed along dutifully and they walked along the seawall when the priest heard a once familiar voice call out his name.

"Good morning, Father Coniglio. It's been years since I've seen you here."

The voice was that of an old friend. Father Coniglio turned to be greeted by Rabbi Morton Zuckerman of the Temple Beth Abraham. It had been years since they had last talked to each other. He returned the greeting to the small and portly man with the gray beard. "Good morning to you, Rabbi. It has been years."

Rabbi Zuckerman leaned over and petted the top of Shagtyme's head. "What a stout lad you have here. How long have you had him?"

"Just over a year. He actually belongs to my associate, Father Wesley."

"I heard you had an assistant. Things must be going well at St. Theresa's if the cardinal saw fit to send you some help."

"Things are getting better at St. Theresa's. How's business at Temple Beth Abraham?"

"Fantastic. Let's sit on the seawall and talk. You know, the way we did in the past."

"Yes. Let's do that," Father Coniglio answered.

Rabbi Zuckerman was the same age as Father Coniglio and the two had been friends for nearly thirty years. Over that time span they had often sat on this seawall and discussed many different topics, rarely agreeing on any subject. But they never left one another on unfriendly terms. Their disagreements became a way of life for the two men of God. But those lively conversations came to a halt six years ago when Father Coniglio became dispirited with his daily existence and rarely left the grounds of St. Theresa's. It filled Rabbi Zuckerman's heart with joy to see his old friend enjoying life again.

Across from where they sat was a lounge called Rose's—formerly known as Maxine's. The establishment demanded Shagtyme's attention. The dog watched as the front door opened and a middle-aged man exited dragging a barrel. In his wake was a young German shepherd and as they both disappeared into an alley next to Rose's, Shagtyme began to bark and pull on his leash.

"What is it, Shagtyme?" Father Coniglio asked, as if he expected the dog to answer.

"I think his hormones just got lit up," Rabbi Zuckerman chided.

"What are you talking about?"

"Didn't you see the other dog that came out of that bar across the street?"

"No, I didn't."

"Well, the dog did. What did you say his name is, Shagtyme?"

"Yeah. Father Wesley named him. I know the name sounds kinda tacky but it isn't."

The man on the opposite side of the street reemerged from the alley and stopped. "C'mon, Love Muffin. We don't have all day," he shouted. The dog came running out of the alley and scampered back into the bar followed by the man.

"Love Muffin, huh? Figures a Catholic dog would be attracted to another dog with the name of Love Muffin," the rabbi commented, trying to spike their conversation with some subtle humor.

Father Coniglio seemed to take the rabbi's ribbing seriously. "What's wrong with that? Are you trying to tell me a Jewish dog would be trained to be more selective?"

Rabbi Zuckerman laughed. "Father, I'm glad to see you haven't changed. I should get going, though. I hope we'll be seeing more of each other in the future."

Father Coniglio nodded. "I hope so too," he said.

Father Coniglio continued to sit on the seawall, enjoying a gentle breeze that had begun to blow in off the ocean. After a few minutes he turned his head to the right and noticed a woman rummaging through a trash barrel, searching for what appeared to be cans or bottles.

She had a haggard look about her. The woman's face was drawn and had a weather-beaten appearance. Her hair was unwashed and looked as though it had been that way for some time. She held a green trash bag in her right hand to store the cans and bottles she found. The next barrel she would come across was less than ten feet from Father Coniglio.

As she approached the trash container, Father Coniglio studied the woman closely. Trying to determine her age was not easy. It was possible she could be in her fifties or she could be in her seventies. A tough life had taken its toll on her. "Good morning," Father Coniglio said as she began sifting through the barrel.

The woman looked up, startled as if she had been unaware that he was sitting there. "Good morning to you," she replied in a hesitating manner. As she spoke Father Coniglio noticed one of her front teeth was missing.

Shagtyme barked and the woman backed up a step, not knowing whether the dog was friendly or not. "Don't be afraid," Father Coniglio tried to assure her. "He won't bite you."

"Yeah, sure. I've heard that one before, only to find out differently."

"No. I mean it. Come over here and give him a pat on the head. He likes people."

"I think I'll pass," she said. The woman then began studying the priest very suspiciously. "You're Father Coniglio, aren't you?" she finally asked.

"I am. I'm sorry, have we met? Do we know each other?"

"No," she said with emphasis. "What makes you think that way?"

"I'm sorry. I didn't mean to upset you. Since you knew me I figured we must have met."

"We haven't." The woman continued to keep her distance from the priest and the dog.

"Why don't you sit next to me? You look as though you could use a friend." Father Coniglio proceeded to pat the spot on the seawall next to him. The woman seemed to welcome his invitation, although she moved with trepidation, still fearful of the dog.

As the woman sat on the seawall, Shagtyme proved the old priest to be right. The dog walked over and placed his head on the woman's lap. She, in turn, cautiously began to stroke the fur on his head, not quite convinced the dog wouldn't snap at her if she made a wrong move. "I've never known of a priest owning a dog. Is this something new?" she went on as she continued to run her right hand along the dog's head.

"Not really," he answered. "He actually belongs to an associate of mine. His name is Father Wesley. Do you know him?"

"No," she said even more emphatically.

"Are you Catholic?" he asked.

"I was born Catholic, but I haven't been to church in years."

"How many years?" Father Coniglio pried.

"Since I was about ten."

"It's never too late, you know."

"I don't think God is any hurry to have me in his ranks. I have a history and it's not a pretty past."

"Don't sell yourself short. God is very forgiving."

"Yeah, sure he is," she responded, sarcastically.

"Do you have a family?" Father Coniglio felt it was necessary to get off the subject of her fallen virtues and move onto something else.

"I have a son. Why do you ask?" her voice was steeped in suspicion.

"No reason. You seem to be a very insecure person."

"I am by nature. But since you asked I'll tell you. My son and I have grown apart. We haven't seen or talked to each other in years."

"That's sad."

"It is, but I have no one to blame but myself. My son has grown up to be a responsible man but with no thanks to me. I was a terrible mother. As a baby I paid little attention to him. If it wasn't for a cousin I had by the name of Anne Marie Wells he might not have survived his early years."

Father Coniglio knew the name of *Anne Marie Wells*. He couldn't recall when or where he had met her, but he knew he had.

"I'm sorry to hear that, but at least you're big enough to own up to it." He didn't dare go any further with this conversation. He wanted to ask her son's name but decided against it, knowing there was little chance she would tell him. Their little chat at the seawall was starting to make Father Coniglio feel uncomfortable.

The woman raised herself off the wall. "It was nice talking to you," she said as she prepared to leave.

"I enjoyed talking to you, too."

The woman began to walk away. She had taken about five steps when Father Coniglio called out to her. "Miss! You never told me your name."

The woman turned. "It's Joan," she shouted back his way.

"Joan what?"

"Just Joan." She then resumed walking, headed towards the next barrel.

CHAPTER
SIXTEEN

Father Coniglio continued to walk the beach on a daily basis, when the weather cooperated, in what was left of the summer. Each day he would look for Joan, but he never did see her. There had been something haunting about the woman and what she had said about Anne Marie Wells. He decided to keep his chance meeting with the woman to himself. She was his little mystery and he was determined to solve the case on his own.

His strolls along the beach always included the company of Shagtyme. He'd also stop and talk to Alfredo and Salvi. But the majority of the time he spent on the beach in the fading summer sun was spent talking to his old friend, Rabbi Zuckerman. They were two old pals who enjoyed the company of one another. Their daily chats along the seawall gave them some precious time to enjoy in one of the few summers they had left.

The prelate's daily sojourns down to the seaside started out as two-hour affairs. But they soon expanded to four hours. He would leave the grounds of St. Theresa's around nine in the morning and return by one in the afternoon. He was usually exhausted by the time he returned to the rectory. On most days he would skip lunch in lieu of a two-hour nap. The afternoon snooze he came to relish, soon started producing dreams of a woman. With his mind at ease his memory had a chance to do a recall for him. In his subconscious he was resolving the mystery which plagued him.

It pleased Father Wesley to see how Father Coniglio was enjoying life again. Those stories about a faulty memory no longer concerned him. All the old man needed was a respite from the strain running St. Theresa's brought, and Father Wesley was grateful he had been able to provide it. The parishioners, as a whole, had picked up on the change in their pastor as well and dared not tamper with it. If there was a pressing problem, the St. Theresa's faithful now brought it to the attention of Father Wesley.

———

It was a Friday morning in early September. Father Coniglio and Shagtyme had left for the beach ten minutes earlier. Father Wesley decided to take advantage of the opportunity and read his daily office in the first pew of the church. He was alone for about five minutes when he heard someone enter the place. He turned to see who it was. The person walking down the center aisle, headed in his direction, was Anna Gregorio. The young curate could tell by the expression on her face that something was bothering Grimaldi's daughter.

"Father, is it possible to talk with you?" she asked as she stopped next to him.

"Of course," he replied. He then moved a few feet over so she could join him in the pew.

As she sat down Anna began to cry. Father Wesley gave her a few seconds before speaking. "Anna, what's troubling you?"

She looked at him, her tears flowing freely. "Father, I've done something terrible. I have to tell someone or else I'm going to lose my mind. I wish I had the guts to put a gun inside my mouth and just pull the trigger."

"Anna, that's a loser's way out. If you've done something wrong then you simply have to own up to it. Ending your life is not the answer." Father Wesley was beginning to get an ugly feeling as to what the gist of this conversation was meant to be and he sensed heartache.

"They call you the *cool* priest, you know, the one in touch with reality. I need your help. I need it really bad." Anna was pleading.

"I'll help if I can," Father Wesley assured her.

"You know I'm pregnant?"

"I do." Father Wesley felt his stomach beginning to churn. He had a queer feeling as to what was coming next.

"What's the Church's view on abortion? Is it still a no-no?"

"It is." Now he knew where this conversation was headed.

"Aren't there certain circumstances when exceptions are made?"

"Anna, you are talking in circles. Something is bothering you about this pregnancy. I can't wave a magic wand and make everything right. I can only counsel you. Put your trust in me. What you say here today stays here."

Anna began to sob again. "I'm a disgrace. An absolute disgrace," she stammered through her tears.

The priest put his left arm around her shoulders. "Anna, let's start from the beginning. Allow me to understand what you are going through. So far all you've asked of me is to give you an answer of *yes*, as if it would cleanse your soul of whatever sin you have committed."

Anna leaned her head forward before glancing to her right at Father Wesley. "You're tougher than I thought you'd be," she told him.

"Anna, why don't you just tell me what is bothering you."

Anna reached for Father Wesley's left hand and gripped it tightly. She took a deep breath and began. "Father, I don't believe this baby is my Arthur's."

A lump built in Father Wesley's throat. "I see. So this is your way of confessing you had sex with another man?" He was careful to avoid the word *adultery*.

"It was just a one-time thing. I'm so ashamed it ever happened. It should have never happened, but it did."

Now Father Wesley had a duty to give guidance to her, but he had never run into a situation like this in his short tenure in the priesthood. He was at a loss as to what to say but he had to at least try.

"This is tough, real tough. Father, I'm thirty-three and I'm not exactly a raving beauty. I've been a success professionally, I've made some good money as a dental hygienist but my personal life has not been so great. I think I got married out of desperation before it got too late. I've paid the price for settling. My Arthur stinks as a lover. If we get into a romantic situation at night he has to get it over with fast so he can watch a game or get the scores on TV. All he really wants to do is sit around and swill down beer and watch whatever sporting event is on television."

"What about the other man?" Father Wesley hated to press her on the issue but what recourse did he have.

"That's where it gets kind of weird and unforgivable. I don't know what made me do what I did but I did do it. I was at a bachelorette party and they had a male stripper. There was a raffle and I won. I don't want to get into what could have been done or should have been done. I was angry with my life and I had been drinking at the party and… well, I think you know what I'm getting at. I was starving for affection. I settled for unbridled lust because it was right there to be had. I never thought something like this was going to happen."

"So you think this man is the father of your child?" This was getting interesting.

"It goes much deeper than that, Father. Much deeper."

"How so?" Father Wesley demanded to know.

"The male stripper was black. Try and lecture me on that one. My husband and father are Neanderthals when it comes to race relations. They think people should be with their own kind. I've tried to convince myself it is Arthur's baby but I know I've been only trying to fool myself. Now I'm scared."

A sudden surge came over Father Wesley. This situation was bad enough without hearing this news. Often an unwanted interracial child is headed towards a life bereft of acceptance and filled with discord as soon as he or she emerges from the womb. He wanted to tell her to go and abort the child. Then, as quickly as the thought entered his mind, a semblance of reason came to him. "What if it is Arthur's baby?" he asked.

"Father, don't be foolish. We've tried, or at least I have, with no results. Then, I go to bed just one-time with this other guy and, boom, I'm pregnant! It simply doesn't add up."

"So what are you going to do?" Father Wesley insisted on knowing.

"I'm going to abort this child."

"And what are you going to tell your husband and parents as to what happened?"

"I don't know. I'll think of something." Anna stood up as if to leave. As she did so Father Wesley's head ached with vivid memories.

"Anna, before you run off and do something you will surely come to regret, I'd like to tell you a story. It might help you get a better grip on the decision you are trying to make. Please, come sit and hear me out."

Anna did as he asked. She was trying to keep an open mind on the subject, for the decision she had to render was tormenting her. Coming from a devout Catholic family, Anna was schooled on Catholic doctrine to the point of being overwhelmed by it. She feared the repercussions which were sure to come in the next life. She took her seat in the pew and listened to what Father Wesley had to say.

"Anna, there was once a boy born out of wedlock. His mother was such a degenerate she was unable to name the father of the child. Her pregnancy period was a travesty. She did not abort the child because of her own selfish reasons. However, she did everything in her power to destroy that child. She continued to drink and smoke and lead the most immoral life imaginable. Despite it all, the child was born and, thanks to the grace of God, was healthy. But his problems continued. His childhood was one of total neglect and it eventually caught up with him as he moved into adolescence. He fought back because of that unwanted feeling. He hated his mother. He hated himself. He hated God for allowing him to be born. Then one day it all changed. He no longer rued his life. He was grateful to be alive and he made the decision to make the most of the life he had been given.

"What I am trying to say is that whatever decision you make, think of the consequences before you do it. Will you be able to live with yourself? Will you be haunted by the image of a child who was never born but longed to be? Is it necessary for you to deny a life because of a sin you committed? Weigh those questions before you make a decision you must live with for the rest of your life."

Anna appeared to be more distraught. "Father, I don't think you're being fair. What I have to do troubles me deeply and what you just said makes it more difficult. You can't imagine the pain, misery, despair and shame that goes with it. If I have this baby and it turns out to be black, my Arthur will take a gun and blow the top of my head off. He's typical Italian. Very headstrong."

"And what if the baby is his? If he's typically Italian he'll be drunk with pride."

"You really want to believe in that remote possibility, don't you?"

"I just can't overlook the possibility."

"I have to."

"Anna, why did you come here if your mind was already made up? Were you seeking advice or were you hoping I would agree with you and condone your action so you could have some peace of mind?"

"I don't know. Maybe I was just looking for someone to hear me out. I must have been out of my mind to think someone else could provide an answer for me. I appreciate the fact you took the time to hear what I had to say without lambasting me with horror stories of what awaits me in the bastions of hell."

Anna, again, got up to leave. "One second, Anna," Father Wesley implored. "I don't have to describe hellish experiences for you because you are already going through it. Anna, a marriage is based on trust and honesty. Most people violate those basics. Aborting a child is bad enough. But the emotional dishonesty you will have perpetrated will destroy you just as much. You'll always fear that slip of the tongue from someone who knows your secret. However, that will seem minor compared to the pall of deceit and sorrow you will carry within yourself. The course you chart today will determine if you become the woman you aspired to be or the woman you strive not to be."

"Are you suggesting I tell Arthur the whole story?"

"I'm not suggesting a thing. What you do is your decision. What I'm trying to say is every person is different. Believe it or not, some people can find it within themselves to live with the deceit and dishonesty wreaked on them, and of course there are those who cannot. Life is based on what is good and what is bad. We cannot know one without knowing the other. Granted, if you tell Arthur there is no way of predicting how he will react. It will take time for him to heal. But if he truly loves and cares for you he will never turn his back on you. Your soul is already fractured by the remorse you have brought on yourself. Don't break your heart as well."

"I think you're going overboard."

"I beg to differ with you. I wasn't always a priest. I know, all too well, what emotional torture can do to a person."

"Good-bye, Father," Anna said as she stepped out of the pew and into the center aisle. She was ten steps away when Father Wesley again called out to her.

"Anna, one last thing."

Anna turned. "What now?" she replied, as if agitated.

"I'm not on the outside looking in, as you seem to think."

"Oh, really," she responded in a snarly voice.

"The story I told you."

"Yeah, what about it?"

"The child in that story was me. I've been there, Anna."

The look on Anna's face became one of astonishment. She knew the priest had a past but never thought of it as being as horrific as he had depicted. Father Wesley had tried to make her feel guilty and had not succeeded until he unveiled his own tarnished past. Her mind was now a jumble of thoughts.

—⚭—

At one o'clock that afternoon Father Coniglio returned from the beach. He attached Shagtyme's leash to the front railing of the rectory. He was tired but there was something on his mind and it needed attending before he napped. He wandered into the backyard where he found Grimaldi at work mowing the lawn. "Grimaldi," he screeched as he cupped his hands to overcome the sound of the lawnmower. "I need to talk to you, right now!"

The caretaker killed the engine on the lawnmower and hurriedly made his way towards the priest. "What is it?" he asked as he mopped the sweat from his brow while swatting at the flies his perspiration attracted.

"Grimaldi, where do we keep the sacramental records?"

"It depends on what you are looking for. I've stored the old records in the basement of the church. Some of the more recent stuff is in your computer. I think Mildred has been working on it for a while, trying to update it."

"I'm not interested in anything recent. I want to go back to the day I took over St. Theresa's."

"Father, that's quite a few ledgers. What do you want me to do with them?"

"Just bring a couple of ledgers at a time to my room. Once I get through with them you can return them to the church basement and bring me some more until I find what I'm looking for."

"Whatever you say. What sacrament do I start with?"

Father Coniglio had to stop and think for a moment. That was a good question. He thought of what Joan had to say about how Anne Marie Wells had cared for her son, making sure his early years followed a somewhat regular life. He was beginning to think he might have hit a dead end before he even started. If he had met Anne Marie at a First Communion or Confirmation ceremony then there was no record of it. "Damn," he cursed himself. He did not know Joan's last name and he never asked her son's name. Aside from Anne Marie Wells' name he had nothing to go on. He was about to tell Grimaldi to forget the whole idea when he decided, *What the hell*, "Grimaldi, bring me the baptismal records." It was a long shot but he was going to give it a try.

A half hour later Grimaldi trudged up the stairs to Father Coniglio's room. The four ledgers he carried were dusty and the particles flying in the air from the old sacramental volumes caused the caretaker to wheeze. As he placed the ledgers at the foot of Father Coniglio's bed he said, "Here they are. Books number one, two, three and four. You wouldn't believe the crap I had to climb over to get my hands on them. I hope what you're looking for, you find fast."

"So do I," the old priest answered as he sat on the edge of the bed and prepared to go through book number one. "Thank you, Grimaldi. It's going to take me some time to go through these so I might as well get started. I'll let you know when I need the others."

Father Coniglio was tired but he was also anxious to get started on this project. He figured he would give it twenty minutes, nap for an hour, and then pick up from there. However, the cleric's quest for a quick answer did come to a swift resolve. He spent eight minutes going down the columns listing *godmothers* when he came across the name of Anne Marie Wells.

There was a notation under the listing. He looked at the entry of the child in question and was stunned when he saw the name of Paul Kevin Wesley listed. In the blink of an eye it came back to him. The priest remembered the woman and how she had pleaded with him to do a righteous act and eradicate the humiliation the boy was being forced to endure. The memory flooded his mind. The Baptism was held on a Friday night and the following morning the child made his First Communion. It seemed so ironic to Father Coniglio. The young boy he had helped had come back, in a way, to repay his debt by being the guiding light St. Theresa's had been lacking.

Then a disturbing thought crept into the old priest's thinking. It bothered Father Coniglio to know that Father Wesley was demonstrating to be an excellent priest yet he was showing a shallow trait in the matter demanding his utmost attention. It didn't matter that Joan Wesley had proven to be a deplorable mother. It was Father Coniglio's belief that her son should be reaching out to help her until she was out of reach. The old priest was sure if Father Wesley didn't recognize his shortcoming, the day was going to dawn when he would be beset with grief for the small-minded behavior he had exhibited when it came to his mother.

The tired priest closed the ledger and tossed it on a chair. He had solved his mystery, but in doing so, he had uncovered a troubling scenario concerning his associate. Right now it was too much to focus on. He dropped his exhausted body on the bed to take a much needed nap.

CHAPTER
SEVENTEEN

The streets were quiet. It was early September and the children were back in school. But the silence prevailing around the grounds of St. Theresa's was discomforting. Grimaldi came and went about his business, hardly saying a word to anyone on the premises. Something gnawed at him. Yet, the grief he carried he carried alone. His co-worker and friend, Mildred, was the first to notice the change in him. Grimaldi, in what seemed to be a self-imposed state of isolation, avoided her inquiries. The emotional pain he was enduring he was intent on enduring alone.

The housekeeper, concerned about his despondency, brought it to the attention of the two priests. Both men admitted that they had failed to notice any change in Grimaldi's disposition. Father Coniglio took it upon himself to deal with the matter since he knew the man the best. He felt the St. Theresa's caretaker might be more apt to confide in him than Father Wesley. The old priest was right but for the wrong reason.

Father Coniglio waited a day before confronting Grimaldi. It was a Thursday morning. The old priest was tending to his garden when he saw Grimaldi emerge from the rectory basement with a hose and sprinkler. He watched as the caretaker went about the chore of setting it up. This was about the time of day when Father Coniglio went for his walk with Shagtyme. But today it was going to have to wait. He was going to try and be of some help to his old friend.

"Yo, Grimaldi, are you going to water the lawn?"

What a stupid question, Grimaldi thought. Of course he was going to water the lawn. What did the dimwitted old priest think he was doing with a garden hose and sprinkler in his hands.

"Yes, Father, it could use a good drink."

As Father Coniglio came out of the garden he was carrying a basket of tomatoes. Grimaldi spotted the basket and went along with the small talk routine. "How's your garden coming along? Those tomatoes certainly look good."

"I think I'm finally going to have a bumper crop," Father Coniglio proudly boasted as he walked past Grimaldi to the kitchen door of the rectory. Once there he turned and said, "Grimaldi, when you get the chance can I talk to you?"

"Sure. We can talk right now if you like."

The two men sat on the back steps. There was no suspicion in Grimaldi's mind as to why the old priest wanted to speak to him. "What is it, Father?"

"Grimaldi, you have us all worried. You don't seem to be yourself. If you have a problem and need some help, then this is the place to be. It's one of the reasons Father Wesley and I are here."

Grimaldi had to turn his head away and stare at the side of the church. *This had to be Mildred's interference*, he thought. *Why couldn't she mind her own business and stop meddling in other people's affairs.* Grimaldi had always believed he could have walked around with an arm missing and Father Coniglio would not take notice unless Mildred pointed it out to him.

"Grimaldi, you don't have to say a word. I just want you to know you have friends, people you can count on." The old priest was doing his best to be tactful.

Grimaldi grunted. "I wish you could be of help but one of you priests has already done enough damage."

"What was that?" Father Coniglio wasn't sure he heard Grimaldi correctly. What could Father Wesley have done or said to place Grimaldi in such a sullen state? Suddenly he was more interested in Grimaldi's problem than he dare let on. He was certain whatever Father Wesley had done he did with the best of intentions.

Grimaldi wrestled with the question for a few seconds. He finally decided to bare his soul to Father Coniglio—a priest he could trust.

"It's my Anna, Father. She and her husband have split up. I think everything would have been fine if Father Wesley hadn't butted in and told her what to do. I'm only telling you this because you are going to hear about it sooner or later, so you might as well hear it from me."

"And what did Father Wesley say or do to cause the breakup of Anna's marriage?"

"Father, it's very difficult to explain."

"That's all right. Just take your time. Maybe I can help where Father Wesley failed."

"That's impossible. The damage has already been done."

"Damage? This sounds serious."

"It is. As serious as it gets. Father, my Anna, it seems…this is kinda hard to tell you."

"Grimaldi, I'm your friend. I'm here for you. I've heard it all in my years as a priest. Nothing you tell me is going to send me into a state of shock."

Grimaldi looked at him, queerly, as if to say, *That's what you think.*

"Father, my Anna had sex with another man," he said as rapidly as possible.

Grimaldi waited for a few seconds to see what Father Coniglio's reaction would be. All the old priest said was, "And?"

"And Father Wesley said she should tell her husband all about it, so she could have peace with herself. Well, she has peace all right, a piece of loneliness. She's pregnant and without a husband."

Father Coniglio had run into a few cases such as this over the years, but he never imagined someone such as Grimaldi going through this kind of ordeal. Considering what a devout Catholic the man was, he knew the hurt Grimaldi was bearing. He wondered if there was something he could say to ease his pain.

"Did this act of infidelity occur while they were married?" Father Coniglio was old fashioned and naïve so his obvious question did not seem out of place.

"Yes," Grimaldi answered. "Anna has brought disgrace upon our family. Why couldn't Father Wesley stay out of it? It was her sin. Why did he have to become a part of the problem and the humiliation that goes along with it?"

"Did Anna tell you all this?"

Grimaldi broke into an hysterical laugh. "Are you kidding. My once sweet Anna would rather slit her throat than tell her father she had been a whore."

"So it was Arthur who told you."

"Of course it was. He wanted to make it clear as to why he was walking out on her."

Grimaldi's contemptuous attitude towards his daughter was making Father Coniglio angry. It was his view that Father Wesley had done no wrong. He did what was required of him. He also had a suspicious notion that Father Wesley knew a lot more than Grimaldi realized. If Anna had come to him then it was because the guilt she was bearing was becoming intolerable.

"Grimaldi, we are talking about your daughter. Don't be so disdainful towards her. Anna came to Father Wesley seeking help and I don't think he let her down. She committed a grievous sin and the weight of it was too much for her to carry by herself. Anna came clean so she wouldn't have to live with this dark secret for the rest of her life. Give her a break and stand by her. Damn it, Grimaldi, no one is perfect."

"I know that, Father. I'm not going to turn my back on her but the grief attached to what she's done is killing me."

"It's killing you? Then maybe she would be better off dead. That way she wouldn't serve as an embarrassment to you."

"Jesus, no. Don't say that, Father."

"Then get your priorities straight. Stop thinking about Antonio and start thinking about Anna. If you don't it will be you who is killing her—slowly and methodically. You're damning her soul as if you were playing God."

"I wish you wouldn't put it that way."

"I have no choice. You are being pigheaded and selfish. You're worried more about your own pride than the pain your daughter is going through. Life is full of challenges. Anna made a mistake and now she is trying to do something right about it, despite the humiliation she must go through. Yet all she gets for doing the right thing is a cold shoulder. Her husband leaves her and her father treats her with contempt. I realize the sin she has committed has inflicted great pain on others. But she has found it within herself to find strength while those around her exhibit weakness. She's in a fragile state. Right now, she could use her father more than she ever did before."

Grimaldi shook his head as though he were trying to clear it. "You make it sound so simple. But there is something else that bothers me."

"And what might that be?"

"It's the baby. What if…what if it's…what if it's not…"

"What if it's not Arthur's?" Father Coniglio completed the question Grimaldi was having trouble saying.

"Yes."

"This affair Anna was involved in. Was it ongoing or just a one-time thing?"

"I assume it was just once or at least that's what she told her husband. But once was enough for him."

"It seems rather remote that a one-time fling would end up in conception."

"But it happens, Father. Considering the troubles they were having it leaves me very concerned, I think it might help us—"

"Grimaldi, don't even think about it. If you're talking about abortion it is not the answer."

"Father, I have to admit the thought has crossed my mind."

"I see. Let's get rid of the nuisance before it brings more shame upon us. I hate to be so puritanical about matters but if God chose for Anna to become pregnant in such a way then there has to be a reason. Maybe the child is meant to test your faith. I believe Jesus once said: 'The exalted will be humbled and the humbled will be exalted.'"

"But, Father, it doesn't seem fair to bring an unwanted child into this world. If this baby is the end result of an adulterous act think of the anguish the poor thing will have to endure. Does that seem right?"

"That's where you come in, Grimaldi. No matter who the father is, the child is still your grandchild. If you show love, then it is …" Father

Coniglio had a brief thought of Joan and Father Wesley… "you'd be surprised how some of those unwanted children turn out."

"I wish I was as strong as you expect me to be. Maybe in time I'll find that strength. Right now I don't have it."

"Time is something you do have. Make the most of it."

Father Coniglio left Grimaldi to think about what he had said. He moved to the front yard and unchained Shagtyme. There was still time to take his morning walk along the beach.

When Father Coniglio returned from his walk it was lunch time. As he entered the kitchen, Father Wesley was sitting at the table munching on a tuna sandwich. The old priest was carrying the basket of tomatoes which he had left on the steps during his talk with Grimaldi.

"How was your walk?" Father Wesley asked as he watched the older priest place the basket on the kitchen counter.

"Fine," he said as he turned to face his associate. "Father, can I see you in my office?"

"Certainly." Father Wesley had a queer feeling as to what this was about since Mildred had told him about Father Coniglio's little chat with Grimaldi.

Once in the office Father Coniglio closed the door and sat at his desk, while Father Wesley sat in the big black armchair. It was Father Coniglio who spoke first.

"Father, I had the chance to speak with Grimaldi this morning to see what was making him so withdrawn of late. Apparently, you already know. How come you didn't say anything to me about it?"

"Does this concern Anna?"

"You know it does," the old priest snapped.

"She took me into her confidence. It wasn't a confession but it sure sounded like one. I gave her my word not to talk about the subject and I intend to keep it."

"That's very noble of you and I understand. But now the problem is beginning to magnify. Grimaldi is a frustrated man. It's up to us to lend assistance to the Grimaldi family. Why don't we pool our resources so we can do whatever we can in their time of need."

Father Wesley wondered how much Anna had told her father. *Had she bared all? What course of action was she now prepared to take?* He knew how the story developed. Now he needed to know what kind of ending she had in mind.

"Why don't you tell me what Grimaldi told you?" Father Wesley asked.

"Cute, Father, cute. You're not going to show your hand until you've seen mine."

"Something like that," Father Wesley replied with a wry smile.

"Have it your way. Grimaldi is a distraught man. Anna had sex with another man in the past few months. She told her husband and he couldn't handle what she had to say and has since left her. Grimaldi is also fearful that the baby she is carrying might not be her husband's. Now is there anything you can add to the story?"

Father Wesley sat in silence for a few seconds. Obviously Anna had abandoned the abortion idea. A sense of guilt began to run through him. If he had broken with Catholic philosophy and told her to have the abortion then this whole mess could have been avoided. Being so righteous had placed such a heavy weight on Anna's shoulders that it dragged her down. He felt totally responsible. Being a priest brought some crosses to bear.

"What Grimaldi told you is the same story Anna passed on to me. However, I didn't know her husband had left her." Since she had apparently skipped the thought of having an abortion he was not going to mention it. He, also, was not going to disclose the fact that the man she had been intimate with was black. Hopefully there wouldn't be some living and breathing evidence of her adulterous transgression in the future.

"There is nothing you can add?" Father Coniglio asked, certain the younger priest had managed to get more details out of Grimaldi's daughter.

"Nothing whatsoever, Father."

"Well, where does that leave us? Any suggestions?"

Father Wesley scratched his chin. "There is not too much we can do. I hate to use a cliché but *time will cure what ails them*. At least Anna and her father are reaching out. We have to make sure to stand by them and have an attentive ear when they have something to say."

"I guess that is all we can do. Let's hope we've seen the worst of this situation."

A sickening feeling came to Father Wesley's stomach. "I certainly hope you're right," he told the older priest. "If we're finished here I think I'll go outside and see if Shagtyme remembers me."

"Go ahead, Father. I'm going to take my nap."

—⟋⟍—

Father Wesley was in the front yard reacquainting himself with Shagtyme when the police car pulled up in front of the rectory. It was Officer Kilcullen. "Father, can I speak with you?" he asked as he emerged from the squad car.

"Sure," the priest answered as he walked over to the wrought iron fence, Shagtyme, playfully, tagging along. "What's up?"

"Father, I'd like you to keep an eye out for anyone acting strangely in the neighborhood. We've got a pervert floating around. In the past few days he's exposed himself to some young girls. Started masturbating in front of one of them."

Father Wesley's face developed a troubled look. In his personal renaissance period he had learned to be compassionate but there was no toleration in his life for any demented individual who preyed on children.

"What else can you tell me about this deviate? Has he been spotted around here?"

"Not yet. Three days ago we had an incident over in Beachton. Earlier today he showed up by the shopping plaza near the expressway. Let's hope we catch him before he floats into this area."

"Do you have any idea what he looks like?"

"Not much. Older man, thin, around seventy. One of the kids said he smelled like beer."

"No big surprise there," Father Wesley noted. "That's what it takes for one of these clowns to get up their courage."

"Now, Father, I don't want you taking this matter into your own hands, like you did with those goons from the beach. If you see someone suspicious just let us know and we'll handle it."

An unabashed grin came to Father Wesley's face. "Officer Kilcullen, I get the impression you hope you get to him before I do. I'm a man of God. What kind of harm do you think I might direct this sicko's way?"

Kilcullen looked at Shagtyme before saying another word. "Father, between you and that dog, I feel the wrath of God might be greatly expedited."

Father Wesley gave Officer Kilcullen a wink and told him, "You're right. You better catch him before we do."

EIGHTEEN

"I'm telling you we can do it. What are you afraid of?" Danny Corrigan was trying to convince Freddy Brandt as they sat on the backstairs of Brandt's home on Shurtleff Street.

"I just don't want to screw around with that priest," Freddy answered as he lit a cigarette. "He can be a mean bastard, you know."

"Forget the priest, I'm talking about the dog. I've watched them. Their routine never changes. Every morning the old priest takes the dog for a walk along the beach. At night the other priest usually does the same thing. We can be in and out and they'll never know it was us." Danny Corrigan was hellbent to carry out his vendetta against Father Wesley.

"Why do you want to get the dog drunk?" Freddy felt Danny's idea was ludicrous. "I'm not in favor of wasting good money on booze to watch a dog pass out."

"That's when it gets even better. Once he gets good and stiff we unleash him. He won't bother us once he's juiced." Danny had his plan well-calculated.

"What happens then?" Freddy asked.

"Who cares. Maybe he gets run over by a bus. I don't give a damn. I want to get even with that priest for what he did to us." Danny seemed very committed to evening the score with Father Wesley.

"Danny, it's been months. Why not just forget it?"

"I'm not going to forget about it. That priest made idiots out of us. I'm going to get even with him. If this fails I'll find another way. I want to take something away from him that means something."

"Why don't you just blow up his church?" Freddy suggested, jokingly.

"If I knew how, I would," Danny answered, seriously.

"You're beginning to worry me with this kind of talk."

Danny was becoming agitated. "Do you stand up to take a piss or do you have to sit down? I'm beginning to wonder what kind of man you are."

Freddy took the remark as an insult. He raised himself off the steps and flicked the cigarette on to the walkway leading to the house. "Alright, Mister Smartass, I'm with you. Just one thing, though.

"What's that?"

"If the dog gets hurt he does it on his own. We don't lead him into having an accident."

Danny smiled as he stood up and extended his right hand. "It's a deal. We do nothing to really harm the dog."

Freddy reluctantly shook Danny's hand before saying, "I just hope the priest doesn't figure out who got his dog loaded. If he ever does, our days are numbered."

"Don't worry," Danny guaranteed him. "He's never going to know."

"This had better work," Freddy fired back in his direction.

"It will," Danny reassured him.

"When does it go down?"

"Tonight." Danny smiled as if in a state of euphoria.

Just after one on that same afternoon Joan Wesley was perusing through the trash barrels when she found her pot of gold. She now did her shopping on the beach early in the morning and after one in the afternoon. She knew Father Coniglio's schedule, and she was going to do what she had to do to avoid him. She didn't care about herself—hell, she had given up on her life a long time ago. But she did care about her son and the shame which could rain down on him if Father Coniglio ever found out she was his associate's mother.

Joan Wesley was alone in life and she understood why. But now she had a prize in her hand. She was feeling as though God had smiled down on her. In her hand was a nearly full fifth of vodka. She knew better than to drink it, she had already done enough damage to her liver, but at the moment she didn't care.

The bottle was probably dumped in the trash receptacle by some teen trying to avoid a confrontation or arrest by the police. That kid's misfortune had turned out to be Joan Wesley's good fortune. She kissed the bottle before saying, "Mr. Smirnoff, you and I are going to have a grand old time." She placed the bottle in her trash bag and made a quick retreat to her dingy living quarters, which she rented courtesy of the State's welfare system. She was no longer interested in being lonely. She now had a companion to help her make it through the night.

Once home Joan placed the bottle on the nightstand and stared at it as though it were a false idol. She soon settled into bed, knowing the bottle and its contents would carry her through the rest of the day. Just the sight of the cheap bottle of booze lifted her spirits. She had been warned that any further drinking could do her body immense harm. The years of alcohol abuse had wreaked havoc on her liver and stomach lining. Those organs were now like charred battlefields, its remnants tattered, torn and inflamed. Further abuse could kill her and she knew it. But Joan didn't care. She was willing to take the chance. The bottle created too great a temptation and she was unable to resist. She loosened the cap and took her first sip.

Joan gritted her teeth as the straight vodka made its way down her throat and into her stomach, where it settled like a sea aflame. She snuggled the bottle against her bosom and leaned back against the headboard. Her eyes closed and she thought of her life and the dismal failure it had been. Joan was convinced no act of penance was going to save her from what she had done.

The only positive thing she could claim in her life was her son. She thought of what he had become after a shaky start because of her repulsive ways, which had led him into a life of shame. Thank God for Anne Marie, she reflected. Her cousin had lifted him from that cesspool Joan called life. If Anne Marie had not been around there was no telling what might have become of him. Joan Wesley was sure her cousin had a place in heaven because of what she had given of herself to Joan's little Paul.

Joan took another sip from the bottle and the burning sensation took her breath away. Her stomach was turning into an inferno. She hugged the bottle a little tighter. At this hour in her life it was good to be with an old friend.

—◆◆◆—

Danny and Freddy stood on the railroad bridge waiting. It was getting late in the day and they were wondering if their prank was going to have to be postponed for a day. But after a few minutes of anxious deliberation Father Wesley left the premises, through the front gate, and headed off towards the beach with Shagtyme by his side. Danny and Freddy were in business.

Once the priest and dog were out of sight the two wiseass teens started walking briskly towards the rectory. "Give it to me!" Danny demanded as they walked along.

Freddy reached into his jacket and took out a pint of gin, 100 proof, and a can of ginger ale. "Don't waste it all on the dog," he said as he handed the bottle and can to Danny.

"Don't worry about it," Danny responded as he stuffed the bottle and can of soda in his jacket pocket. "This should be enjoyable to watch."

Once they reached the front gate to the rectory they stopped. There didn't seem to be anyone around to witness their act of defiance. Once they were sure no one was watching them, Danny hurdled the fence and, as he made his way to Shagtyme's water bowl, took the cap off the bottle.

There was about an ounce of water in the bowl and Danny dumped it on the lawn, before pouring the gin into the bowl with just enough ginger ale to give it flavor. Once finished he made a hasty retreat following the same route he had taken to the bowl. His little act of daring took all of fifteen seconds.

"What do we do now?" Freddy wanted to know when Danny rejoined him on the sidewalk.

"Now it's just a matter of time. The priest will be back with the dog in about an hour. He leaves him chained outside for a while. We'll be back before then to unleash him."

Danny had done his homework. He had studied the schedule of Father Wesley and Father Coniglio for about two weeks. Danny knew the priests' itineraries as well as they did.

As he had predicted Father Wesley was back in an hour. The priest placed Shagtyme on the yard chain and was about to replenish the animal's water bowl when he noticed it was already full. He just assumed Grimaldi had filled it before heading home. Father Wesley left it at that and retired to the rectory.

Shagtyme sniffed the bowl. It emitted a scent he was unfamiliar with but it looked like water. He lapped at it and soon all of the demon fluid was out of the bowl and settling into his system. The large dog's legs became shaky and he was feeling tired. He laid down on the grass and nodded off.

Soon thereafter, Danny and Freddy returned. Freddy was disappointed to see Shagtyme sleeping. "Great," he said. "Now he's sleeping it off. Looks like that plan of yours boomeranged."

"Maybe not," Danny replied. He again hurdled the fence and tiptoed over to Shagtyme's slumbering body. As he reached the dog, Shagtyme lifted his head. His sudden consciousness startled Danny and his guard stiffened. He then looked into the dog's eyes. They had a starry glaze to them and the animal seemed friendly.

Danny glanced over at the bowl. It had been licked dry. He could hear a snarl about to emit from Shagtyme as he petted him on the top of the head. "Nice dog," he repeated over and over. Shagtyme seemed to sense a friend and started licking Danny's right hand. The teen was careful not to antagonize the animal. He knew the liquor would keep him mellow, but he wasn't sure if a sudden jolt or unusual movement might distort what the dog was feeling and, somehow, make him vicious.

With a great degree of caution, Danny unleashed the buckle on Shagtyme's collar. This was all he could ask for. What happened next was up to the massive German shepherd.

Danny slinked his way back to the gate. Once he reached the spot he opened it. He was pleasantly surprised to find the gate had been well-lubricated and did not squeak. Thus far he had not disturbed a soul other than Shagtyme. He was feeling good about himself and the lowly act he and Freddy had managed to pull off. He made certain to leave the gate open.

"What happens now?" Freddy asked of his cohort.

"Who knows? It's up to the dog."

"What about us? What do you want to do now?" Freddy inquired in a tone that indicated they had spent enough of the night getting a dog drunk.

"Let's head down to the beach. Maybe you can get somewhere with that Rachel chick who seems to like you?"

"Now you're starting to make some sense. Let's get the hell out of here before that priest sees us."

Danny and Freddy took about twenty steps when they noticed Shagtyme come stumbling through the gate. "He's following us. Was that part of your plan as well?" Freddy asked, deliriously.

"No, it wasn't, but don't worry," a relaxed Danny answered. "Let him follow us to the beach. He's moving kinda slow so it should be easy to lose him in the crowd. He's in a lovable mood right now so maybe he'll make some new friends."

"This whole idea of yours sucks. I don't know how I let you talk me into this godforsaken farce."

"You worry too much. He's so drunk right now his legs probably won't get him to the beach."

"What if that doesn't happen? What if people notice that a drunk dog is following us? He's going to implicate us and that priest is going to have our asses. Like I said, your plan sucks.

"You know something, you're actually scared of the priest. That priest's not going to do anything unless he can prove we got the dog drunk."

"It sucks. It sucks. It sucks," Freddy kept reiterating. While they argued they didn't realize there were a set of eyes watching their every move. Across the street, in a rundown three-story tenement house, was Phu Luong staring out his second floor living room window. He watched as the two teenagers walked along, continuing to bicker, with Shagtyme following behind.

Once they reached the rotary at the beach Freddy put another question to Danny. "Okay, smartass, which way do we go now?"

"Let's see, the old priest takes him all over the place. The other priest always takes him to the right."

"Then what are we supposed to do? Walk into the ocean?"

"You're beginning to piss me off with your snide remarks," Danny let Freddy know.

"Then get your act together. This dog is following us like the plague. He's going to follow one of us home and what do we do then? I don't want that priest knocking on my door looking for his dog."

Danny was about to give Freddy another sarcastic response when he noticed Shagtyme's snoot was in the air. The dog abandoned them and started to roam towards the north end of the beach.

"Hey, look at that," Danny exclaimed. "He smells food and he's going to find it."

"Good," Freddy countered. "Now let's get out of here before he has a change of heart." Danny and Freddy then started running down the south end of the beach.

—⋙—

The doorbell to the rectory began to ring incessantly and there was a continuous knock on the door to go along with it. Father Coniglio was sitting in the living room by himself. He was thinking about retiring a little earlier than usual for the night when the clamoring began. "Who in heaven's name can that be?" he said to himself.

He opened the door. It was Phu Luong and he was out of breath from the quick sprint he had made to the rectory. "Where... where is Father...Father Wesley?" he asked through panting gasps.

"Phu Luong, relax. What's the problem?"

"It's...it's Shagtyme."

"What do you mean, It's Shagtyme? Isn't he in the front yard? Father Wesley was just about to go get him."

"No, Father, those kids got him."

"What kids?"

"Father Wesley knows who they are. Where is he?"

"He's in his office at the moment." Father Coniglio turned and called out to him. "Father Wesley, can you get out here."

Father Wesley opened the door to his office. "What is it?"

"It's Shagtyme. I think he's been taken for what could be a harmful stroll," Father Coniglio conveyed.

Father Wesley came rushing out of his office and saw Phu Luong standing in the doorway. "What do you mean he's been taken for a stroll?" the younger priest said in a stern voice.

"It was those kids," Phu Luong told him. "You know the ones who were bothering me at school. They took Shagtyme down towards the beach."

"Are you sure it was Shagtyme? He wouldn't leave with just anyone."

"Father, he looked funny. He couldn't walk straight. Those kids were arguing about him."

Father Wesley rushed past Phu Luong and Father Coniglio and ran to the front yard. Shagtyme was, indeed, gone. The thought of the filled water bowl struck him. He picked up the now empty bowl and gave it a sniff. There was a faint odor of alcohol. "Those bastards," he screamed into the night air.

He could hear the phone ringing in the rectory, but at the moment his mind was locked onto what sadistic fate those two punks had designed for his dog. He had let them off easy the first time but now they were going to pay for their madcap caprice. Shagtyme was the closest living thing he had that he could call family. If anyone harmed the animal, they had a price to pay and Father Wesley, priest or not, was willing to seek revenge.

"Father, there is a call for you," Father Coniglio hollered from the front door. "It's Bryan Fogarty and he says it's important."

Father Wesley was in no mood to talk to anyone and that included Bryan Fogarty. Then his thoughts centered on the beach! Yes, of course, those two clowns had taken his dog to the beach and Fogarty had found him. He rushed back into the rectory and grabbed the phone out of Father Coniglio's hand. "Yeah, what is it?" he said into the receiver.

"Father, this is Bryan, Bryan Fogarty."

"Yes, Bryan, I know it's you. What's the problem?"

"Well, Father, it's your dog."

"My dog," he said somewhat anxiously. "Is he all right? Where is he?" Father Wesley tried not to think of the worst. Yet, that was all he could imagine. Those two juvenile delinquents had taken advantage of the inebriated state they had placed Shagtyme in and had drowned him in the surf.

"Father, I'm down here at Rose's, you know the old Maxine's. Your dog's in the back of the place in a drunken stupor."

Father Wesley let out a huge sigh of relief. "Then he's all right?" he finally managed to say.

"Oh, he's fine. He's doing so fine that we can't get near him. Love Muffin won't allow it."

"Love Muffin?"

"Yeah. She's the watchdog for this place. They were co-mingling, if you know what I mean, and now your dog's passed out and Love Muffin won't let anyone near him. Looks like true love to me."

Father Wesley fell back on the couch with the phone still pressed against his ear. He was now at ease. "I'm sorry, Bryan. I didn't mean to be so curt with you but it seems a couple of wise guys decided to get Shagtyme loaded."

"I understand, Father. Now we have to figure out a way to separate these two. Can you get down here? By the way, who's Curt?"

Father Wesley broke into a relieved laugh. "I'll be there before you know it. I'll explain what *curt* means when I get there."

As he hung up the phone Father Wesley could feel the palpitations his heart had produced slowing down. Everything was back to normal. Those two buffoons had failed in their attempt to get even with him through his dog. Shagtyme was safe. Love Muffin was seeing to it.

Relieved, Father Wesley passed on the story Bryan Fogarty had told him to Father Coniglio and Phu Luong. When Father Coniglio heard mention of Love Muffin he immediately recalled that day on the beach with Rabbi Zuckerman and Joan the bag lady. Father Coniglio had a story of his own to tell and he did, describing for Father Wesley the time Shagtyme and Love Muffin first came across each other. He offered his services to go down to Rose's and retrieve the dog. The old priest was specific in his details involving the dogs, but careful not to mention the chance meeting he had with his associate's mother.

Father Wesley was quick to pick up on his fellow priest's offer. But he did so with an ulterior motive in mind. He wasn't too eager to walk into Rose's after all these years. He was fearful of finding his mother there.

CHAPTER

NINETEEN

Anna Gregorio unlatched the front gate leading to the rectory and began the walk to the front door, praying she had timed her visit correctly. Her father had just returned home for lunch, so he should be absent from the grounds for another half hour. She had heard him say that Father Coniglio always took a nap in the afternoon. Now she hoped Father Wesley was available to speak with her. Perhaps she should have called for an appointment, she thought. Well, it was too late to dwell on that fact.

Shagtyme was not in the front yard as seemed to be the custom, but she could hear the dog barking as she approached. Since the inebriation prank Father Wesley had decided to now chain his dog in the backyard. He had not forgotten the incident but being a priest, he thought it wise to turn the other cheek. It wasn't right, he felt, for a man of the cloth to become involved in a vendetta. However, he wasn't sure he would be able to maintain that righteous attitude should Freddy and Danny try another sinister act in the future.

It was a struggle for Anna to make it up the walkway. Each step seemed to be an effort. She had cast her lot in life and the decision she had made had much to do with what Father Wesley had said to her. He had struck a nerve and made her look at her inner self. The thought of aborting her baby, no matter who the father was, turned her soul inside out. She had to find peace with herself, despite the tremendous amount of pain and disappointment she had inflicted on those around her. She was unable to find it within her inner makeup to take the easy way out. Anna came to the decision that she could not live with the ghost of an aborted child. Whatever her sin, Anna managed to take the proper initiative and commit herself to having this child.

Mildred answered the door. "Good afternoon, Anna. What can I do for you?"

"I'd like to see Father Wesley, if he's not busy. I don't want to be a bother."

"Both Father Wesley and Father Coniglio are in. Father Coniglio is napping. But I believe Father Wesley is available."

"I don't want to speak to Father Coniglio. I came to see Father Wesley," Anna answered as if annoyed with Mildred. *What the hell was wrong with her?* Anna mused. She had specifically asked for Father Wesley.

"Please come in," Mildred said as she opened the door wider to allow her to enter the rectory.

What was so hard about that, Anna felt like saying. The pressure she was under seemed to be building and she was beginning to wonder if this was such a good idea.

Anna took a step inside but moved no farther. Mildred urged her to take a seat but she declined. The housekeeper did not make the offer twice. She left Anna standing just inside the doorway as she went to Father Wesley's office to see if he was available to talk with Grimaldi's daughter.

The rap came to the door. "Mildred?" he called out.

"Yes, Father, it is. You have a visitor," Mildred continued as she opened the door.

"Who is it?"

"It's Anna Gregorio. She'd like to speak with you."

Father Wesley placed his reading glasses on the desk. A gratified feeling began to swell within him. He had hoped she might seek him out a second time.

"She said not to disturb you if you're busy."

The priest stood up from behind the desk. "I am not busy. Will you please show Anna in?"

"All right, Father. I just wanted to make sure."

"You've done that. Now send Anna in."

Mildred returned to the living room where she still found Anna standing by the door, as if she were preparing to make a quick getaway. "Father Wesley will see you," the housekeeper told her. Anna then followed the housekeeper to the young priest's office.

"Anna, it's so nice to see you again. What can I do for you?" he asked as she entered his office.

"Father, I've come to ask a favor of you."

"Certainly. I'll do whatever I can. Why don't you have a seat and we'll talk," he said as he closed the door behind them.

"I'm sorry, I heard about your husband leaving you," he said as he returned to his seat behind the desk. "I'm sorry it had to come to that. I had hoped and prayed he would be somewhat more understanding, but we don't always get what we hope and pray for. But I'm also happy to see you have reconsidered the abortion idea. Now what can I do for you?"

"Father, I know my father has told Father Coniglio of my situation. He knows of the conversation we had earlier. That leads me to assume that Father Coniglio has talked to you about it. If so, how much did you tell him? Did you explain the whole story to him?"

"No, Anna, I didn't. I told you your secret was safe with me. I only verified what your father told Father Coniglio. That's all."

Upon hearing what the priest had to say, Anna relaxed. She was now fairly certain Father Wesley was a man she could trust.

"Father, I thank you for keeping my indiscretion to yourself. Now, that brings me to the reason I came to see you. I need a friend and so far you have proven to be the only one I have." Anna seemed to be having a little trouble saying what she came here to ask of the priest.

"Anna, I am your friend. You can count on me. Now why don't you just tell me what it is you need from me."

Tears began to run down Anna's cheeks. This was humbling and it was taking its toll. "Father, can you be in the delivery room with me when the baby is born? If my worst fear is realized on that day, I'm going to need a hand to hold. Tell me I can count on you being there."

Anna had become a forlorn soul and Father Wesley was full of empathy for her. He felt partly responsible for the lonely road she traveled. He had no intention of abandoning Anna in her hour of need. "Anna, it would be my privilege to be in the delivery room with you. When is your due date?"

The tears now flowed freely down Anna's cheeks. It was so comforting to know she had a friend to be at her side in what could be her darkest hour. "March 2nd," she answered, rather simply.

"I'll clear my calendar. We have a date," he promised.

"Thank you, Father. Thank you so very much for being considerate and understanding. You have no idea how much this means to me."

"Anna, I have to ask you this question and I think you know what it is."

"I know where you're headed, and the answer is *no*. I haven't told Arthur or my parents about the possibility the child might be..." Anna was having trouble saying aloud what she feared the most; that the baby's skin color would be a testament to the sin she had committed.

"Anna, I hate to be so righteous about the matter, but you can't put it off forever. Your parents and your husband have the right to know or else they are going to be in for the biggest shock of their lives."

"Father, I've become like you. I'm now a believer in miracles. I'm gambling that the baby will be Arthur's and therefore I won't have to cross that bridge."

A major risk, Father Wesley thought. Anna's prayers were probably loaded with concessions to make her sin venial in the eyes of God. *Let the baby be Arthur's and I'll never sin again* is the deal she is probably proposing. Didn't we all make comparable pleas to the Almighty when the situation seemed untenable?

"Anna, have you talked to your husband?" Father Wesley wanted to get a better grip on what was going on in her head.

"I've tried but gotten nowhere. You should hear the vile names he calls me."

Father Wesley shook his head in dismay. "That's a shame," he told her. He didn't know Arthur Gregorio, so it was impossible for him to get a read on the man.

Their business done, Father Wesley escorted Anna to the front gate and watched as she walked away. He couldn't help but feel bad for her. She had taken on the bravery routine because of what he had said was the Christian way of handling her delicate matter, and now she was paying the price for her courage. Everyone Anna cared for was shutting her out.

"Was she seeking your Solomon-like wisdom again?" The cynical voice was that of Grimaldi. Father Wesley turned to see him coming from the backyard with Shagtyme on his leash.

"Father, I've got the sprinkler going in the back so we either put Shagtyme out front or in the house."

"Let me have him," Father Wesley answered as he took the leash from Grimaldi's hand.

"So, Father, what was my daughter looking for this time?"

"She came seeking a friend, someone you haven't been of late. It bothers me to see you treat your daughter this way."

"She has brought disgrace to our family. What do you expect from me?"

"I expect you to be a caring father. I expect you to stand by her. She made a mistake and she's atoning for it. Do you intend to hold this against her for the rest of her life? We all commit sins. Have you never sinned, Grimaldi?"

"Never a sin of that magnitude."

"Where is it written that one sin is greater than another?"

"Father, you're playing with words."

"Am I? Well, let me try these words on you. Perhaps you don't have the capacity to forget but you do have the capacity to forgive. Grimaldi, I know you. Your pride has been hurt but in time, you'll do what is right."

"Maybe," he said, unconvincingly.

At that precise moment Shagtyme began to bark and started pulling on his leash as if he wanted to be freed. "What's wrong with him?" Grimaldi asked as if Father Wesley knew the answer.

"I don't know," Father Wesley replied. He squatted down hoping to calm the dog but Shagtyme kept pulling on the chain. The children were now running down the street on their way home from school.

There was something wrong and Shagtyme sensed it. The dog had never acted this way in the past.

"Father, he's going to rip that chain right out of your hands," Grimaldi said, anxiously.

"You're right. Let's see what's bothering him." Father Wesley then worked his way along the chain and unsnapped the clip on his collar. As soon as Father Wesley set him free Shagtyme took off, leaping the fence, and running in the direction of the Lincoln School.

"C'mon, Grimaldi, let's follow him. I may need you to help corral him."

Shagtyme rushed into the traffic, dodging the cars artfully. Two cars, trying to avoid the large dog, sideswiped each other as Shagtyme reached the other side of the street. His powerful legs carried him across the railroad bridge and he saw little Jenna running towards him. She was screaming the canine's name out, imploring his help. She was wearing a powder blue sweater and it had been ripped around her left shoulder. Shagtyme rushed past her, chasing a man who was now boarding a bus. "Shagtyme," she cried out. "Don't leave me!"

The dog stopped and looked back at Jenna. He then glanced back at the bus which was pulling away. The man was now out of the dog's reach. Shagtyme made his retreat to Jenna.

Father Wesley, running at a frantic pace, was about five yards in front of Grimaldi. Once he reached Jenna he dropped to one knee and put his arm around her. "Sweetheart, what happened?" he asked as he searched to regain his breath.

"It was awful, Father," she answered in a quivering voice as she clung to Shagtyme.

Father Wesley took notice of the torn sweater. "Did someone bother you?" he asked.

Jenna nodded. "Shagtyme saved me, though. He scared him."

Grimaldi caught up to Father Wesley and in a panting and wheezing voice asked, "What happened?"

"That's what I'm trying to find out," the priest said as he looked over his shoulder at Grimaldi. "What did he say? Did he do anything?" Father Wesley asked as he looked back at Jenna's blue eyes.

"I was coming out of school and he asked me if I wanted a twinkie."

"What did you say?"

"I said 'yeah.' I like twinkies. I took the package and opened it and then ate it. Then he asked me if I wanted another twinkie. I said 'yeah.' He then asked me what I liked most about twinkies and I said 'the cream.' He then said I would like his twinkie." Jenna began to shake as she related what happened.

"Then?" Father Wesley asked, his voice shaking. He didn't like putting her through this inquisition but he now knew the molester Kilcullen had spoken of was now working the streets of St. Theresa's.

Jenna was ashamed. She didn't want to tell Father Wesley what had happened. She just wanted the horrible thought out of her mind. The priest immediately sensed the problem she was experiencing.

"Jenna, I know you're having trouble telling me what happened, but you have to do it. Shagtyme came to help you and I came to help Shagtyme. Don't worry for a second. Shagtyme and I are going to find this man before he can do anything bad again."

"Do you promise?"

Father Wesley gestured with his index fingers. "Cross my heart," he told her.

Jenna gave Shagtyme a tighter squeeze. She felt she needed the dog for protection so this horrible act would never happen to her again.

"He took his thing out and told me to put it in my mouth. He said it had cream in it and I would really like it. I ran and he tried to grab me and he ripped my sweater. But I got away and that's when Shagtyme came running up the street."

"Where did he go?"

"He got on the bus. Shagtyme was going to chase him but I stopped him."

"Why'd you do that?"

"I was scared. Shagtyme won't let anyone hurt me."

Father Wesley paused to reflect on the situation before him. He felt sick to his stomach over what had happened. Perversion had crept its way within St. Theresa's boundaries and was now threatening her parishioners. He was intent on seeing that there would be no more perverted acts perpetrated on the good people of this parish.

"Jenna, I don't want you to stop and talk to or accept anything from people you don't know. There are a lot of bad people around and some of them want to harm little children. You've got to promise me you won't ever stop and talk to someone you don't know, ever again. Promise me."

"I won't, Father, but I knew this man."

"What? You know him?"

"Yeah, I don't know his name but I've seen him in the church."

Father Wesley's anger was rapidly reaching a point of no restraint. The damn pervert was a member of the parish. That did it. He was going to track this swine down and see to it that the depraved degenerate received his just due.

"Jenna, I want you to go to the rectory and stay there until I get back. Take Shagtyme with you. No one will bother you with him by your side."

"Okay, Father," she answered in an obedient tone. "Come on Shagtyme," she said as she began to pull on the dog's collar to leave. Little Jenna Napoli was feeling safe again.

Grimaldi looked at Father Wesley and asked, "Do we have a sick puppy floating around the neighborhood?"

"It seems that way," the priest answered as he stared off into the distance, wondering where the deviate was going to strike next.

"Well, Father—please pardon my French—but I'll rip the balls off the creep if I catch him. It makes my blood boil to know there are sick people wanting to do these things to kids. What's wrong with them?"

A sorry expression came to Father Wesley's face. It was all right if you were free of sin to toss down the gauntlet and champion the victim's rights. Grimaldi was being quite narrow-minded in Father Wesley's way of thinking. Jenna's days of sin were still ahead of her. She was still pure, but the day was not that far away when she, too, was going to succumb to the temptations of the flesh. Everyone was subject to human imperfection, be it of the mind or flesh, and Jenna was not to be an exception. The odds became greater, in her case, growing up in this neighborhood. Father Wesley wondered if Grimaldi would remember this day should Jenna Napoli's fall from grace occur.

"Father," the voice said, snapping the priest out of his semi-trance.

Father Wesley turned to his left and saw Murph, the Paine police officer. There was a commotion in the street because of the automobile accident which had occurred. "I hate to do this to you but your dog was on the loose again and apparently was the cause of this accident." Murph handed the priest the citation. "Shagtyme, right?"

Father Wesley took the ticket from the police officer. Now he had something new to agitate him. "That's correct but we had a near episode of child molestation here. Shagtyme prevented it from happening."

"We did not receive a call about a child being molested. We did, however, receive a report of two cars colliding with each other when the dog dashed across the street."

Father Wesley took the citation and stuffed it in his shirt pocket. "Nice to see you're on top of things," he said in an upsetting manner.

"I beg your pardon?" Murph didn't care for Father Wesley's attitude.

"Forget it." Father Wesley and Grimaldi then started back towards the rectory.

The street was abuzz with activity because of the accident Shagtyme was guilty of causing. As the two men approached the rectory, Father Wesley noticed Jenna was on the front lawn playing with Shagtyme. He also took notice of Father Coniglio talking to Bryan Fogarty. They were standing on the front walk of the church where Bryan had parked his motorcycle. They were engaged in what seemed to be a heavy discussion. Father Wesley was beginning to detest this day. Bryan would not be speaking to Father Coniglio unless it concerned him. A queasy feeling came over the priest. He just knew this wasn't good.

As he crossed the street in the direction of the church, he observed Father Coniglio and Bryan shaking hands before his old friend made a hasty exit, jumping on his bike and taking off. Father Wesley meandered towards Father Coniglio. The old priest remained stationed in front of the church, his hands crossed, waiting for his associate to join him. The younger priest was getting bad vibes about whatever had taken place between Father Coniglio and Bryan Fogarty. As he neared Father Coniglio he asked, "What's going on?"

"Father, can I see you in my office?" The old priest had a somber look on his face.

Father Wesley nodded. He had no idea what had taken place but whatever it was, it had given him an unsettling feeling in the pit of his stomach.

———m———

"Father, won't you please sit down," Father Coniglio said in a hushed voice as he sat at his desk. Father Coniglio stared into Father Wesley's aquatic eyes. He had no inkling as to how the younger priest was going to react to the sad news he had to pass on to him.

"Father, I have some tragic news to report to you. About an hour ago a woman was found dead in an apartment down by the beach..."

As Father Coniglio uttered the words, Father Wesley's pulse quickened, and his mouth became dry. The day which had always been in the back of his mind was at hand. He wasn't sure if he should be smug or should he cry. He did neither.

"...that woman's name was Joan Wesley. I believe she was your mother. Bryan came here to tell us the sad news before the police found out who she was, and her relationship to you."

Father Wesley dropped his head down and stared at the floor. "How did she die?" he asked, as if he didn't know.

"She suffocated in her own blood and vomit."

"Was her death attributed to alcohol?"

"There was an empty vodka bottle in her bed."

Father Wesley looked up at Father Coniglio, a sad and tired gaze in his eyes. "So she died the way she lived. I always believed this was the way she would go." He seemed to be fighting whatever emotion he should be showing and this bothered the older prelate.

"Father, I want you to know that I met your mother a few weeks ago while walking the beach. I didn't know who she was at the time, but I did come to find out. Father, I know she was a disappointment to you but try not to judge her too harshly. I'll admit she was a downtrodden soul but in our brief encounter I found her to be a sad creature, sad because of what she had not taken advantage of during her time on earth."

Father Wesley shook his head in despair. "You're being kind, Father, but I know differently. My mother led an unsavory lifestyle, a lifestyle that only had room for the weakest of God's creations. I know you find it strange that I have not shed a tear. But then, what have I lost? I was no light in her life. I was a hindrance."

Father Coniglio was hard-pressed to explain to his associate how he felt, but he was going to try. "I think you're wrong. I think she was proud of you."

"She sure had a funny way of showing it," Father Wesley answered, his voice ringing with cynicism.

"That's where you are remiss, Father. Your mother was extremely proud of you and what you have accomplished in your life. What disappointment she knew in life centered around herself and the shame she brought to you. It was impossible for her to reveal how she truly felt. It's a sad footnote to a life, but it's true."

"Father, it's as if you are eulogizing her. You're finding good where good did not exist."

"What I'm trying to say to you, Father, is don't make the same mistake. Let her pass into the next life with the assurance that even if there is no love in your heart there is forgiveness. You are a bigger person than the one you are trying to portray. Take heed of what I'm saying or you might be regretting it for the rest of your life."

Father Wesley was perturbed by what Father Coniglio had to say. He did not consider the old priest's lone casual encounter with his mother to amount to much. What did he know of the anguish and embarrassment he was forced to go through as a child? The old priest knew nothing of the foul truth he had to face and how he fought back with the physical attributes God had given him. *Yes,* he assured himself, *Father Coniglio could not possibly understand the bitterness which ravished his heart and soul.*

"Father, I'll bury my mother. But I'll do it without the slightest trace of remorse in my heart. Love is something to be gained and appreciated. It is not a virtue that can be summoned for a splinter of time or a moment of grief. Don't ask of me what I am incapable of doing."

Father Wesley did not wait for a rebuttal from Father Coniglio. He had made his point and left, abruptly. The old priest remained seated and pondered what Father Wesley was experiencing. He honestly believed that under his hard façade was a man of torment. The older priest could only pray that Father Wesley came to grips with the anguish which bedeviled him before he placed his mother in the ground.

Meanwhile, Father Wesley returned to his room. He was finally rid of the link which had made his life so miserable. That being the case, why did he not feel better about himself?

Then he thought of Grimaldi and the tears came forth. He had preached God's tenets but now found he was unable to practice them. He felt like a fraud. He thought he had put his mother aside many years ago, but he hadn't. Now it was time for him to find the strength which was warranted so his mother could rest in peace.

CHAPTER
TWENTY

Two days later Joan Wesley's funeral was held at St. Theresa's. There were more than one hundred people in attendance, but not one could lay claim to being a friend of the deceased. Those people on hand came out of respect for Father Wesley. He was a priest who had proven to be a friend. Thanks to her son's popularity Joan Wesley was receiving a dignified sendoff to the hereafter.

Father Wesley appreciated the respect so many of his fellow parishioners were exhibiting. He expected his mother's funeral to be a lonely and sad affair, with nary a soul attending. The loyal and understanding friends he had come to know saved this ritual from becoming a sad embarrassment.

Father Wesley celebrated the Mass with Phu Luong serving as the altar server. Father Coniglio stood off to the side, in the sacristy, wondering what kind of eulogy his associate was going to deliver. In a way he prayed for this day to be over so the memory of Joan Wesley could be buried with her.

Finally the time was at hand and Father Wesley approached the lectern. As he did so a lump built in Father Coniglio's throat. His palms began to sweat and his heart began to beat at a frantic pace. The old priest bowed his head and offered a prayer for the forlorn soul of Joan Wesley. He had a queer feeling he would be the only one doing so on this day. He crossed his fingers and made a silent plea to the God above, asking for Joan Wesley's son to be gracious as he bid her farewell.

Father Wesley scanned the crowd before him. Intensity burned within him which he had never known before. As a man of the cloth it was expected of him to show compassion, yet he was having trouble doing so. It pained him to know it was his mother who was to be the victim of his lack of mercy. If he ever needed the Lord's hand on his shoulder then this was the moment.

"I thank you all for finding the time to join me in this personal moment of grief. Before us rests a woman. A woman who was scorned in life. Many of you did not know her but did know of her. Her life was one of decadence and self-abuse, a salacious lifestyle which was appalling to all. Many would call it the waste of a life. A person who preferred to walk in the dark rather than the light. But I have been forced to look at her life differently.

"As a man of God I must stop and examine each soul that comes before me. I must take notice of the seeds of immorality and behold the bitter fruit that begs the question—why? I cannot castigate a soul and deem it irretrievable until the question has been answered.

"Now, you ask, what good can be found in the soul of the person reposing before us? I asked the same question with a great deal of pain and repugnance, for the life I explored had a link to me. A sordid person who brought shame and humiliation my way but, in a strange sense, passed on strength and provided an insight to a life that might have entrapped me, if it had not been for her. In an odd way she sacrificed her soul for mine. You might laugh at what I have to say but you will listen. My words will probably astound you, but heed what I have to say. Before you is a child of God, who was also an instrument of the Almighty.

"She was the savior of your daughters. Her role in life was cast to be a lewd one. Her mere presence, in the eyes of many, made parents more fervent and better Christians. She was to be a living reminder for what one should not be. It is a sad legacy but one that must be passed. If her unholy presence turned a stomach but spared a soul from a similar fate, then there was an ounce of good to be found in her life. Therefore, with a heavy heart, and a trace of sorrow, I say good-bye to my mother.

I know, somehow, she has reaped a reward that only God can justify. It torments me to know I understand her better in death than I did in life."

Father Wesley removed himself from the lectern, unsure of where the words had come from, but grateful they had. Still, there were no tears on his part. Somberness filled the church. Father Coniglio heaved a sigh of relief and uncrossed his fingers. Grimaldi's cheeks became moist. Father Wesley's words made him realize that he could not do to his daughter what Joan Wesley had done to her son. Father Wesley, in a few words, had verified and restructured the faith of those inside the tiny church on Everton Street. He found good in a woman whose legacy should have been one of contempt. Those who had gathered had done so out of respect to Father Wesley. As they left this house of worship they felt privileged to have been a part of it.

Joan Wesley's casket was wheeled down the center aisle of the church. Bryan Fogarty and five of his rebellious cohorts from the beach served as pallbearers. Father Wesley had asked this favor of his old friend since they were part of the breed his mother had known so well. He stood at the foot of the altar, his hands folded, and watched as his mother was taken from this House of God. In a gentle whisper he said: "Go in peace."

Father Coniglio walked over to the troubled priest's side. "That was nice," he said. "You didn't disappoint me. Your mother was right when she said she was proud of you. Don't ever be ashamed to admit she was your mother."

Father Wesley turned to look at Father Coniglio, his cheeks glistening with the tears he was trying to hide. "I don't know where the words came from. They were just there," he explained.

"The words came from your heart," Father Coniglio assured him.

"I just hope she's not resting in the bowels of hell," Father Wesley said in a voice trembling with fear.

Father Coniglio placed his frail left arm around the younger priest's shoulder. It was a comforting feeling to Father Wesley and he felt like crumbling into the older priest's embrace and weeping endlessly. Yet, he had to remain strong. There was a certain part of him that was not going to allow his feelings to show.

"Rest at ease, my young friend," Father Coniglio consoled him. "If God had any decision to make about your mother's destiny you helped Him make that decision in the last hour. Now go and bury your mother. There is nothing else you can do with the dead. The plight of the deceased is out of your hands. Turn your concern to the living, those around you who now demand your attention."

A sad smile came to Father Wesley's face. Thanks to Father Coniglio, he felt as though a tremendous burden had been lifted from his shoulders.

———⟨ɯ⟩———

It was two hours later when Father Wesley returned from the cemetery. Emotionally drained from the experiences of the past few days, he went straight to his office. The rectory was extremely quiet at the moment, and he just assumed Father Coniglio and Shagtyme went out for their daily walk. He also had no idea where Mildred and Grimaldi were and frankly, he didn't care. He rested his head on the top of the desk.

A few minutes later he heard a commotion which seemed to be coming from the kitchen. He could hear Father Coniglio's voice and he was ranting. "It's a damn shame. A damn shame, I'm telling you," he kept bellowing over and over.

Father Wesley raised himself from the desk and headed towards the kitchen to see what was troubling the old priest.

Father Coniglio was pacing back and forth and there was no doubt he was upset. Mildred was sitting at the kitchen table. She had not said a word. She was serving as his sounding board. "It's a tragedy, a damn tragedy," he was now shouting.

Father Wesley stepped forward into the kitchen. "What's a tragedy?" he asked.

Father Coniglio turned to look at his associate, a nasty scowl on his face. "It's Temple Beth Abraham. Some arsonist burned it to the ground."

"That certainly is a tragedy. Are you sure it was arson?"

"Of course it was arson," Father Coniglio answered, tersely. "The fire department has labeled the fire as suspicious. I'd have to say that usually means arson. It was an anti-Semitic act of violence against the Jewish community of Paine."

"Have you spoken to Rabbi Zuckerman?"

"Not yet, but I will."

"Isn't Temple Beth Abraham the only synagogue in the city?"

"It is. If I know Rabbi Zuckerman, he'll have the place rebuilt as quickly as possible. In the meantime they're going to have to find a place they can use as a house of worship."

"Did they save the Torah?"

"I don't know that either. Boy, this whole incident has me fuming."

It had been less than three hours since Father Coniglio had consoled him. Now it was Father Wesley's turn to do the same for the old priest who had become a close friend.

"Father, try and relax. I understand how this fire has upset you but if you don't try and calm down you're going to blow a blood vessel."

"I can't calm down," he shouted. "In fact, I'm going to try and reach Rabbi Zuckerman right now!" Father Coniglio stormed out of the kitchen. Father Wesley and Mildred could hear his office door slam shut after he entered it.

"He thinks the world of Rabbi Zuckerman. They have been friends for years," the housekeeper felt compelled to tell Father Wesley as she raised herself from the kitchen table.

"I understand," Father Wesley replied. "But I hate to see him take it so personally. He's acting as though someone had torched this place."

"That's just the way he is. You're not going to change him at this stage in his life."

"That, too, I understand."

Changing the subject, Mildred asked Father Wesley if he had eaten. He was hungry but he only wanted a salad. It was too warm to eat anything heavy.

Father Wesley was sitting at the kitchen table eating the tossed salad Mildred had made him when Father Coniglio returned to the kitchen ten minutes later. "I talked to Rabbi Zuckerman. He's going to drop by later this afternoon and fill us in on what happened and what his plans are. Maybe we can be of some help."

Father Wesley looked at him, quizzically. Through a mouthful of lettuce he said: "What kind of help can we offer? We certainly don't have any money to pass his way."

"How do I know, Father. But if we can be of some assistance to our Jewish brethren then we will be. Say, that salad looks good. Are those my tomatoes?"

Father Wesley glanced at Mildred, a dumbfounded look on his face. "Yes, they are," Mildred answered for him. "Would you like a salad of your own?"

"I'd love one," the old priest answered as he pulled out a chair and sat down at the kitchen table, before returning his attention to his associate. "Father, I want you to join Rabbi Zuckerman and me when he drops by later this afternoon."

"I'd be happy to, but why do you need me?"

"Three heads are better than two. Also, you might come up with one of your off the wall ideas that just might work."

"Glad to see you have such faith in me."

"Father, to be honest with you, you never cease to amaze me. Just when I think you are about to run out of steam you prove me wrong. You have an uncanny way of finding an answer if there is one to be had."

"I'm not so sure about that," Father Wesley answered, embarrassed by Father Coniglio's sudden boost of confidence in him.

Mildred placed the salad in front of the old priest. He took his fork and stabbed the utensil into a slice of tomato. A satisfied expression came to his face as he chewed on it. "This is great," he said with pride. "I just knew it was going to be a bumper crop this year."

—〰—

At 4:30 that afternoon Rabbi Zuckerman arrived at the St. Theresa's rectory. Father Coniglio anxiously awaited his arrival and was the one to greet him at the door. He had been sitting in the living room for an hour, counting the minutes until his old friend showed up.

Father Coniglio immediately ushered the short and rotund rabbi to his office. Once his friend was seated he summoned Father Wesley from his room. As soon as the younger priest joined them, he instructed Mildred they were not to be disturbed unless it was absolutely necessary. It was time to get down to brass tacks. Father Coniglio was beginning to feel as though they were actually going to get something accomplished.

Father Wesley and Rabbi Zuckerman exchanged handshakes. It was the first time they had met, although Rabbi Zuckerman was well aware of Father Wesley's impact on St. Theresa's. "So sorry to hear about your mother," the rabbi said.

"Thank you," he answered, sincerely.

"Gentlemen, why don't we get right to it," Father Coniglio said as if he were giving a command. Rabbi Zuckerman's dilemma had his old juices flowing.

Father Coniglio sat behind his desk, hands folded, looking as though he were presiding over a high-level meeting. The pensive look on his face told the two clergymen before him they were not leaving this room until they had matters under control.

"Rabbi, fill us in. What has transpired over the course of the day? Where do you stand at the moment? I know you, Morton. You are not going to allow any moss to grow beneath you."

Father Coniglio seemed to be engrossed in zeal as he spoke to his Jewish counterpart. His unearthed fervor did not catch Father Wesley by surprise but the same could not be said for the rabbi. Father Coniglio's ardor was not something he expected to encounter.

The rabbi cleared his throat. He wasn't sure what this meeting was going to accomplish but he was willing to give it a try. "Right now, it's going kind of slow."

"In what way?" Father Coniglio wanted to know.

"Well, right now we know it was arson."

"Aha!" Father Coniglio exclaimed, as though he were playing the role of *Sherlock Holmes*. His piercing glare turned to Father Wesley. "What did I tell you," he said in a self-gratifying manner.

"You did, Father," his associate answered, further stoking the fires of commitment Father Coniglio seemed intent on showing his Hebrew friend.

"How did they come to the arson conclusion?" was Father Coniglio's next question.

"Rather simply," the rabbi responded. "Once the smoldering was under control the fire department brought in a dog especially trained to sniff out those things. They ended up finding an incendiary device that had set off the blaze. What happens next is sort of in the air."

"It was anti-Semitic, wasn't it?" Father Coniglio needed to know.

"I don't think so."

"What makes you say that?"

"They would have left a calling card, at least according to the police."

"What do you think?" Father Coniglio asked of Father Wesley.

"I think the police are right," he was quick to respond. "If these were Jew bashers; they'd let you know about it."

"How so?" Father Coniglio asked, as if Father Wesley were an expert on the subject.

"Father, please. You know, as well as I do, that if this was ethnically motivated those responsible, would have burned a swastika, or something equally demeaning, on the lawn as well."

"So if it's not anti-Semitic then what are they after?" Father Coniglio was all questions.

"Maybe I can answer that," Rabbi Zuckerman interjected. "There's been a land development company, Old Colony Real Estate, looking to make some investments in the community. There has been talk amongst my congregation about building a new and more modern synagogue, on the large parcel of land we own that abuts the land we currently occupy, one with the amenities we now lack, especially a day care center. Whoever decided to burn the place must have heard the rumor because I was approached about the prospect of selling the land on which the temple sits. I told them I wasn't interested. Now, I don't want to go around accusing anyone of setting fires but that sure looks like a convenient way to try and turn a *not interested* into an *interested*."

"It sure does," Father Coniglio agreed. "I don't suppose there is any way of proving they're responsible, if they indeed are."

"You can forget about that happening. If they were, indeed, involved in some sinister plot against the temple you can bet their tracks were covered long before the first flame was sparked." The truth of his own words did not set well with the rabbi.

"What do you think your next move will be?" Father Coniglio asked the beleaguered rabbi.

"That's where it gets murky."

"What are you saying?"

"It's the insurance company, the police, and the fire department. They have to conduct a complete and comprehensive investigation. If it were up to me, I'd have the temple rebuilt as soon as possible, if it were not for this bureaucracy nonsense."

"Your congregation, Rabbi. You're going to need a house of worship. What are you going to do until the red tape is resolved?" Father Coniglio was genuinely concerned.

"So far that has proven to be a problem. I've inquired around about renting some halls but I don't seem to be getting anywhere. They all seemed to be booked."

"I find that hard to believe," Father Wesley chimed in. "Are you sure it doesn't have something to do with the fact that no one wants to rent their building to a bunch of Jews who want to turn it into a synagogue. Not to mention, they are probably fearful that they are setting themselves up for a little fire drill of their own, from some nut who does not appreciate the kind act of a good Samaritan.

"I thought you didn't think the fire was ethnic related?" Father Coniglio said.

"I don't. But that doesn't mean there might not be some Jew haters out there who think it was and might just like to finish off the job themselves."

"I suppose that thought has crossed some sicko's mind," Rabbi Zuckerman was moved to say, dejectedly.

"Hey! I've got an idea," Father Coniglio said, excitedly.

"And it is?" the rabbi asked.

"St. Matthew's has that CCD recreation hall they built a few years ago. I think it's large enough to house your congregation."

A stabbing expression came to the rabbi's face. "I have explored that possibility, as well. I spoke to Monsignor Cosgrove just over an hour ago, and he is willing to let us use the facility for a thousand dollars a day. However, we cannot use the hall until eight o'clock or until their evening Masses are completed on those Saturdays. The monsignor was concerned about a congregation…parking problem."

"A parking problem! A thousand bucks a day! What humanitarians! They're nothing but a bunch of Philistines, as far as I'm concerned," an agitated Father Wesley said as he abruptly stood.

"Father, relax. It makes me angry as well. But right now, as we speak, it's the only alternative I have."

"That may be the case but they shouldn't be trying to take advantage of you. We may be of different faiths but we worship the same God. We should be there for one another, rather than trying to capitalize on the other's misfortune." Father Wesley was clearly upset, figuring Father Moore was probably behind the attempt, on the part of the staff at St. Matthew's, to impede the progress Rabbi Zuckerman and the good people of Temple Beth Abraham were trying to make, until he received what he wanted out of the deal.

"Unless you have a better suggestion then that's the way it's going to be. The money doesn't bother me. We can well afford it. What does bother me is being forced to provide a service so late in the day. But until something better comes along that's the way it has to be."

A devilish smile came to Father Wesley's face. Father Coniglio knew that expression. "Father, I can tell by that look on your face that something is rattling around in that brain of yours. What gives?"

Father Wesley began pacing back and forth, his arms crossed, his right index finger pressed against his lips. What he thought might be an endeavor of complexity didn't seem as bizarre now that he had a few moments to dwell on it. He stopped his pacing and pointed his finger at both men. His mind was made up.

"If the rabbi is up to bending the rules so can we. Why don't we let Rabbi Zuckerman use St. Theresa's on the Saturdays he needs until his temple is rebuilt. We only use the church for confessions on Saturday and we can adjust that schedule, accordingly. What do you say, Rabbi? It wouldn't cost you a nickel."

"Oh…I don't know," the rabbi responded, somewhat flustered by Father Wesley's suggestion. "It seems a little unorthodox. I mean, would you celebrate a Mass in a mosque?"

"I would if I had to," Father Wesley let him know.

Rabbi Zuckerman looked at Father Coniglio. The Jewish clergyman was warming up to the idea. But the suggestion meant little if Father Coniglio refused to buy into it. St. Theresa's was still his church. "So what do you think?" the rabbi asked.

Father Coniglio leaned back in his chair, his left hand covering his mouth. He nodded slowly before saying, "It's okay with me. The place is yours for as many Saturdays as you need it."

"Then that settles it!" Father Wesley exclaimed. He extended his right hand to Rabbi Zuckerman. "Welcome to St. Theresa's, Rabbi. A church which recognizes all denominations."

Rabbi Zuckerman took the young priest's hand and shook it but there was a look of distress on his face. "I just hope this doesn't backfire on us. You spoke of it earlier, Father. I pray St. Theresa's doesn't become a target because of your humane ways." The rabbi's distress was real.

"Rabbi, we can't live in fear. We cannot buckle under to intimidation. If we succumb to such pressure, we might as well padlock the doors and board up the windows. We'd be of no use to anyone."

The rabbi shook his head in amazement. "I heard you were a go-getter."

The meeting adjourned and the three men left Father Coniglio's office. As they did so Father Coniglio asked his fellow priest, "What do you think the chancery is going to say about all this?"

"Don't worry about the chancery," Father Wesley reassured him. "I can handle them."

Fourteen days came and went and not much was made of the fact that Temple Beth Abraham was now operating out of St. Theresa's. There was an article written about the unique relationship being forged by the two faiths in the *Paine Journal,* a local newspaper, but that was the extent of it. The lack of notoriety pleased the two priests and the rabbi. The less fanfare the better. The trio of clergymen didn't want this issue becoming a bigger topic than it was. Even the chancery had yet to get involved. Father Wesley had written an email to Father Moore's office about the unique bond developed by the two faiths, but he had not heard back from the cardinal's secretary. But Father Wesley was no fool; he knew it was just a matter of time until he heard from the man and the displeasure he was sure to vent.

CHAPTER

TWENTY-ONE

It was Sunday afternoon, two weeks since the two faiths agreed to share St. Theresa's as a base of operation. The little church on Everton Street was now quiet after a hectic weekend. Father Wesley had the church to himself since Father Coniglio was taking his nap.

He was seated in the first pew, lost in his thoughts. He found the quiet church to be so peaceful. Shagtyme was with him, stretched out on the floor of the center aisle. The dog seemed to be enjoying the still of the moment as much as his master.

Twenty minutes had passed, and Father Wesley used the time to reflect on his fifteen months at St. Theresa's. It was his point of view that it had been time well spent. He didn't know how the cardinal felt about his days at his old friend's church but he did know how his secretary felt. A contentious smile crept across his face as he thought of his adversary at the chancery.

While lost in thought, the front door of the church opened. Father Wesley didn't hear it but Shagtyme did. The dog raised his head and looked back across his body from his prone position. A woman had entered St. Theresa's and the dog watched as she stopped and stared at the empty pews before her, as if she were trying to make the decision as to where to kneel and pray.

Shagtyme's arousal caught Father Wesley's attention. When he turned and saw the woman a sense of relief rushed through him. Over the past several days he had become extremely edgy, fearing some kind of reprisal against St. Theresa's for opening its doors to the worshippers of Temple Beth Abraham. The woman looked harmless. He did not consider her to be any part of a dissident group.

Father Wesley turned his attention away from the woman, but he could hear her footsteps approaching. As the woman neared the pew, Shagtyme sat up and her pace slowed. She took three additional steps and stopped. The woman was wary of the dog.

"Hello, Father. It's been a while," she said from a distance of twenty feet.

A chill ran through Father Wesley; he knew the voice. It pained him to hear it again for he remembered the last time they had spoken. Yet, he knew this day was going to dawn sooner or later. Today was that day. It was the voice of Ruth Ann Travers.

He turned his head slowly and gazed at her. The years had not been kind to his old girlfriend. She appeared to be weary and drawn. She had also put on about twenty to thirty pounds. This was not the picture he had painted in his mind of her, should they meet again. The person he was seeing saddened him.

"Ruth Ann, what a pleasant surprise to see you. It has been a long time."

Ruth Ann stared at Father Wesley for a moment and tried to remember the reckless and carefree man she had once called her lover. It was hard for her to fathom the fact he was now a man of God. It all seemed so out of context.

She wondered if she still had a flame burning inside her for this man. She also wondered what had become of the feelings he had once professed for her. This was a day Ruth Ann also rued but it was long overdue. "May I sit down?" she asked.

"But of course," Father Wesley said as he slid over three feet in the pew so she could join him. "Don't mind the dog. He's friendly," he went on as she daintily stepped past the animal and moved into the pew.

"I hope so," she answered in return. "You and that dog have become legends in the streets. His name is Shagtyme, isn't it?"

"It is."

"It's funny. Years ago you were also a legend in the streets but it was a legend of a different nature. Now you return and become a symbol of what is good and right. Did you know the people of this parish consider you a gift from God?"

"No, I didn't. Where did you hear that nonsense?"

"It's what they're saying in the streets. Is the trust these people seem to have in you for real?"

A nagging thought came to Father Wesley as Ruth Ann uttered the words. He could only think of the day when he was assigned to St. Theresa's. He felt like such a *Judas*. He knew he had better change the subject before he started becoming despondent because of the role he knew he was playing.

"Enough about me. Tell me about yourself. How has your life been? I understand you have a daughter."

"How do you know that?"

"Sharon Beasley came by to see me about a year ago. She told me."

"I see. Well, if you've talked to Sharon then you know my life has not been a bed of roses."

"Yes. She did tell me about some of the hardships you've been forced to endure. I know your daughter's name is Rachel and you were married and now divorced. Sharon also told me you were having some problems with your daughter."

"Sharon has a big mouth," Ruth Ann said, angrily.

"Don't be upset with her. She was concerned about you. Why don't you tell me about your daughter? How old is she?"

This conversation was becoming more difficult by the minute but Rachel was one of the reasons she was here. She needed her old boyfriend's help since he was now a priest. But Ruth Ann knew once she told him of Rachel, it was going to grieve him much like she had grieved him fourteen years earlier. "She's thirteen going on thirty," Ruth Ann told him.

Thirteen! Wow! he was thinking to himself. She didn't waste any time getting herself pregnant after leaving him. This was a lot for the priest to stomach in one sitting but he was going to have to do it.

"So what seems to be the problem with Rachel?"

Ruth Ann took a swallow and began. "I can't control her. She hangs out on the beach with a gang. Most of the kids she hangs with are a good four or five years older than her. What's becoming of her scares me. I could use your help."

A sheepish grin came to Father Wesley's face. "Sounds like a girl I once knew."

"Yes, I know, and look what's become of me. I don't want the same thing happening to her."

"What makes you think I can be of any help?"

"Because you know what it's like on both sides of the fence. Those people she hangs out with on the beach know all about you and your history. I think, in a strange way, they admire you. In you, they think they see a way out when they're ready to make the commitment. I know it sounds crazy but that's how their minds work."

Father Wesley shook his head in dismay, before taking her hands in his and squeezing them. "You make me sound like some kind of hero, which I'm not. Maybe, from afar, those kids look at me in such a light but if I was to try and interfere in their lives it'd be a whole different story. That includes Rachel."

"So what you're saying is that you are not even willing to try."

"What I'm saying is that Rachel can't be helped until she wants to be. Perhaps there is something else in her life that is causing her to rebel. What about your ex-husband? Doesn't he care about the direction his daughter's life is taking?"

Ruth Ann bowed her head, as if in a state of shame. "Her father isn't around. There is nothing he can do," she informed him.

Father Wesley looked at Ruth Ann, his mind now steeped in suspicion. He was trying to imagine what kind of shallow individual she had married. How could any man turn his back on a child because of a divorce? He knew such men existed and, apparently, Ruth Ann had found one. He then thought of Anna Gregorio and her predicament. He had to get a better handle on these matters if he hoped to be of any help to either woman.

"I don't suppose you want to tell me who Rachel's father is."

"I don't think it's necessary."

"I see."

This was difficult. Oh, how she wanted to tell him the truth.

"Will you please try and help me? I'm not expecting any miracles. I was just hoping you might be the person she'd listen to and come to realize that what she is doing with her life is wrong."

"Ruth Ann, let's keep in mind she is only thirteen. All children go through a rebellious period. I know we did. It's probably nothing more than a phase and she'll get over it."

"You know better than that. You know what the beach crowd is like and how easy it is to become a piece of crud. You've been there. The only difference is that God smiled down on you and showed you a way out. Maybe he did so with the idea you could return and help those who can't help themselves."

"Never knew you to be so philosophical," Father Wesley remarked.

"Never thought I'd be talking to you like this myself. But I've had some time to think about it and I truly believe that you were sent back here for a reason. The good you've done in your short time is already quite apparent."

"How's that?" Father Wesley was anxious to hear what his old girlfriend had to say. He also wanted to find out what she now thought of him. He had it in his mind that Ruth Ann now regretted the day she shut him out of her life. He knew he was trying to even the score by forcing her into admitting her mistake and thus gaining a measure of self-gratification which he believed he deserved. Ruth Ann had done him wrong and he wanted her to know it and hurt over it.

"The Christmas party you put together for the children in the parish is one example. That act of generosity opened the eyes of the people of St. Theresa's to believe you were not going to allow their church to be yanked out from underneath them. The people of St. Theresa's believe in you but, more importantly, they trust in you. You've taken a tired old church and raised it from its deathbed."

What Ruth Ann had to say was not what Father Wesley wanted to hear. He was trying to make her hurt and she was praising him. He was also getting tired of these glowing accolades which kept coming his way. Sometimes those flowery compliments directed at him made him want to sing out what a fraud he was. Now the insidious feeling tormented him as he realized that Ruth Ann, the only person he had ever loved, was now one of those ardent believers in him. He was gradually starting to feel as though he were cursed. The priest was going to try and do himself in.

"I think the parishioners of St. Theresa's read too much into my tenure and make too big a deal out of some of the things that have happened since I've been here. But, enough about me. How can I help you with Rachel?"

"Just talk to her. See if you can get through to her. Deep down inside she's a good kid. She's just confused. Life has not been kind to her and she's angry about it. But I don't think she's a hopeless cause. All she needs is some simple direction from a person she can trust."

"And you believe I'm that person?"

"Yes, I do."

Ruth Ann's belief in him was winning Father Wesley over, but he wondered just how much good he could do. If Rachel was anything like her mother then he might stand a chance of getting through to her. If she wasn't, then he didn't know what to expect. But he had to make it clear to himself that whatever he tried to do, he did for the benefit of Rachel and not because he was out to impress Ruth Ann.

"I'll talk to her. However, allow me to do it my way. I assume she won't come to see me, so I'll have to seek her out. Where on the beach am I most likely to find her?"

A sorry but relieved smile came to Ruth Ann's face. She was feeling lucky that God had sent this man back into her life at a time when she could use his help. Then the sin she carried began to bite at her from within. If only she could tell him the truth. But the truth carried pain with it and she didn't want to hurt this man any more.

"On the seawall near a place called Rose's. It's the old Maxine's."

The thought of going near Maxine's—or Rose's as it was now called—pained him but it was a pain he would have to endure. "Then I'll track her down," he said.

"Thank you. I hope this doesn't violate any rules," she said as she leaned over and planted a kiss on his cheek.

"None that I know of," he replied as he recalled those bygone days when their kisses were of a much more passionate nature.

"I must be going," she said as she arose from the pew. "It was nice seeing you again."

Father Wesley, remaining seated, said, "It was nice seeing you, too. I'll be in touch."

Ruth Ann stepped out of the pew and was about to walk down the aisle when she stopped. "Oh, I heard about your mother's passing. You're a changed man, so I assume you are more considerate and more forgiving of the lifestyle she employed. I'm sorry."

"Thank you," he said. That was gracious of her, he thought, since Ruth Ann was the one person who knew how much he despised his mother because of the way she lived her life. She seemed to understand him better now, and what he might be going through.

He continued to watch as she walked down the aisle and exited the church. He wasn't sure what he expected to feel once they did meet. But now that the time had come and gone he was sure his feelings for Ruth Ann remained ambiguous.

CHAPTER

TWENTY-TWO

It was another hot Indian summer day as the black Audi made its way down Everton Street. The vehicle came to a halt on the opposite side of the street from the church. Sixteen days had passed since St. Theresa's had become the temporary home of Temple Beth Abraham.

During that period Father Wesley had become extremely tense. Two weeks and not a word from the chancery or, to be more precise, Father Moore. In addition, Father Wesley had not made his weekly personal phone call to the cardinal's secretary, since dispatching the email explaining the decision he and Father Coniglio had rendered concerning Temple Beth Abraham. He knew the man had to be hot under the collar. The spirit of humanitarianism being exhibited at St. Theresa's was being looked upon with scorn by the cardinal's zealous assistant; of that, Father Wesley was fairly certain. This exhibition of being a good Samaritan also had to be proving to be a public relations nightmare for Father Moore and a major hindrance in his plan to bring St. Theresa's down.

The driver's side door of the black Audi opened and the hot air clashed with the air conditioning inside the vehicle. Father Moore emerged from the automobile and his face became flushed by the suffocating heat. In a matter of seconds he began to perspire and his breathing became labored. He was dressed in his black priestly garb and the dark color of the clothes retained the heat. The white collar around his neck seemed too tight and he felt like ripping it off to relieve the prickly irritation it was causing. *What was it about this place,* he wondered? Whenever he came to St. Theresa's the weather seemed to serve as a detriment.

Father Moore's pace quickened as he crossed the street and made his way up the walkway to the rectory. He could hear voices coming from the backyard. The voices were those of Father Coniglio and Grimaldi having another spirited conversation about the old priest's garden. He also heard the barking of a dog. Had to be the mutt Father Wesley had adopted, he surmised.

Inside the rectory Mildred was busy vacuuming the living room rug when she heard the front doorbell ring. The distraction it caused put her in an irritable mood. She hated to be disturbed while doing housework.

Upon answering the door her eyes met those of Father Moore. The sight of the scrawny priest gave her stomach a sinking feeling. She remembered him from his earlier visit with the cardinal, and there was something about the man she disliked. As for Father Moore, he vaguely remembered the woman and had forgotten her name as soon as they had been introduced during that initial visit.

"Good morning, Father," Mildred said with a trace of anxiety in her voice.

"And good morning to you," Father Moore replied. "I'm sorry but your name escapes me."

"It's Mildred," she said, warily.

"It's nice to see you again, Mildred," the sinister priest responded through untruthful teeth.

Mildred cast a cursory smile his way but her mind was becoming one tangled web. She was sure his visit was not of a friendly nature.

"Are you here to see Father Coniglio?"

"No. I'm actually here to see Father Wesley. Is he in?"

"Yes, he is. Won't you please come in. He's in his office. Have a seat and I'll tell him you're here."

"Please, do so," he said as he walked past the housekeeper and took a seat in the living room.

Mildred hastily made her way to Father Wesley's office. The door was closed so she knocked and opened it before he could utter a word. "Father, you have a visitor." Mildred's fret was quite evident in her voice.

Father Wesley looked up from a homily he was preparing and asked, "Who is it?"

"It's that Father Moore from the chancery."

Father Wesley leaned back in his chair. He didn't relish this impromptu meeting but in a way he was relieved. This was inevitable so he was anxious to be done with it. With the thought now fresh in his mind, an impish smile found a way to his face. He and Father Moore had something of importance to discuss.

"Send the good father in, Mildred. Let's not make the man wait," he told her, his voice ringing with self-assurance.

Mildred smiled. The priest's cunning grin seemed to be infectious and Mildred returned to the living room, not feeling so leery of the intimidating priest.

Father Wesley stood up from behind his desk as Father Moore entered the room. "What an unexpected surprise. What brings you to St. Theresa's?" Father Wesley forced himself to say.

Father Moore closed the door behind him and motioned for Father Wesley to sit back down. This was Father Moore's indicator that this meeting was of a serious nature. He was not here to exchange pleasantries. "Sit down, Father. We have to talk," he told his fellow priest as he, too, took a seat.

"All right," Father Wesley responded. "I know you're not here for the fun of it. So let's skip the theatrics which usually precedes one of your diatribes." Father Wesley was setting his own ground rules. This was to be a knock-down, drag-out affair.

Father Moore's eyes locked onto the face of Father Wesley and a look of loathing came over him. It seemed as though the scorn he held for Father Wesley intensified with each successive meeting he had with the man. Father Moore abhorred the lack of respect and defiant manner Father Wesley directed towards him, and the office he represented in the archdiocese. Plus, he had to admit, the man had turned out to be a more formidable foe than he thought he was capable of being. It had become a battle of wills between the two prelates but Father Moore knew, in the end, it would be he as the winner because of his station in the chancery. The only problem for Father Moore was that he was unwilling to wait. His patience was wearing thin because of Father Wesley's daring do when it came to the day-to-day operation of St. Theresa's.

Father Coniglio had proven to be the fly in the ointment. The cardinal's secretary had expected the old priest to be out of the picture by now, and the fate of St. Theresa's securely in his grasp. But it wasn't happening. Father Coniglio was defying the odds and Father Moore was placing the blame on Father Wesley for giving the old priest a second wind. Father Wesley was not carrying out the assignment he had been given, and Father Moore was getting tired of playing the waiting game because of Father Wesley's insubordinate ways.

"Okay, Father, we'll play by your rules," Father Moore said, snidely.

Father Wesley's response was only that of a satisfied smile. He nodded for Father Moore to get on with it.

"Father, you have proven to be a major disappointment. You were given an assignment to carry out here at St. Theresa's. But you have knowingly disregarded those instructions and marched to your own beat. Do you agree with what I'm saying?"

"I do not," Father Wesley answered with an irksome smile gracing his face.

Father Moore began to smolder a little more. "Father, how can you sit there and say such a thing, when you know you were sent here to be a caretaker of a sick and dying parish. Your unmitigated gall makes me…"

Father Moore was unable to finish what he had to say. Father Wesley's deportment had him so flushed he was afraid he might say something he would later regret. Instead, he asked him, "Really, Father, what do you have to say for yourself?"

"Plenty," Father Wesley declared. "For one thing, you say I was told to come back here and be a caretaker. That is true, but I also recall the cardinal saying: 'I want you to prove me wrong. Go back to St. Theresa's and make it flourish.' Perhaps you recall the conversation?"

Father Moore said nothing so Father Wesley went on.

"Now, that's two completely different directives I had been given. I decided to follow through on the *flourish* one." Father Wesley observed the agitation on Father Moore's face and his facial features became somewhat contorted. He enjoyed playing this little game. Plus, he had a little something else to pass Father Moore's way that should make his day a complete bummer.

Father Moore was reading into what his fellow priest was doing and he didn't care for it. He had not come here to lose a war of words. "Father, why is it that I feel as though you love jerking me around. It has become a sport for you, hasn't it?"

"I'm afraid I'm going to have to plead *guilty* to the charge. How did you know?" Father Wesley responded with a sense of pride. He felt confident that he had Father Moore on the run. But he wasn't going to get cocky about it.

"By that irritating smirk on your face, that's how. Now, let me tell you something, Father. You may have taken what the cardinal had to say literally, but it is not what he meant. He was trying to be tactful so you wouldn't feel so guilty about what he was asking you to do. But the truth of the matter is this: St. Theresa's is going to close in the not too distant future, no matter how hard you try to turn it around. You've done a good job here, Father, but don't get the wrong idea. St. Theresa's is going to become part of St. Matthew's and there is nothing you can do about it."

"Is that so," Father Wesley replied, his face now taking on a stern look. "Let me tell you something about a church and its parishioners. A church is like a part of your family. You take it away or harm it in some manner and you've done irrevocable harm to yourself. The family will stand up and avenge its loss. That is what's going to happen at St. Theresa's should you turn your back on her now that she has righted herself. The church, the parish, will become a public relations nightmare for you."

"Then it's a public relations nightmare we will learn to live with."

"Father, I believe you are speaking strictly for yourself and not the cardinal in making such a proclamation. I think it is you who has misinterpreted what His Eminence had to say concerning St. Theresa's."

"Father, you think what you want. None of your grandstanding schemes are going to work. You can organize all the Christmas parties you want to impress your parishioners. You can be the trendy priest by owning a dog and spending your own money to fix a roof on a dilapidated church. I let you get away with that much thus far. But now, Father, you have crossed over that fine line. Who gave you the authority to allow a Jewish congregation to use a Catholic church as their place of worship? It is unheard of."

"It is? I thought we were here to help serve one another, regardless of our faith."

"We are. But, Father, I know for a fact that St. Matthew's offered Rabbi Zuckerman the opportunity to use their recreation hall as a makeshift synagogue. It seems more fitting in my way of thinking."

"I'm sure it does," Father Wesley answered. Father Moore was headed exactly in the direction he wanted. "St. Matthew's offer was quite generous, if Temple Beth Abraham paid a nifty stipend of a thousand dollars a week and rearranged their schedule, so it didn't conflict with St. Matthew's. I think our offer, although not financially rewarding, far exceeds what St. Matthew's had to put on the table."

"Father, a thousand dollars is not all that much money. They can well afford it. Why was it necessary for you to be so charitable? The only thing you had to gain out of it was my wrath."

"Once again you are right on target," the annoying smile reappearing on Father Wesley's face as he spoke. "And while we're discussing Temple Beth Abraham let me ask you a few questions concerning the fire which ravaged the place."

Father Moore was taken back. "What questions? You're making it sound as though I had something to do with the fire."

"Father, there are some questions that need to be answered and I think you are the man to do it."

"I have no idea as to what you are talking about." Father Moore appeared to be genuinely mystified by what Father Wesley was saying.

Father Wesley slid open the top drawer of his desk and produced a manila folder. "Father, I've been doing some checking and some strange coincidences have arisen."

"Father, can you just say whatever it is you have to say." Father Moore was beginning to become unnerved. He knew Father Wesley smelled a rat.

"Okay, Father. It seems that in the recent past three churches have been closed. Our Lady of the Sea in Germantown was condemned and

St. Kevin's in Dorchester and the Sacred Heart in Montrose burned to the ground. Now, you say, what do these three churches have in common with Temple Beth Abraham? My research shows me that the three Catholic churches were replaced by high-rise retirement buildings. It was good for the archdiocese to do it this way because of the glut of churches there now are. However, what is missed in the translation is that all three retirement complexes were developed and are currently run by Old Colony Real Estate. A real score for that company, considering the obstacles they managed to sidestep since Church and State are separated and that means no taxes are involved."

Father Wesley paused to see if what he had to say was having an impact on Father Moore. The cardinal's associate didn't disappoint him. The priest was beginning to sweat.

"Now, Old Colony Real Estate approached Rabbi Zuckerman about selling the land on which Temple Beth Abraham sits. It was a business move on their part. There was some talk of a new synagogue being built, so maybe the land where the old one was located was available. That's where it gets interesting."

Again Father Wesley stopped to check out Father Moore's expression. The priest's face now had a steely glare about it. Father Wesley had the man's undivided attention.

"St. Kevin's and the Sacred Heart go up in smoke and Old Colony is there to capitalize. Then Temple Beth Abraham burns to the ground and who has been hanging around ready to lend their assistance? Why Old Colony Real estate, that's who."

Father Moore began to do a slow burn. He knew nothing about Old Colony Real Estate taking an interest in Temple Beth Abraham. Someone might have been getting a little too greedy, but who was it? The *who* was a major concern to Father Moore.

"Father, allow me to interrupt you for a moment. Are you accusing me of being involved in the burning of two churches and a synagogue? If you are, you better have something to back it up." There he had said it. Father Moore wanted to know just how much Father Wesley had uncovered.

"I'm not accusing you of lighting the match but I have to believe you have some…shall we say…interest in what Old Colony Real Estate has to gain."

The bastard knows was the thought which immediately came to the mind of Father Moore. Now it was mandatory for him to find out what was going on with the burning of Temple Beth Abraham. Suddenly, St. Theresa's looked as though it were drifting farther and farther from his reach.

"What interest?" Father Moore asked, knowing what the answer was going to be.

"Father, it seems a certain James Moore is the Chief Executive Officer of Old Colony Real Estate. I believe you know the man. Am I correct?"

"All right, he's my brother. So what. Sure, I took some liberties with the situation involving those closed churches. Call it a conflict of interest if you want, but you're not going to get very far with it. So I practiced a little nepotism. Who hasn't done something like that if given the opportunity?"

"Oh, Father, I don't take issue with you because you took advantage of the opportunity presented to you to fatten the family coffers. In fact, I consider the move to be very enterprising. However, I will take issue with you should I find out that Old Colony had anything to do with the burning of those sacred buildings. As I said, I am not accusing you or anyone of wrongdoing. But I am warning you. I'm on the watch now. Another mysterious fire and I stop looking the other way. There is only one way for you to rid yourself of me. And, Father, for all your faults and self-serving ideals, you do not strike me as a man who would allow himself to be cast in a criminal light."

"Are you done?" was the only response Father Moore could muster.
"I am."

"Then I'll be leaving," Father Moore told him, not sure of what to do next. His thoughts flashed back to that day at the chancery, when he and the cardinal wanted to make sure the man, they selected for this covert assignment, would not come back to hold a loaded gun at their heads for personal gain. Well, thanks to the zeal he had developed, Father

Wesley was doing just that. Only the gun was now pointed strictly at the head of Father Moore.

———⚏———

Father Coniglio was entering the rectory from his hour in the garden as Father Moore was leaving. He looked at Mildred and asked, "What's he doing here?"

"I don't know. He came here to speak to Father Wesley and now he appears to be leaving in a huff. You know, there's something about him I don't like. I don't think he can be trusted."

"My sentiments, exactly," Father Coniglio responded with a smile. It was easy to tell that whatever Father Wesley and Father Moore had been discussing had not turned out to Father Moore's liking. He had to admit the cardinal's decision to send him a helping hand was working out rather nicely.

———⚏———

Once he returned to the chancery, Father Moore immediately put in a call to his brother's office. Although it irked him, St. Theresa's was going to have to come off the *Hit List,* at least as long as Father Coniglio was alive. They were also going to have to be careful in how they dealt with the property involved. Matters were getting slightly out of hand.

"John, so good to hear from you," James replied to the sound of his brother's voice.

Father Moore skipped any small talk and cut right to the core of the matter. "James, forgo whatever plans you have devised for the demise of St. Theresa's."

"Is there a problem, my big brother?"

"There is, and right now any damage done to St. Theresa's could prove to be extremely dangerous. Just back off the St. Theresa's assignment until I give you the word."

"I'll try but I don't know if it can be done. The wheels have been set in motion; a last minute postponement could cost me some credibility, not to mention money. What seems to be upsetting the applecart?"

"It's that damn Father Wesley. He's on to us. What, in heaven's name, went on with the burning of Temple Beth Abraham? I had no idea you were involved."

This was a bit embarrassing for James. He knew what happened with the Temple Beth Abraham burning and he had been hoping his brother never found out about it. "Father John, please believe me when I tell you this, but I did not authorize anyone to burn the Jews' synagogue. My man told me that they were thinking of closing the place down and building another one nearby, so I had one of my people approach them and ask about the place. I came to find out it was not for sale. That should have been the end of it, and it was as far as I was concerned. Trust me. I had nothing to do with the place burning down."

"I see," Father Moore replied. "Well, no matter what, we're now in to it up to our eyeballs. This guy you have working on the St. Theresa's project; is there the off chance he might have been working on his own to try and sweeten the pot for you? If that should prove to be the case I suggest you get rid of him."

"It's not that easy, my brother. You see, he subcontracts to get his end of the job done. He doesn't want to get his hands too dirty."

"James, I don't like what I'm hearing. You're getting too many people involved. You make sure whoever it is you're working with knows we are not in the business of greed. Do you understand?"

"Yeah. Try and relax, will you. Things are going to be fine. I'll see to it that no one operates on their own initiative."

"You do that," Father Moore told his brother before hanging up.

CHAPTER
TWENTY-THREE

"Hey, Fogarty, get your sorry carcass over here. I've got something to talk to you about." It was the voice of the slovenly Arthur Gregorio calling out to Bryan Fogarty, as the biker walked through the front door of Rose's.

"Drunk again, I see," Fogarty said to Johnny Rogers, the owner of Rose's and on this night a bartender.

"Yeah, he is, and he's really starting to annoy some of the other customers. He used to be such an annoying yet, somehow, pleasant drunk to be around. But since leaving his wife he has become one surly individual. I'm telling you, Bryan, he keeps this stuff up I'm going to throw him out of the place, and I won't let him back in until he gets his act back together."

"Any idea why he wants to see me?"

"Yeah. He's been waiting for you. He's got some kind of beef with Paulie."

"You mean Father Paul?"

"The one and only. Keeps saying he is a meddlesome pain in the ass. I told him if anyone knows anything about the father then you're the man. I warned him that Paul Wesley was once a tough S-O-B and, just because he's now a priest, doesn't mean he isn't tough anymore."

"And?"

"And he doesn't seem to care."

"Why don't you tell him you can't run his tab any higher."

"Therein lies another problem. Suddenly, he has plenty of cash. Claims he came into a windfall."

"Okay, I'll talk to him. I'm kinda curious to see what he wants."

As Bryan approached the man, Gregorio motioned for him to take the bar stool next to him. "Let me buy you a beer," he said as Fogarty took his seat.

That gesture alone put Bryan on alert. Arthur Gregorio never bought anyone a drink. He never had the money. "Yeah, I'll have a Budweiser." Bryan wasn't going to pass on the opportunity while it was available.

"A Budweiser for my friend and I'll have another Heineken," he told Rogers.

"Okay Arthur, or are you Arturo these days? I can never get that straight. What do you want to see me about?"

"Call me Arthur. The only people who call me Arturo are my dumbass in-laws, stupid guineas that they are."

"All right, Arthur, what is it you wanted to talk to me about? Johnny says it has something to do with Father Wesley."

"It does. These stories about him being a tough guy before becoming a priest. How true are they?"

"They're true." It was beginning to sound as if Arthur Gregorio was intending to duke it out with Father Wesley, which Bryan Fogarty found amusing.

"Do you think he'd ever fight again? I mean now that he's a priest."

Bryan sensed this conversation was going to turn into a Mulberry bush exercise, so he took it right to Gregorio. "Just what are you getting at Arthur? You got a problem with the father?"

"Yeah, I do, and I just wanted to know how he might respond to getting his brain bashed in."

Fogarty broke into a hearty laugh. "Get his brain bashed in, you say. Gregorio, let me tell you something. You should count your lucky stars Father Paul is who he is these days and not likely to use his fists. If he ever did, he'd kick your sorry butt from here to Timbuktu."

"Oh, really."

"Yeah, really. Now what's this all about?"

"He should have kept his mouth shut. He interfered in my life and he's going to pay for it."

"How'd he do that?" Fogarty was going to get to the bottom of whatever was bothering Arthur Gregorio.

"None of your business." Gregorio was equally determined to keep Bryan from knowing anything.

"This has something to do with your marriage, doesn't it? Did he give a little counseling you didn't agree with so now you want to kick his ass? Good luck to you."

"If he had just kept his mouth shut everything would have taken care of itself. But, no, he had to get involved. Suddenly he's Mr. Pious and Mighty. From the stories I hear about him on the beach he was no saint in his day."

"No, he wasn't. Maybe that's why he's the man to listen to when there is a problem. Obviously your problem has something to do with Anna. Why else would you be sitting here and bitching?"

"Think you know it all, don't you? Well, let me tell you something. When I end up getting divorced it'll be because of that man."

"Wait a minute. Are you trying to tell me something Father Paul said to Anna is the reason you and your wife split up? Come on, what do I look like, the village idiot?"

Arthur had to pause and make sure what he said next was right. After all it was going to be a lie so he was going to have to remember it.

"Ah...no. We were having our troubles and he didn't help matters by getting involved."

"So you're saying if Father Wesley didn't get involved with something to do with Anna, you and her wouldn't be getting divorced. What'd he do? Tell her you're a deadbeat and could do a lot better?"

"You're a smartass. Do you know that?"

"Then explain it to me, Arthur. I think I have a right to know. You're talking about kicking the crap out of a priest, a priest who happens to be a friend of mine. I think it's my duty, as a friend, to look out for him. Maybe, if I talk to him, he can explain what's going on between you two."

Jesus, no, was Arthur's thinking. So far no one, except for family and Father Wesley, knew of Anna's transgression. He didn't know if

Father Wesley would share his wife's secret with Fogarty and he wasn't prepared to take the chance. Arthur would have to let Fogarty know just enough to satisfy him but not enough to embarrass himself in the process. A wife sleeping around is humiliation enough. The possibility of her getting pregnant by her lover takes it beyond forgivable bounds.

"Well, Fogarty, if you can keep this under your hat, I'd appreciate it."

"Sure, Arthur. I'm not the least bit interested in spreading your dirty laundry throughout the streets."

"Who said it's dirty!" Arthur did his best to get miffed. "Anna and I were on a collision course right from the moment we got married. We decided to go our separate ways. But, unfortunately, she ended up getting pregnant just before we came to that decision."

"So how does Father Wesley fit into the mix?" Bryan felt as though Arthur Gregorio was making the story up as he went along.

"I wanted her to have an abortion and she was willing. That is until Father Wesley stuck his nose into our affairs and told her to handle the situation differently. Pure Catholic bull, if you know what I mean."

Something wasn't registering quite right with Fogarty. If Anna was so willing to have an abortion, why did she drag Father Wesley into it? No, Gregorio wasn't telling him everything, and Fogarty really didn't have the right to know. But he did have the right to protect Father Wesley from Arthur Gregorio's wrath. Gregorio didn't have to spit it out to him that he thought Anna might be carrying another man's child. Fogarty had been around enough to know when somebody was trying to conceal something. If that were the case Arthur Gregorio was carrying a vengeance in his heart for a man who had done what could only be expected of him. But Arthur didn't look at it that way. Arthur's pride was telling him he couldn't win, so Father Wesley be damned. Arthur was going to have to recognize this child as his own or let the world know that his wife had been unfaithful to him. A simple abortion, with a concocted story of a miscarriage, would have made his life so much easier. Anna taking heed of Father Wesley's advice had made his life pure misery.

"Arthur, what you just told me sure doesn't seem as though it warrants going after Father Wesley's head." Bryan was hoping to catch him in his lie.

"Maybe not to you, but it does to me. I'm going to have to support this kid for the rest of my life. That's what pisses me off. If that priest had kept to his own business, then I wouldn't have this problem. Damn, I need to get out of here and buy some smokes."

Fogarty watched as Gregorio took a wad of money from his pants pocket to pay his bar bill before leaving to buy some cigarettes. The slovenly bastard did have a bundle of cash on him.

"Say, Arthur, that's a fistful of money you have there. Where'd you come by it? You've never had two nickels to rub together."

"Oh, this," Gregorio began to answer. He stared at the bills as though the money was betraying him. "It's...it's the profit I reaped from selling Anna's car." Another lie he was going to have to remember.

"You sold Anna's car and she let you keep the cash?"

"Yeah, it's my share. It's the least the bitch could have done for me."

Later that night Father Wesley sat alone in the living room of the rectory watching the late news. Father Coniglio had retired two hours earlier. Now that he had forced Father Moore's hand he was enjoying some quiet time. For the first time since being assigned to St. Theresa's he felt the parish was safe from the lecherous hands of the cardinal's secretary. Then the phone rang.

"Hello, Father Wesley speaking."

"Father, it's Bryan. You got a minute to talk?"

"Sure. Is there a problem? It can't be Shagtyme getting loaded again. Last time I checked he was asleep on the kitchen floor."

Fogarty laughed. "No, it's not Shagtyme. I'm calling about you."

"Me? What about me?"

"Father, I've been down here at Rose's all night and I've had to listen to Arthur Gregorio bellyaching about you interfering in his life. It has something to do with whatever you said to his wife about a pregnancy. He's out to get you so I thought I should warn you."

"Thanks, Bryan, I can handle it. Is he still there?"

"No. He left about ten minutes ago, rip-roaring drunk. All of a sudden the guy's got a few bucks and he's spending it like a drunken sailor."

"That's strange. I was led to believe he didn't make much. He sells used cars, right?"

"Yeah, and clunkers at that. Says he sold Anna's car and that's how he got the money."

"That's the car I sold Anna a year ago. I guess she needs the money for more important matters right now."

"Well, I just wanted to let you know about him"

"I appreciate your concern but I'm sure I can handle Arthur Gregorio."

"I'm sure you can too. Just thought you should know."

"Bryan, on another subject, I was wondering if I could ask another favor of you."

"I hope you don't want me to promise to be Santa Claus again."

"No," the priest replied through a muffled chuckle before turning serious. "I had a visit the other day from Ruth Ann. She has a daughter she's having trouble with."

"Rachel."

"You know her?" the priest asked.

"I know of her. She hangs out on the seawall with a group of kids. They are trying to prove they're a tough bunch, just like we did. But, Father, these are different times. If she's not careful she could find herself in some serious shit. Oh, I didn't mean to say that."

"It's all right. Let me get back to Rachel. Ruth Ann wants me to speak to her."

"Father, save your strength. This kid's not going to listen. She's got a massive chip on her shoulder and I can't think of anyone who might be able to dislodge it."

"Do you have any idea what's bothering her?"

"It's her life. She hates it and she wants everybody to know it."

"Okay. Then can you tell me this. Ruth Ann said she's divorced but she wouldn't tell me her ex-husband's name. Maybe you can find it out for me? I'll look this guy up and see if he is part of the problem. Surely he knows of the rough time his daughter is going through."

There was dead silence on the line.

"Bryan? Are you still there?"

"Yes, Father, I am."

"Something's bothering you. What is it?"

"Father…I don't know how to tell you this…but…"

"But what?"

"Father, Ruth Ann is not divorced. She tells everyone she is but she's never been married. I'd have thought she would have been honest with you about her situation."

"That can't be. I talked to Sharon Beasley when I first arrived here and she told me Ruth Ann was divorced."

"She probably told you that because that's what Ruth Ann wants everyone to believe. Sharon obviously abided with her wishes, figuring Ruth Ann would tell you the truth on her own."

Father Wesley was dumbfounded by what he was hearing but he did remember Sharon telling him: *What she did to you hurts her as much as it hurts you.*

"Bryan, I have to go now. Thanks for calling and making me aware of the Arthur Gregorio problem." Father Wesley was now in need of some desperate quality time with himself in order to deal with his thoughts.

"Father, are you going to be all right?" Bryan Fogarty was concerned. He knew what his longtime friend was thinking since he had wondered the same thing.

"Right now, Bryan, I'm not sure."

CHAPTER
TWENTY-FOUR

Father Wesley sat alone, in the last pew of the church. He was having a problem dealing with what Bryan Fogarty had told him the previous night. He wanted to dismiss the crazy thought floating around in his head, but he was unable. It all seemed to add up, and the more he thought about it the more he became convinced he was Rachel's father.

He reconstructed everything he and Ruth Ann had gone through, as it had happened, over and over in his mind until his head hurt. The end result, each time, pointed towards him. He was Rachel's father and now that he was a priest Ruth Ann could not bring herself to tell him the truth. Father Wesley bristled with anger at the thought. She had no right keeping this information from him. She had done him wrong fourteen years ago and she was still doing him wrong today. He had the right to know the truth no matter how damaging it seemed to be.

He continued to fume as Rabbi Zuckerman entered the church. He was looking for Father Wesley for he had good news to pass his way. He was unaware of the predicament the curate now found himself in.

"Father Wesley," he called out upon spotting him and settling into the pew in front of the priest. "I bring good news with me." It was then he noticed the troubled look on the young priest's face. It was plain to see his newfound friend was wrestling with a personal dilemma.

"Oh, Rabbi Zuckerman. Good news, you say. What is it?"

"I've come to tell you that the work on the new temple has commenced, so it won't be long before we'll be back in business. I intend to make this a speedy project. We'll have our doors reopened before you know it."

"That is good news," Father Wesley replied in an unenthusiastic tone. "How do you expect to get it done so fast?"

"I've got them working around the clock and with the promise of some additional income as an incentive…well, you know how that works."

"Yes, I do."

"I thought I should let you know, since you were the one responsible for providing me with the motivation to jumpstart this project. Thanks to you and Father Coniglio's generosity my congregation, including myself, didn't have any time to feel sorry for ourselves. Talking about feeling sorry for one's self. You don't look too chipper. Can I be of any help?"

"Is it that obvious?"

"It is, my friend. It is not good to keep our troubles locked within if there are those around us who can help. Are you in need of help, Father?

"Rabbi, I could have used that so-called help years ago. I've just now found out that the sins of my youth, have left me with a certain amount of guilt and responsibility that cannot be washed away, or healed by the passage of time. No, Rabbi, I am a man of disgrace, and it continues to live within me today."

"I find that hard to believe. You are a good man, a righteous man. What brings you to be so hard on yourself? Surely, whatever haunts you now seems dark but in time you will rise above it. You have already done it, if what I hear of your younger days is correct."

"Yes, that would be accurate, Rabbi, if it were not for a living reminder of those past transgressions. I am still paying for the sins I committed as a reckless young man and will continue to pay until I am an old man. I have come to realize I am a fraud. But, until yesterday, I didn't realize just how big a fraud."

Father Wesley's rather indelicate way of describing himself gave the Rabbi an unsettling feeling. Undoubtedly, he thought, the man was being too hard on himself. But he spoke of a *living reminder* and it had to mean he had come across something not in his best interests. Yet, surely, the price he was asking himself to pay was far greater than the sin committed. Rabbi Zuckerman felt it to be his obligation to convey this belief to his Catholic counterpart.

"Father, I cannot imagine a man with such good and noble intentions, such as your own, to be frowned upon in the eyes of God. The good you have performed here at St. Theresa's far outweighs the bad you might have perpetrated in the past. Go easy on yourself. I'm sure you have already been forgiven by the one who counts the most."

"Think so?"

"Yes, Father, I think so. Unless you can prove otherwise, I'd have to say you are being far too harsh on yourself. I have a willing ear if you need to vent the horrors that now inhabit you. As a man of the cloth you are asked to bear a lot for the good of mankind. The weight becomes much heavier when you have to do it alone and you begin to lose sight of the good you have accomplished."

A weak smile came to Father Wesley's face. "You are a good man, but perhaps too much of a romantic," he told the rabbi. "I don't think you understand the full context of how my soul is being ravaged. You cannot possibly understand the severity of the sins I am being asked to commit and bear. If you did you would not be so gracious and kind in your judgment of me."

"Now it is sins you are being asked to commit?" the rabbi questioned.

"Yes, sins. The betrayal of a man who has proven to be more than an associate. A man who has become a close friend."

"Then come clean, young man," Rabbi Zuckerman demanded.

It was time, Father Wesley was convinced, to reveal himself for the phony he truly was. It seemed rather ironic that as a Catholic priest he would be making his *confession* to a Jewish rabbi.

"Rabbi, what I am about to tell you is disturbing but it must remain between the two of us for the time being. Any disclosure of the true reason for my being assigned here at St. Theresa's could prove to be detrimental to Father Coniglio. I think you will agree once I've told you the secret I keep."

Secret? What Father Wesley spoke of had Rabbi Zuckerman intrigued. He enjoyed a good mystery and the clandestine shroud Father

Wesley seemed to be hiding behind certainly had his curiosity aroused. "Go on," he told the priest.

"Rabbi, I was not dispatched to St. Theresa's as a breath of fresh air to help alleviate the workload that was wearing down Father Coniglio. Instead, I was sent here to nursemaid a sick and dying prelate, so the cardinal could have peace with himself for the oversights he had committed regarding a good friend, namely Father Coniglio. The anguish which tormented Cardinal Burke's soul was transferred to mine and I consider it to be a selfish act on his part."

Rabbi Zuckerman pondered what Father Wesley had to say for a moment. He had a feeling he knew what the young priest was putting himself through and it wasn't fair. He was right in his assessment of the cardinal but that, too, Rabbi Zuckerman understood. Yet, it was apparent Father Wesley had ignored whatever directive had been passed his way about how to conduct himself in his assignment at St. Theresa's. There was more to his *Wolf in Sheep's Clothing* story than met the eye. There was something else bothering Father Wesley.

"Father, I still say you are being unfair to yourself. You were assigned here to administer over a dying parish until the necessary time came along and the place was shut down. It would bother any self-respecting cleric to be asked to take on such an assignment. But, Father, you didn't just take it on. You did more than that, much more. You have given new life to this parish and nothing you say can refute that fact. You have given back to St. Theresa's her legacy and I'd be willing to bet that even the cardinal is thrilled with what you have accomplished."

The cardinal, maybe, but not Father Moore. Father Wesley didn't dare go onto that discussion and the possibility that Father Moore's brother may have been involved in the burning of the rabbi's temple. Right now the survival of St. Theresa's was being held over Father Moore's head in return for not saying a word about the burning of Temple Beth Abraham. It was better to leave the subject alone.

"Rabbi, your words are kind and somewhat uplifting. I'll try and take heed of what you have to say."

"Father, if I may, I believe something else is torturing you. This act of contrition you just made, regarding your tenure here at St. Theresa's, is masking an even greater pain. You don't have to talk about it if you don't feel up to it. But I know it's there. What about those sins from your youth that you are still paying for?"

Again the weak smile graced Father Wesley's face. "You are a very perceptive man, Rabbi. You're right. I have to tell someone, for my heart is indeed heavy with grief. I wonder if you'll have the same high regard for me once I've told you this story."

"Go on," was all the rabbi said.

"It goes back to my hellion days along the beach. I had a girlfriend by the name of Ruth Ann Travers. We had a fight one day when she told me she was moving away and she never wanted to see me again. No reason given. Just that she didn't want me in her life any longer. On that night, I took her decision hard and tried to drown it in alcohol. The end result of that ill-fated night was the death of a close friend and the loss of my eyesight. All because I couldn't handle losing a girl. But it was more than that. Until that night I hadn't realized how much I truly loved her. Again, I was being selfish for not acknowledging my feelings until she was gone."

"It's not a unique scenario, Father. Many others have traveled down that road of despair."

"I know. The memory of her was one of the reasons I balked at being reassigned here. But it proved to be all right until recently. She came to see me, asking for help with her daughter. I thought our prior relationship made me a bad choice for the job. You see, Rabbi, she had told me she had been married but was now divorced. Then, last night, I discovered she had lied. She had never married. You start doing the arithmetic and you realize that the day she walked out of my life she did so with a child in her womb. I believe it to be my child."

"Then why walk out on you?" a stunned but still supportive Rabbi Zuckerman asked him. "You were an able-bodied man, capable of supporting a family. That leads me to think you might be overreacting as to who is the father of this child."

"You might think that way but there is more. Ruth Ann was dedicated to me. She'd never do anything like what you are suggesting behind my back. You also have to realize she was only seventeen at the time. Her parents hated me and everything I stood for. Looking back I would have hated that person, too. I was a real reprobate. They could have sent me to jail for statutory rape but I believe Ruth Ann cut a deal with her parents. She traded me for the baby. The family bought into it and agreed to move and that would really force me out of the picture. Her parents probably thought I'd just forget her and move onto somebody else."

"So where does that leave you now?" the rabbi wanted to know.

"What do you mean?"

"What I mean is: what are you going to do now? You can't just sit here and brood about the situation for the rest of your life. You have an agenda to meet. If you believe you are the father of this child, then it behooves you to find out for sure. Go to Ruth Ann and put the question to her. By the way, what's the girl's name?"

"Rachel."

Suddenly, Rabbi Zuckerman developed a very quizzical look on his face. "Ruth and Rachel," he mumbled. "Father, those are biblical Jewish names. Is Ruth Ann by any chance Jewish?"

"Yeah, her family was Jewish but she never owned up to the faith. She was named after both her grandmothers; Ruth was her maternal grandmother's name and Ann was her paternal grandmother's name. As far as I know her family were not practicing Jews."

"That doesn't matter. There might be someone who is a member of my temple who may have known them. Do you recall her parents' names?"

"Her father's name is Alan and her mother Miriam."

"Hmm," Rabbi Zuckerman mumbled as he crossed his arms and rubbed his chin. "I'm willing to bet we can get to the bottom of this. I've got a strong feeling that someone who attends Temple Beth Abraham has the answers you need to set your mind straight. A lot of Jewish families are very strait-laced when it comes to the lineage of their descendants. They frown on gentiles becoming part of the mix and will do whatever it takes to hide the fact. That may have been Ruth Ann's parents way of concealing what they considered a black mark against their family name, by taking their daughter and granddaughter away, so their new friends knew nothing about their past and the blemish their daughter brought against their good family name."

Good Lord, Father Wesley thought. This sounded too much like the fiasco involving Grimaldi and Anna.

"What's going on in here?" The voice of Father Coniglio interrupted their conversation and caught the two men by surprise as he entered the church with Shagtyme in tow.

"Oh, Father, you snuck up on us. I was just telling Father Wesley that the reconstruction of Temple Beth Abraham is now underway, and your traveling tabernacle of Jews now see a light at the end of the tunnel and will be leaving St. Theresa's soon."

"That's marvelous news," Father Coniglio commented, oblivious to the actual subject Rabbi Zuckerman and Father Wesley were discussing. But the same could not be said about Shagtyme. The dog sensed his master's distress and snuggled his trusty head on the priest's lap.

"Good boy," Father Wesley was moved to say as he pet the top of Shagtyme's head and his thoughts drifted back to Ruth Ann and Rachel. The rabbi suggested he confront Ruth Ann on the subject but he knew she'd never tell him the truth, not after all these years. But he was determined to find out Rachel's true lineage, if only to save his own sanity.

———ɯ———

Meanwhile, down on the beach, a meeting of a different nature was taking place. There was a sense of urgency in the air, and the two major players had convened in the hope of warding off any repercussions that could foul up their plans.

The white Lexus pulled off the parkway and parked in a parallel fashion against the seawall. James Moore emerged from the vehicle and looked around. The person he had to see was on the opposite side of the street, sitting on a park bench with another man who James did not know.

It was a pleasant October day and there were a few hearty souls on the beach, not ready to give up on the summerlike conditions. James, dressed in a drab gray business suit, looked somewhat out of place as he walked over to the seawall, found an isolated spot and sat. It was the signal for the man on the other side of the parkway to join him.

James was facing the ocean, a soft and gentle breeze blowing in his face. When the other man joined him, he too sat on the wall but faced the opposite direction. They were to discuss their business in this manner.

"Okay," the man began. "Why the sudden urgency that requires us to meet? I hope you're not still pissed off about that Temple Beth Abraham thing. I told you it was a mistake and I don't want to belabor the point."

"Well, you're going to have to. Your brilliant plan to hand me the property Temple Beth Abraham sits on, as a consolation prize, turned out to be a booby prize. We are out of business for the time being."

"Out of business! Have you suddenly lost your affection for consecrated land that has turned a nifty profit for you? Or has the fact that a church and a synagogue, in the same neighborhood, and the prospect of burning just weeks apart, tampered your lust for money?"

James did a slow burn. He was seething, realizing millions of dollars could be lost because of greed. Temple Beth Abraham had come back to haunt them, big time!

"Again, just what did you hope to gain by burning the place? All I could hope to get from that parcel of land was the demolition rights, should they decide to rebuild. Unlike St. Theresa's that place was not slated to close. I never should have told you about my interest in the temple. Now we're implicated because of your poor judgment."

"What do you mean implicated?"

"The new priest at St. Theresa's is onto us. He's willing to keep his mouth shut as long as St. Theresa's doesn't go up in smoke."

"Father Wesley?"

"Yes, Father Wesley. He and my brother have some kind of feud going on between them. I guess my brother overplayed his hand and this Father Wesley, realizing how much my brother wanted the church closed, started snooping around. Someone told him about Old Colony's interest in the Jewish place. Then it burns down. He starts looking at the Catholic churches that also burned and he starts putting two and two together. It leaves us standing around with our pants down and if we're not careful someone is going to sneak up behind us and stick it to us but good."

"So what do you want from me?"

"You know what I want. Get to the man with the matches and tell him everything is off. You tell this guy if St. Theresa's goes up then I'll find him and I'll see to it that he, too, goes up in flames. We are going to have to find another way of acquiring St. Theresa's."

"I doubt if we can get the money back from him. In fact, he might demand the rest of the payment. He's a lazy bastard, and St. Theresa's was proving to be a quick score. He might threaten us with trouble if he isn't paid in full."

James was getting even hotter under the collar hearing this tale. This faux pas was already costing him $5,000 in up-front money. There was no way he was going to cough up the $15,000 that had been promised upon completion of the torching of St. Theresa's.

"You listen to me, and you listen good. You tell this psycho you are dealing with that all bets are off. He can keep his retainer, but that's it. He's not getting another nickel and if he decides to try some bullying tactics, or threatens to drop a dime on us, I'll see to it that he soon takes up residence with Satan himself."

James left it at that and made a quick retreat to the Lexus, leaving the man he had been talking to sitting on the wall trying to put it together. James's co-conspirator was Alfredo and he now had a major problem on his hands. He slowly made his way back across the parkway to rejoin Salvi on the park bench.

"What'd he have to say?" Salvi wanted to know.

"We've got to cool our heels for the time being. It seems Father Wesley knows what's going on and any harm brought St. Theresa's way is going to result with him blowing the whistle on Old Colony. Why did that meathead have to go and burn Temple Beth Abraham?"

"Because when he heard it could soon be included in the package, he decided to go for it. You know, show that he's an eager beaver. Now he's expecting to be paid for it," Salvi hated to say.

"He's not getting paid for something we didn't ask for. Is this guy stable?"

"You know what he is. He's a lazy bum. What do we do with him now?"

"We tell him the church is out of the picture. He gets to keep his retainer but that's it. No more money. I don't care how much ranting he makes."

"Alfredo, he might do that church just for the hell of it."

"What?"

"The word on the street is that he and his wife are splitting up and the wife is pregnant. She was going to get an abortion until Father Wesley talked her out of it. Now he's pissed because he's going to be stuck supporting the kid. He wants to get even. The retainer might just be enough of an incentive."

"Just what we need, a loose cannon," Alfredo muttered. "Well, he's going to have to be convinced not to do anything stupid, because the people we are dealing with are not a pack of boy scouts. This is not just the Catholic Church we're talking about. We're talking about people who are trying to make a score at the Church's expense, and they are not about to let some penny ante crook derail what they have going. I've already saved his ass by not letting Moore know he was the one who decided to torch Temple Beth Abraham. I'm not going to be able to save him again should he decide to go after St. Theresa's to settle a score. Wars have been fought over land and lives lost because of it. The same thing is going to happen to Gregorio if he decides to interfere in Old Colony's plan to gain St. Theresa's."

CHAPTER
TWENTY-FIVE

"That's her, over there. The little one with her hair in a ponytail. Cute thing, even with the braces." It was Bryan Fogarty pointing out Rachel to Father Wesley. The priest and the biker were standing under the pavilion, about 150 feet from where the group of teenagers had gathered.

Rachel Travers was a petite young girl, barely five feet tall. She was wearing skin tight jeans as she straddled a boy against the seawall. Just observing her convinced Father Wesley that Ruth Ann had not been exaggerating when she spoke to him about her daughter. If someone didn't step in now and offer some guidance, Rachel was going to drown in this cesspool of white trash. Father Wesley was certain of that fact since he had once been there.

"So that's little Rachel, just into her teens but trying to be so much older. I wonder what her rush is?" the priest asked his old friend as he scrutinized her every move.

"Probably the same as ours. In a hurry to be older and once they get there they wonder what in the world was their thinking," Fogarty answered.

"Yeah, but these times are different. Look at the jeans she's wearing. I would think they didn't make them that tight. They look as though they've been painted on her. She's asking for trouble being dressed like that."

Bryan was somewhat amused by the outlook of Father Wesley. It didn't seem that long ago when he, too, traversed this beach looking to score with every female he encountered. He finally found what he was looking for when he hooked up with Ruth Ann. Bryan thought his prelate friend might be more prone to understand, considering he had once worn the same shoes. But Bryan Fogarty was not aware of the personal dilemma that was wreaking havoc with Father Wesley's soul.

"Bryan, that kid she's teasing must be four or five years older than her. Ruth Ann has got to get a better grasp on her daughter's situation or else she's going to become a very young grandmother." Father Wesley could feel his anger building as he noticed that Rachel's boyfriend was Freddy Brandt.

"I thought that's why she came to you," Fogarty answered, unabashed. "You seem to have a short memory. What's the age difference between you and Ruth Ann?"

"I see what you're getting at, Bryan, but it's not the same. These kids today don't know what they are dealing with."

"And we did?"

"All right, Bryan, I'll concede the point to you. But having been there we should know better. Because of that experience we should be doing everything we can, to keep our children out of harm's way."

"Excellent point, Father. But consider the environment. What you, me and Ruth Ann grew up in is still haunting this beach, just waiting to claim its next victim. You were lucky, you found a way out. Ruth Ann and I cannot say the same thing. Although older and supposedly wiser, Ruth Ann and I are not the better because of it. I chose to stay because I wanted to. Ruth Ann is here because she's trapped."

"But Ruth Ann got out. You have no idea as to why she came back?"

"None whatsoever," Fogarty answered. "She returned a few years ago. That's all I know. Maybe she had a falling out with her parents and returned to the only place she felt comfortable."

"You mean to come back and atone for her sin?"

"Something like that."

"Tell me, Bryan, since you know about Ruth Ann having never married do you know who Rachel's father is?"

"Nope. Rachel likes to refute her mother's story about her being married. But she is tight-lipped about her father, if she knows who he is."

Bryan glanced Rachel's way and then quickly back at Father Wesley. "I see what you're getting at. I'll be honest with you, I thought of it myself. But, for some reason, if it is the truth, Ruth Ann chose to keep it a secret. Now the question is: why? Why just walk away and not tell you? Why keep this secret to herself? If she's hurting it's her own fault. And if you're hurting it's her fault."

"Bryan, I'm not hurting but I am full of wonder. I'll help anyone I can, provided they want to be helped. But, in the case of Rachel, I am going to have to provide her with direction whether she wants it or not. I'm a priest foremost."

"Father, you have to deal with the other scenario as well. Ruth Ann's sudden disappearance, forcing you to accept a lifestyle that otherwise would have eluded you, and then the two of you suddenly reappearing, and Ruth Ann with a daughter the same age as the time gap. It all seems to lead to the conclusion that you are Rachel's father. But you need more than that. You need proof. The best way to get that proof is to go to Ruth Ann and ask her."

"Bryan, if she was reluctant to tell me back then, what makes you think she is going to tell me now? It doesn't matter that I am now a priest. She's kept this secret so long she has no choice other than to keep it forever."

Bryan shook his head. "You know, you two used to have some pretty good arguments back when we were younger. The two of you were stubborn then and you're still stubborn today. Or shall I say stupid?"

"Both," Father Wesley replied, a small smile finding its way to his face. He then looked at his watch. "Good Lord, it's getting late. It's almost five and I promised Anna Gregorio I'd go to her birthing class with her this evening at six. I'll have to settle this Rachel matter on another day. How often is she down here?"

"Every day. Listen, Father, before you run off. You mentioned Anna Gregorio. Have you given any thought as to what to do regarding her charming husband who seems to have it out for you?"

"I'm not going to do anything. If he's looking for trouble then he's going to have to bring it to me. I'm not going to go looking for him. I think what you heard him say the other day had more to do with his frustration and intoxication than it did with any vendetta he's planning to stage against me." Father Wesley then thought of Anna and her possible mixed-race child and he knew the words he spoke could possibly boomerang on him.

"Well, Father, you still gotta watch your back. When it comes to you the guy is a loony tune."

—⁂—

Behind the smoky and tinted front window of Rose's, Arthur Gregorio watched as Father Wesley and Bryan Fogarty shook hands and went their separate ways. The priest was headed back in the direction of St. Theresa's. Fogarty was walking towards Rose's. Gregorio quickly retreated to a seat at the corner of the bar, which afforded him the opportunity to intercept Fogarty as he came through the front door.

As Fogarty walked in the place, he immediately saw Gregorio. Upon spotting him, Fogarty knew Gregorio was waiting for him, since the man usually sat on the other side of the bar. Fogarty could only think of one reason Gregorio would want to speak with him. He had to have noticed him talking to the priest on the pavilion. That being the case he knew exactly where Gregorio's conversation was going to go, and he was not intent on listening to the man's tale of how Father Wesley had intruded in his life. This time Fogarty thought he might snap if Gregorio launched another verbal attack on the good ethics of his friend.

"Hey, Fogarty. Saw you across the street with the priest. I hope you weren't talking about me."

Fogarty smiled. "What if we were?" he asked, baiting Gregorio to show his hand.

"Fogarty, I've got no gripe with you. But don't piss me off. I know you and the priest are tight. If I find out you and he are—"

"You're going to do what?" Fogarty interjected.

"Well, I guess I'll have to get a little rough with you."

What was he saying? Gregorio knew he was no match for Fogarty. Even if he was fortunate to beat the man with a lucky punch he would then have to answer to his beer guzzling cronies. No, that had been a dumb remark for Arthur Gregorio to make.

Fogarty enjoyed the stupidity Gregorio was displaying. He leaned against the edge of the bar, his face just inches from Gregorio's. "So now you want to get tough with me. Let me tell you something, you dumb bastard. You're long on balls, I'll give you that, but you're coming up short on brains. If you want a piece of me then I'm more than willing to take you on. Let's go outside and settle this matter once and for all."

It was going to take some fast talking by Gregorio to get out of the position he had placed himself in. He had no intention of fighting Fogarty, nor the priest. He had a more meaningful way of hurting the meddlesome cleric.

"Look it, Bryan, I've got no beef with you. What's making my piss boil is strictly between me and the priest. Now if you'll excuse me, I have a business meeting to attend."

"A business meeting! What are you, a high roller all of a sudden?"

"I've got some things in the fire," was all he had to say. He was getting out of Rose's while his face and teeth were still intact. He had an agenda to meet. Arthur Gregorio was now running low on cash.

—✳—

Once Gregorio was out of Rose's, Johnny Rogers joined Fogarty at the bar. "You two still going at it?" he asked the stocky biker.

"Yeah," he answered as if miffed. "You know something, Johnny. I hope he does go after Father Paul. Priest or not I'd love to see him drop the pretense and just wail away on Gregorio. I know the old Paul would have kicked the living daylights out of that jerk by now. Sometimes what seems to be a good change isn't good at all."

Rogers nodded his agreement but he had his own message to be delivered to Father Wesley. He was counting on Fogarty to be the messenger. "Bryan, next time you see Paulie I want you to tell him something for me."

"Sure. What is it?"

"Tell him that dog of his knocked up Love Muffin. Now she's beginning to get lazy. I've got a feeling she's not going to be of much use around here as a watchdog in the coming weeks."

"So what do you want Father Paul to do? Take her off your hands? Or maybe you want Shagtyme to start paying puppy support?"

"Now, don't get cute with me, Bryan. I just thought he should know. Okay?"

"All right. I'll let him know. Is that it?"

"That's it."

CHAPTER
TWENTY-SIX

Arthur Gregorio was having bad vibes about this meeting on the beach as he walked along the parkway. Salvi had left him a message earlier in the day to meet him at the park bench sometime after five. The advance money he had received was dwindling, and it was his intention to torch St. Theresa's in the next day or two. He hoped this meeting was simply about Salvi and Alfredo getting a little anxious about when the job might be completed. He was trying to convince himself that was the case, but his gut was telling him something else.

As they came into view, Gregorio noticed Salvi and Alfredo in conversation, as if it were any other day. Salvi had a bottle of his homemade wine at the ready, concealed in a brown paper bag. Alfredo, as usual, was looking dapper, as the two of them ogled the girls who walked the beach. Soon even Salvi and Alfredo were going to have to go into hibernation, for winter was not that far away. But, as for today, it was a picture perfect autumn day in New England. Too nice a day to pass on.

"Salvi! Alfredo! Beautiful day, isn't it?" Gregorio called out as he made his way to them. Best to dispense with the small talk, he figured.

"It is," Salvi answered, as he looked up to see Gregorio. It was always Salvi who did the bulk of the talking in these impromptu meetings, although Gregorio knew it was Alfredo who was the brains behind their little two-man operation. "Come. Sit. Can I offer you some wine? We have cups."

"No thanks. I guess you two want to know when I plan to finish off my assignment. I'm going to do it in the next twenty-four to seventy-two hours. I'm starting to run a little low on the dinero so I can use the money." Gregorio smiled, hoping what he said would in turn bring a smile to their faces. It didn't.

"Sit down," Alfredo said, sternly. These guys had proven to be a godsend so Arthur had no intention of ruffling their feathers. But they didn't seem to be in a very gratifying mood. Gregorio figured he might have deliberated one day too many, for their satisfaction, in the disposing of St. Theresa's.

"I know you expected the St. Theresa's matter to be taken care of by now. But, I promise you, in the next day or two she will be no more. You can bank on it."

Alfredo glared at Salvi. It was the cue for Salvi to take over from here. "Arthur, there has been a change in the plans concerning St. Theresa's. We won't be requiring your services any longer. The advance money given to you is yours. Consider it a score, since you didn't do anything to earn it."

What the hell was this all about? Gregorio wondered. These guys had been salivating over the demise of St. Theresa's. Now they were pulling the plug. It didn't add up. But, more important to Gregorio was the $15,000 still owed him for finishing the job. He had made a commitment to these two and he expected to be compensated for it. They weren't going to welch on their end of the agreement. It was his intention to see that St. Theresa's burned to the ground, so Father Wesley hurt like he was hurting, and he expected to be paid for it.

"That's too bad but you guys still owe me money. A deal is a deal," he told them in no uncertain terms.

"Arthur, a deal is a deal but you botched it. You are the one to blame for us not being able to get our hands on St. Theresa's. The burning of Temple Beth Abraham did us in. We all know who is responsible for that stupid move. You think you should be paid for your screw up? You've cost us some big bucks already. Consider yourself to be fortunate that we're letting you keep the retainer. Now get the hell out of here.

And should you utter one word about our dealings then you'll rue the day you did." Salvi was now setting the record straight.

An insolent smirk creased Gregorio's face. He wasn't going to be intimidated by their threats. They might think they were not going to pay him the full allotment on what he was owed, but Arthur thought differently. As Salvi had reiterated, *a deal is a deal,* and Arthur Gregorio was prepared to make one. He had something on the man that should bring him money for today and many days to come.

"I'm not going anywhere until we reach some kind of accord. I have no intention of singing about the burning of any church or synagogue." He then looked directly into Salvi's eyes and told him, "Instead, I'll sing about you."

Salvi immediately developed a guilty look about him. "Wha...what are you talking about?" he asked in a shaky voice.

"I don't know if your friend, Alfredo, wants to know about your little hobby," Gregorio answered with a contemptible snarl on his face.

"I don't know what you're talking about," Salvi was quick to reply.

"Yes you do," Arthur informed him. "And I'll expose your pitiful ass to anyone—and I assure you there are many—who'd be interested in what I have to say."

Salvi was flabbergasted by what he was hearing. He turned to Alfredo and, in a voice that seemed to convey his guilt, said, "Don't believe a word he has to say."

"What about the little Napoli girl? Do you think she'd call me a liar?" Gregorio challenged him.

Alfredo usually stayed free of the actual hiring or firing of their operatives. But what Arthur Gregorio was talking about was no mundane matter. He had something on Salvi. He sensed blackmail on Gregorio's part. The man was going to practice a little extortion and Salvi was his intended mark.

"Salvi, is there any truth to what he is saying?"

"I told you not to believe a word he says."

"But he said something about the Napoli girl." Alfredo looked at Gregorio. "Maybe the Napoli girl is mistaken."

"She isn't and neither am I. You see, Alfredo, I was driving down Everton Street the other day and I saw this child molester running from the scene with that priest's big dog on his tail. He was lucky there was a bus going by and he managed to catch it." The irritating smirk returned to Gregorio's face. "Now, are you ready to square matters?" he continued.

"All right, Arthur. What's it going to take?"

"It's going to take the rest of the money you owe me, that's what it's going to take. I'm not settling for a nickel less."

"I see," Alfredo said as he reached into his pants pocket and produced a roll of bills. "Here's two grand for your troubles. Consider it an extension of your retainer. You see the plans for St. Theresa's are actually on hold for the time being, or until the hullabaloo over Temple Beth Abraham subsides. Consider yourself still on the payroll until the rest of our agreement is completed. Do we have an understanding?"

"What if the money runs out before you give me the go ahead to set the fire?" Gregorio asked as he took the cash from Alfredo's hand.

"Then we have a little room for further negotiating. But, Arthur, try not to spend the money too fast. Your lavish spending could prove to be your undoing."

"You're a wise man, Alfredo." Gregorio then turned and looked at Salvi. "As for you, little man, let me give you some advice. Why don't you go home and give it a good yank."

Alfredo and Salvi did not say a word to each other until Gregorio was well out of earshot. Once he was, Alfredo let loose on Salvi. "You idiot! I thought I knew you. A horny little runt, yes. But a pedophile! You disappoint me, Salvi. You disappoint me in a big way."

"I'm sorry, Alfredo. It's the damn vino. I get a little of the love juice in me and I go crazy. I can't score with the broads on the beach anymore, so something just snapped inside my head. It only happened a couple of times. Now that Gregorio knows, I swear I won't do it again."

"You better make sure you don't," Alfredo warned him. "Now that bloodsucking leech has us over a barrel. He always was a lazy good-for-nothing who didn't want to work. Now he's found a way to capitalize on it."

"So, what are we going to do?"

"You're going to keep your goddamn johnson in your pants. As for Gregorio, well, the man presents a problem. We'll have to find something on him that negates what he has on you."

"What if there is nothing? You know he'll just keep squeezing and squeezing. We've done some rotten things in our time but we've never had to resort to eliminating anyone."

"And, hopefully, that will not be the case now."

—⟪⟫—

"Oh my," Father Coniglio was moved to say as Father Wesley entered the kitchen. "Aren't we the picture of sartorial splendor," he went on, sitting at the table sipping a cup of tea.

Mildred, working at the oven on the meat loaf for the priests' supper, looked over her shoulder and was equally impressed. "Are you planning on leaving the priesthood?" she tried to joke.

Father Wesley, dressed rather nattily, in a powder blue shirt with gray slacks and a gray blazer, was forced to muster a smile at their good-natured ribbing. "No, but I do have a date," he responded to Mildred's question.

"What!" Mildred answered, shocked as if the words she were hearing dripped of scandal.

"Yes," Father Wesley replied, as he sauntered up behind her and playfully placed his arms around her waist and nuzzled the back of her neck with his nose. "I think all of this celibacy has turned me into a boring individual. It's time to step out a little. Don't you agree, Mildred?"

"I do not!" Mildred exclaimed as she wrestled herself away from Father Wesley's playful embrace.

"Relax. Mildred," Father Coniglio chimed in. "Father Wesley is going out for the evening with Anna Gregorio to her birthing class. He has agreed to be her coach."

"Oh, really," Mildred responded. "That's quite nice of you, Father. I feel so bad for that girl. I knew marrying that lout was all wrong for her."

"So, Father, will you be dining with us before you adjourn for the evening?" Father Coniglio asked.

"I can't," he answered as he gazed at his watch. "I told Anna I'd meet her in front of the church at six. I shouldn't be late since she is my ride."

"I'll keep a plate for you in the oven. All you'll have to do is heat it up when you come home,"

"Thank you, Mildred. And I'm sorry if I startled you. But...well... you were there to be had, so I couldn't resist."

Mildred shushed him away with the wave of her dish towel. "Don't be silly. Now go. We all appreciate what you're doing for that poor woman."

Right, Father Wesley thought to himself. If they all knew the truth they might be singing another tune about his act of compassion. Father Wesley regretted the situation he was in but he couldn't turn back. He was in too deep at this point.

As promised, Father Wesley was outside the church waiting for Anna Gregorio at six. And, as promised, Anna's punctuality was just as precise. There were some redeeming qualities to what he was doing and Father Wesley hoped the good feeling of being a helpful person might offset the burdensome guilt he was toting. But that feeling of good virtue was shot out of the water when Anna pulled up alongside the curb. Suddenly there was something terribly wrong. His head became a buzz of uncertainty. It abruptly became necessary for him to uncover everything there was to know about Arthur Gregorio. Anna was driving the car Father Wesley had sold her. The Toyota Camry Arthur had, allegedly, sold. The cash he supposedly received for the automobile was the reason for his sudden deep pockets. Now the priest knew differently.

Father Wesley decided it was best to broach the subject of Anna's estranged husband delicately. The woman was already going through enough distress without adding this to her mountain of woes. But this sick feeling he had developed in his stomach would not go away. There was no getting rid of it until he found out as to how Arthur Gregorio had come by the money he now generously flashed about down on the beach.

"So, Anna, you're looking well this evening," Father Wesley began their conversation as he buckled himself in and the car moved away.

"Thanks to you, Father," she graciously responded. "You agreeing to be at my side is proving to be such a relief. Someday, soon, it will be my duty to come clean and let the world in on the true story about this baby. I'm praying when that day comes those who will be so quick to condemn me will think twice, thanks to your kindness."

"That's a very nice thing for you to say, Anna. Now, tell me, you're what, five months along? Isn't it a little early in the game to be going to birthing classes?"

"Yes, it is, Father. But we're not really going to a birthing class tonight. We're going to an orientation on what to expect when the actual classes begin. With Thanksgiving coming up, and Christmas not that far behind, this is the best time to get the preliminaries out of the way. The actual birthing classes will begin right after the start of the new year."

"I see," Father Wesley said, nodding his head. "So there is time for Arthur to become an active participant if he decides to do so."

Anna looked at the priest, her face drawn with skepticism. *What could he possibly be talking about?* Father Wesley knew Arthur wanted nothing to do with this baby. "Father, I find it strange you should say such a thing. You know Arthur's feelings about this child."

"I understand, Anna, but you never know what tomorrow may bring." There, he was onto the subject of Anna's husband. One hurdle cleared. "Let me ask you this: how did you meet Arthur?"

"In one of those bars down on the beach. I went out with him for a few years and then he suggested we move in together. Well, I couldn't have that, not with my parents, especially my father. I guess you could say I was getting desperate. I was into my thirties and there were no prospects on the horizon so I suggested we get married. Looking back on it, I would have to say it was the dumbest move I've ever made."

"So you're saying there was no love involved?"

"Not really. I didn't want to become an old maid and I wanted to have a family. Arthur, on the other hand, claimed marriage might give him some stability in life. What it gave him was a means to become even lazier."

"Lazier?"

"Oh yeah. You see, Arthur has this proclivity for doing as little work as possible and seeing that he gets paid for it. The job he has now, as a used car salesman, is a veritable joke. He deals in junk. He makes just enough to satisfy his needs: beer and the lottery. By marrying me he had the financial wherewithal to continue his deadbeat lifestyle. I make good money as a dental hygienist. He had the chance to live off me and at the time I didn't really care. But Father, I'm a woman, and being neglected was not part of the deal. The wrong I've done, as far as I'm concerned, is partially Arthur's fault. He didn't want a wife. He wanted a servant and a financial backer. Then this pregnancy thing came along and his immediate concern was if it was going to interfere with my ability to maintain a career. But, as you know, I had a bigger problem to worry about. Thanks to your help I was finally able to confront it. In my father's eyes I'm a major disappointment, but he's learning to live with it. It is my thinking that Arthur made me into that failure. But in the process his pride took a major whack. He'll never forgive me for what I've done to him, and it will take some time for me to forgive him for the way he used me."

Father Wesley could see this was a new and more determined Anna. She was now quite different from that frightened individual who had come to him in the past month, hoping he would condone her inclination to have an abortion. It pleased the priest to see her in this light. But Anna was not his real concern at the moment. He needed to know more about Arthur and how he had come into money he certainly didn't earn through hard work.

"Anna, I don't think you're aware of this, but Arthur is parading around down on the beach with a pocketful of money claiming he made by selling your car. I'm curious as to how he came into this money."

"Probably hit the lottery for a few bucks."

"But why not just tell everyone that, instead of saying it came from selling your car? Most people I can think of enjoy boasting about making a financial score at the State's expense."

"I really don't know, Father, and I really don't care. Do you think Arthur is doing something illegal?"

"You tell me. Do you think he's capable of doing such a thing?"

"Sure, but nothing serious I assure you. He's the kind of guy who might steal a battery out of a car or cigarettes and razor blades out of a store, strictly nickel and dime stuff. If he's claiming he made a few hundred bucks out of the sale of this car it's because he wants people to think he's hurt me in the wallet. None of his friends know what kind of car I drive."

"Anna, we're not talking about pocket change. We're talking about some serious dollars."

Anna had no response and it was evident by the expression on her face that she was now trying to figure out what her husband was involved in. As for Father Wesley, he had this terrible feeling Arthur Gregorio had moved up the ladder in his felonious way of conducting business, from a punk two-bit thief to a major player. But at whose expense? It was time for Father Wesley to start looking at Arthur Gregorio from a nefarious point of view. He could no longer dismiss the man as an annoyance because of some insolent remarks made while drinking. Anna talked about his pride taking a major hit. Father Wesley knew the worst had yet to come.

"Anna, have you told your parents or Arthur about the possibility that your baby could be...you know?"

"Not yet," she remarked in a sheepish way. "I'm hoping the tot will be just dark enough so I can pass him or her off as being Sicilian," she tried to joke.

"Anna, be serious. You've come this far. Now you must come all the way."

"I'm trying, Father, I really am."

CHAPTER
TWENTY-SEVEN

Rabbi Zuckerman hustled his pace along the walkway leading to the St. Theresa's rectory. It was a dreary and overcast Thursday morning. There was a chill wind blowing in from the direction of the ocean and it created an even colder effect. Rabbi Zuckerman, who detested the winter weather, was dressed in his black car coat, the collar raised to protect his neck and mouth from the elements. It took something important to get him outside in these conditions. Hence, the reason he was here.

In the kitchen of the rectory, Mildred was busy going about her household chores. She welcomed the changing of the seasons. It was her favorite time of year. Thanksgiving, Christmas and the New Year brought out the best in her, and this holiday season promised to be the best in years now that St. Theresa's had taken a turn for the better.

Her work was disrupted by the sudden chime of the front doorbell. "Who can this be?" she muttered as she stopped what she was doing and went to answer the door. Mildred detested any annoyance that disrupted her working regimen. With displeasure splattered across her face she opened the front door and was surprised to see it was Rabbi Zuckerman. She was not told of his dropping by.

"Rabbi Zuckerman, I wasn't informed you were coming here. Father Coniglio is not here at the moment. He's out taking his walk with Shagtyme."

"I'm not here to see Father Coniglio. I'm looking to speak with Father Wesley. Is he in?"

"Yes, he is and I don't think he's busy. Won't you come in? You're shivering. Is it that cold outside?"

"Cold enough for me," he told her as he stepped into the living room while taking his coat off.

"I'm told Saturday will be your last day with us."

"Yes. Our temple, although not completely reconstructed, now has the infrastructure to allow us to resume services while the construction phase continues. I am looking forward to the dedication next week."

"Good morning, Rabbi. You're out and about rather early." It was Father Wesley coming from his office to join them upon hearing the rabbi's voice. He had a pretty good idea as to why he was here. "Why don't we go to my office so we can talk," the priest went on.

"Let's," the rabbi answered.

"So, Rabbi, tell me. I assume you being here is to tell me something," Father Wesley said after closing the door to his office.

"You are correct, Father," the rabbi replied as he took a seat. "I've been asking around about Ruth Ann and her parents and came up with some interesting information."

Father Wesley sat behind his desk and said, "I thought you might. You might as well tell me what you found out."

"It seems Ruth Ann is half Jewish. Her mother, Miriam, is a Hebrew. Her father, Alan, is not. He's an Episcopalian. However, neither one of them practice their faith. When Ruth Ann was born her mother insisted she be raised in the Jewish faith for whatever reason. Ruth Ann's father went along with his wife's wishes. But, apparently, it mattered little since Ruth Ann also became a non-practicing Jew. I'm surprised you didn't know all this when you were seeing her."

"Believe me, Rabbi, back then religion was the furthest thing from our minds. I had a mother I abhorred, while she had parents she claimed didn't understand her."

"Well, I guess they understood her enough to get her out of here when she became pregnant."

"So she was pregnant," Father Wesley exhorted as he sat up straight in his chair. "How about the father?" he asked, nervously, fearful of what he might hear.

"Apparently the family decided to keep the father's identity a secret, and it has remained so. Alan and Miriam felt disgraced by what happened to their daughter. The minute they found out she was pregnant they were going to see that her life changed. The first step in that process was to move away from here. Alan and Miriam feared if she were allowed to keep going the way she was, then food stamps and welfare were not that far behind."

"So we don't know who the father is," Father Wesley muttered in a low voice, his mind trying to sort through the pieces. "Your sources: are they reliable?"

"It's my source, not sources. And yes, she is reliable. Her name is Debra Goldman. She was a close friend of Miriam Travers when the family lived here. She also told me something you should find interesting."

"Such as?"

"The father of Rachel is a Catholic. Debra did know that much."

"Narrowing the field, somewhat," Father Wesley replied, trying his hardest to be glib.

"Father, it is your belief that you are the father of Rachel. I don't want to say I was disbelieving when you first told me how you felt. I just needed a little proof. If everything you told me about your relationship with Ruth Ann is correct, then I've done what you asked of me. You told me to do the arithmetic and I have. I've calculated and recalculated and each time I come up with the same answer. Father, unless you have something else to add to the equation, I have to honestly say it's you. Your responsibilities have leapfrogged to the point where you cannot ignore them. I, once again, implore you to go to Ruth Ann and let her know what you are thinking. You deserve to know the truth."

"And she will tell me I'm wrong and that I don't deserve to know who Rachel's father is. It's like I told you before, Rabbi: she is only going to lie to me. My wearing this white collar will prohibit her from telling me the truth."

"Then do it for Rachel's sake. Don't compound the mistake by allowing Rachel to become a victim because of two headstrong individuals. She, too, has a right to know the truth. Don't allow your unyielding disposition and Ruth Ann's stubborn commitment to cause the child any more harm or shame than she is already experiencing. It's incumbent upon you to convince Ruth Ann of that fact."

Father Wesley buried his face in his hands and shook his head. What was happening to him? First, he had Anna Gregorio's unborn child to worry about. Now, it seemed evident, he had his own daughter's future to think about. Rabbi Zuckerman was right. He had to confront Ruth Ann on the issue and let her know he was not going to settle for anything less than the truth. Sharon Beasley had mentioned something about the shame Ruth Ann was carrying. Well, as he figured it, it was now time for him to let Ruth Ann know there was no shame to be experienced because of Rachel's ignoble conception. It was now time for him to be there for both Ruth Ann and Rachel.

His thoughts were complex. Then, as if out of the blue, came a reflection which seemed haunted and appeared to stand out from the others. There was something wrong about the guilt he was placing upon himself. Something was not adding up in his head. The circumstances involved on that grim day when Ruth Ann walked out of his life now seemed clearer. "*Then we are going to talk,*" he had been told by his best friend. What was it they were going to talk about? Could it be? If this feeling now building within him was right then he had been betrayed. After all these years there was, indeed, a question he needed answered. Only one person had that answer. Suddenly Father Wesley was not so hesitant to confront Ruth Ann.

Father Coniglio and Shagtyme followed their usual route along the seawall. The biting cold from the brisk ocean wind had Father Coniglio thinking his decision to walk the beach on this day had not been a prudent one. But he also felt the days were drawing towards a precious few, when he could afford himself the opportunity to enjoy the peace and tranquility the incoming wash of the sea brought his way. Winter was now on the horizon, and although spring was in its wake, the wintry mix seemed to stay longer than anticipated, keeping those pleasant spring days at what seemed to be an eternal arm's length.

There were still a few hearty souls strolling the shoreline on this day. These were people much like Father Coniglio, enjoying the personal contentment the moment brought with it. Except for the whistling of the wind, with its arctic nip, there was nothing else to share.

Shagtyme led the way, guiding Father Coniglio, as if it were the animal's decision as to where they should venture. As usual Shagtyme led the priest to the same spot, and as was the norm the dog was quiet until they reached their destination. Then, as though it had been scripted, Shagtyme would let out with a loud howl, with Father Coniglio looking on, somewhat amused.

Shagtyme's baying would soon be returned with the wail of another dog. Somewhere behind the building across the street was Love Muffin, in her state of gestation. The two animals appeared to be confirming their commitment.

As Shagtyme and Love Muffin continued their lovesick serenade, Johnny Rogers came out of Rose's dragging three trash bags with him. He was about to take the refuse from last night's revelers to the dumpster, in the adjacent alleyway, when he heard the howling and spotted Father Coniglio across the street with Shagtyme. This was his chance to find out if Bryan Fogarty had passed his message on to Father Wesley about Love Muffin's delicate condition, and Shagtyme's involvement in it.

Normally Rogers was not in the place so early in the day, but last night Arthur Gregorio had been in rare form and Rogers had been forced to let him sleep it off in the office. Arthur Gregorio was not one to allow a golden opportunity pass him by. Rogers knew if Gregorio woke up in an empty bar then he would help himself to a good ration of Heinekens, on the house, while waiting for someone to show up and let him out. Johnny Rogers had no intention of allowing that to happen.

Johnny Rogers had just about had it with Arthur Gregorio's incessant griping. He didn't care how much money the man was now spending in his place. If Gregorio didn't stop with the badmouthing of his wife and Father Wesley—which had many of Rose's customers feeling uncomfortable—then the man could find another place to cry in his beer. It was not going to be at Rose's. It was Rogers's intention to let Gregorio know his feelings as soon as he placed the trash in the receptacle bin. He had left Arthur Gregorio sitting at the bar with a cup of steaming hot coffee before him as he tried to ward off the aftereffects that were telltale signs of the *cocktail flu*.

Above the din of Shagtyme and Love Muffin, Johnny Rogers called over to Father Coniglio to come and join him. If the priests didn't already know of Shagtyme's impending fatherhood then Johnny intended to inform them.

Father Coniglio and Shagtyme crossed the parkway and the priest listened to what Rogers had to say. Once he was finished, the old priest directed a fabricated nasty scowl Shagtyme's way. "Bad dog," he reprimanded the animal, as if the canine should have known better. Shagtyme, aware of the scolding, dropped to the ground and sheepishly looked away.

Father Coniglio and Johnny Rogers continued to exchange in some small talk when a gray Ford Altima came racing down the parkway, coming to a screeching halt alongside the curb where the two men were talking. Sharon Beasley leapt out of the vehicle and immediately pleaded for assistance.

"Johnny, I need your help. We've got to find Ruth Ann's daughter. Something terrible happened."

"Relax, will you," Rogers insisted, trying to calm Sharon down. "Now, tell me what happened. Does it involve Ruth Ann?"

"Yes. She and Rachel had a terrible fight. I don't know what it was about but Rachel ended up stabbing her mother. Ruth Ann's in the hospital and nobody knows where Rachel has gone. Johnny, we've got to find her. We've got to find her before she does some harm to herself."

Sharon was a nervous wreck. Johnny Rogers put his arm around her, hoping to console the woman. Meanwhile, Father Coniglio asked, "Can I be of any help here?"

Rogers turned his head towards the priest. "Father, you better let Father Wesley know what's happened."

"NO!" Sharon screamed. "I think that will make matters worse."

"I don't understand," a confused Father Coniglio said.

"Father, Ruth Ann was Father Wesley's old girlfriend back in the day." Johnny Rogers then refocused his attention on Sharon. "Why don't you think Paulie should know?" he asked her.

"Because I think he might be part of the problem. If I'm right, then Rachel might try and kill him too."

CHAPTER
TWENTY-EIGHT

"What's going on out there?" Gregorio asked Rogers as he reentered Rose's.

"There's been a stabbing," Rogers told him as he went behind the bar.

"Really. Who was stabbed?"

"Ruth Ann Travers, that's who."

"Who's she? Who stabbed her?"

Rogers paused, wondering if he should tell Gregorio anymore. Considering the vendetta he was building against Father Wesley, he questioned if it would be a wise decision to let Gregorio in on what Father Wesley's role in this unfortunate incident might be. But then again, soon word of the stabbing was going to be on the streets so he'd find out that way. Rogers couldn't quite decide as to what to do. Maybe he could tap dance his way around it.

"Ruth Ann Travers is an old friend from my younger days. The police are now looking for her daughter. They think they had an argument over something and Rachel stabbed her."

"Rachel? Not the little thing who hangs out on the seawall with all those other kids?"

"Yes, that's her."

"What'd they argue about?"

"What do you care? It's none of your business anyway."

"Hey, Rogers, I'm just curious. If the daughter stabbed the mother it had to be over something serious."

Rogers decided he didn't want to go any further with this conversation. "Arthur, I've gotta get out of here. I have some things to do and I'm not leaving you here alone. If I do you'll drink all the stock I have in the place."

Gregorio smelled a skunk. "Look it, Rogers, you're not telling me something. What is it?"

"I don't think it's any of your business."

"It isn't. I'm just curious as to why a daughter would stab her mother. You'd be too, if you didn't know. What did the mother do, walk in on the daughter giving some kid a hummer? Or maybe it was the other way around—the daughter walked in on the mother and became repulsed by what she saw and decided to let the old lady have it. You know, that kid is carrying something inside her that needs to come out."

It irked Rogers to hear Gregorio talk that way about an old friend, a person he did not know. Although reluctant to do so, he was tempted to let him know about the relationship between Father Wesley and Ruth Ann. Maybe that's what was needed to really tick off Father Wesley and put Arthur Gregorio in his place. Yes, he was going to do it. Arthur Gregorio deserved to draw the wrath of Paul Wesley, a wrath that once cast fear over this entire stretch of beach.

"Ruth Ann Travers and Father Wesley were pretty close when we were younger. He thought the world of her. Apparently, some of the kids on the beach found out about it and have been riding Rachel hard; claiming she was the bastard child of a priest. I guess she went home and confronted her mother on the issue and when she heard something she didn't want to hear, she stabbed her mother for making her life such agony. Now I've got to get the hell out of here. Rachel's on the loose and we need to find her before anything else happens."

What a hypocrite, Gregorio mused. This priest was dispensing Catholic tenets to his wife on the right and wrong and the moral obligation she carried inside of her. It was pure moral bull. Father Wesley was a phony and it pleased Arthur Gregorio to know he was going to hurt the fraud even more, when he burned his blessed church to the ground.

Father Wesley sat alone in his office trying to deal with his thoughts. Rabbi Zuckerman had left a half hour ago and now Father Wesley was presented with a rather complicated situation. His thought process took him back to the days preceding his accident. He had found less and less time for Ruth Ann. Their romance had been dying, but he didn't realize it until this very moment. Then came the day she closed the door on him. He had led himself to believe his accident, and the loss of Billy Castleman's life, was because of his heartsick response to Ruth Ann's rejection. But now he was convinced it wasn't that way at all.

Ruth Ann's rejection of him had nothing to do with love. It had more to do with her being unfaithful. What he considered to be the breaking of his heart had actually been the shame and fear his girl and his best friend would be forced to bring his way. In retrospect the accident had put a damper on the whole sordid issue and left Ruth Ann free from admitting to the sin she had committed against him. In a left-handed way she had been spared the ordeal of revealing the truth. In the end the only people left suffering were he and Rachel. As a priest, he was required to show forgiveness. As a man, he needed to exhibit anger.

Now, whether he liked it or not, he had to confront Ruth Ann on the matter. The betrayal he now felt seemed as though it were tearing at every fiber of his being. He was feeling angry, and rightly so. It was time to let his former girlfriend know the guilt trip she had forced him to endure for the past fifteen years was over. It was time to let Ruth Ann know she no longer had to keep this dark secret within herself.

"Mildred, tell Father Wesley I want to see him in my office, immediately!" Father Coniglio demanded as he came charging through the kitchen door of the rectory with Sharon Beasley in his wake. Shagtyme had been left outside, chained in the backyard. Mildred had an upsetting feeling as she rushed off to get Father Wesley. First, Rabbi Zuckerman shows up to have a secretive meeting with the young cleric. Now this. The good feeling the housekeeper had been experiencing an hour earlier had evaporated. Something bad was happening, she could feel it in the air.

Father Wesley rushed to the old priest's office, and when he got there he saw Sharon sitting in the armchair. This had to have something to do with Ruth Ann and possibly Rachel. Why else would she be here?

"Father, sit down," Father Coniglio ordered. Father Wesley did as he was told.

"Father, we have a problem on our hands. Sharon has explained to me the predicament involving you and Ruth Ann Travers. Each—"

"Father, with all due respect, I know where you are headed," Father Wesley interrupted as he looked at Sharon. "I don't think I am Rachel's father."

"Whether you are or are not is not important at the moment. That's not the reason I called you in here…"

What Father Coniglio had to say caught Father Wesley off guard. Now he joined Mildred in the bad feeling department. Something was wrong, very wrong.

"…Rachel and her mother had an argument and Ruth Ann is in the hospital. Father, Rachel stabbed her mother with a knife and now she is nowhere to be found."

Stunned, Father Wesley didn't know what to say. Once again he was feeling guilty. Here he was, ready to disavow anything to do with Ruth Ann or Rachel. Once more he had been selfish and this time he knew it. He needed to be stronger this time around.

"Stabbed," he said, weakly. "How so? What happened?"

Father Coniglio stared straight into the eyes of his subordinate. "Father, we thought it might have something to do with you. Sharon can explain it better than I can."

Father Wesley gave his undivided attention to the person he considered to be Ruth Ann's closest friend. If Ruth Ann had disclosed the identity of Rachel's father to anyone, then Sharon was that person. Obviously, Ruth Ann hadn't. Otherwise the thinking wouldn't be that he was, somehow, partly responsible for this tragedy between mother and daughter. But he had to ask.

"Sharon, what happened?"

"Father, Ruth Ann told me Rachel was having some trouble with the kids on the beach. Once you returned, stories began to circulate about the two of you and how close you had been back when we were younger. I guess some of the kids picked up on it and began to razz her about having a priest as a father. It was Ruth Ann's intention to sit her down and explain the whole story to her. But Ruth Ann must've feared the repercussions which might come her way. Why else wouldn't she have explained it to her before now?"

"I think I know why."

"You do?"

"Sharon, who is Rachel's father?"

"I always thought it was you. I told you that married story just to protect Ruth Ann until she had a chance to settle the matter with you. It's the story she wanted people to believe."

"Did she ever say it was me?"

"No, but I figured it was a given. Are you saying you don't think it is you?"

"I don't want to get into it right now. At the moment I have to find out how serious Ruth Ann's condition is and what has happened to Rachel. What hospital is Ruth Ann at?"

"The Lutheran."

"Father, why don't you talk to that policeman friend of yours. Maybe he can lend a hand in the situation," Father Coniglio suggested.

"Kilcullen? I'm sure he's already on the case."

"Father, I have one last question," Sharon asked of Father Wesley. "If you're not Rachel's father then why not just reveal the person's name? Good Lord, it's been a number of years. I think it's time she addressed the truth."

"She didn't for a number of reasons and, sad to say, I'm involved in all of them."

"Then you think you know who Rachel's father is?"

"I have a sneaking suspicion."

The next order of business for Father Wesley was to check in on Ruth Ann's status and locate Rachel. Once Sharon Beasley had left the rectory he, Father Coniglio and Mildred gathered again in the kitchen. They weren't together more than thirty seconds when Grimaldi came charging through the kitchen door, his right arm outstretched, pointed at Father Wesley.

"You are a miserable, intruding son of a bitch," he lashed out.

"Grimaldi, please," Father Coniglio replied before the others could speak. "If there's a problem let's resolve it civilly."."

"I'm sorry, Father, but this son of a…" Grimaldi was turning crimson and was tongue tied.

"Antonio, what's wrong with you?" It was Mildred's turn to chastise the caretaker.

"It's…it's him," he muttered through a staccato voice. "He's finally… he's finally gone and done it."

"Gone and done what?" Father Wesley asked in his own defense.

"You know, you meddling…you meddling zealot of decency."

"Now, Grimaldi, just calm down," Father Coniglio insisted.

The phone rang. "I'll get it," Mildred eagerly volunteered, wanting to get out of the room before all hell rained down on them.

"Grimaldi, please sit down. You too, Father Wesley."

"No," Grimaldi shouted. "Go ahead, Father. Go ahead and tell him what you've done this time. Go ahead and tell him how you've again dragged the good name of Grimaldi through the mud."

"Grimaldi, does this have anything to do with Anna's baby?" Father Wesley wanted to know.

"You know it does. I knew, all along, you getting involved was a big mistake. Now my whole family is paying for it, especially Anna, and she doesn't even realize it yet." Grimaldi then looked at Father Coniglio. "Father, he told Anna to come clean. Let everyone know that the baby might not be her husband's. Let everyone know she could be carrying a black man's baby inside her. Maybe the idea of abortion was a little out of line, and I came to respect the decision she made because of his, so-called, prudent advice. But this I cannot tolerate. We could have discreetly let her have the baby and then put it up for adoption and nobody would have been the wiser. But now the damage has been done, even if she does put the baby up for adoption. Do you know she's actually thinking of telling Arturo about this? That crazy bastard will kill her."

Father Coniglio had to slump into a chair and cover his eyes with his right hand. Once he thought he had it together he said, "Grimaldi, what would have been said if Anna went into the hospital to have the baby and didn't come out with one?"

"We could have said it died or something."

"Grimaldi, I was trying to help Anna. It had nothing to do with dishonoring your family name. Think of your daughter first and your damn pride second." Father Wesley could feel himself getting hot under the collar.

"Get off your mighty horse, will you," Grimaldi fired back. "Joe tough guy, who once patrolled these streets as if they were his own, decides to become a priest. Now he has to make up for all the wrong he has done in his life. Well, while you were making peace with God, you should have left my daughter out of it."

Low blow and Father Wesley felt its vicious sting. He wanted to lash back at him. But he wasn't going to lower himself to that level. He was going to be cool, calm, and above all, collective.

"Enough, gentlemen, enough," Father Coniglio implored. "I've heard just about all I can stomach. Grimaldi, I believe Father Wesley is correct when he says he was acting in Anna's best interest. I also understand the torment you are going through. The answer as to if the baby should be put up for adoption is not yours to make. It's Anna's. If she chooses not to put the baby up for adoption then the question of his or her lineage is going to be right out there for all to see. Maybe Anna's doing the right thing by addressing the matter now."

"She's not keeping it, if I have anything to say about the matter."

"Just a minute, Grimaldi." Father Wesley's voice was an octave or two higher. It was obvious he was becoming enraged. "We are not talking about a pedigree pet that became impregnated by some mutt in the neighborhood. We're talking about your daughter and grandchild. Stop being a pigheaded and stubborn old fool."

"I wouldn't be talking like a pigheaded and stubborn old fool if you had kept your nose out of my family matters."

"Once again, Grimaldi, I must remind you that it was Anna who came to me."

"I hope you are still so pious and righteous once she gets her head caved in by that deadbeat husband of hers."

Father Wesley reflected for a moment. "You've got a point there, Grimaldi. Let me talk to her about letting the public in on her little secret, until she has determined what she intends to do with the baby. I'm with you when it comes to your son-in-law. I don't trust him, either."

Mildred reentered the kitchen. Her face had a confused look about it. "Father, there's a phone call for you. It's Maria Castleman."

Father Coniglio looked up from his slumped over position at the kitchen table. "Tell her I'll have to call her back."

"I'm sorry, Father. I should have been more specific. She wishes to speak to Father Wesley."

CHAPTER
TWENTY-NINE

Walking at a brisk pace, Father Wesley made the three-minute trek to the Castlemans' single family clapboard house on Sagamore Street. It was the priest's first trip to the Castlemans' home since his return to St. Theresa's. The simple two-story, weather-beaten structure was just as he remembered it when he would arrive in his old beat up Thunderbird to pick up Billy for another night of raucous revelry.

All Maria said to Mildred was for Father Wesley to come over to the house, quickly. He was complying with her wishes but as he approached the Castlemans' home he began to feel uneasy. Maria had already forgiven him for what had happened concerning Billy. However, Father Wesley had no idea as to the feelings of Maria's husband, Frank, or their daughter, Heather. Being the one responsible for the death of Billy made him wonder if the rest of the family was going to be as willing to forgive as Maria stated she was. He prayed that Frank and Heather also carried mercy in their hearts.

The priest climbed the rickety three stairs leading to the screened in porch area and Maria was there to greet him at the door. The look on her face was one of intense confusion. The past few days had already proven to be a tangled web of complexity for the cleric, and he had to believe Maria was going to add something to it.

"Father, thank you for coming so quickly," Maria said as she opened the screen door.

"I did as you asked. Now, what's the problem?"

"Please, come to the kitchen with me. We need your help and, hopefully, understanding."

Understanding? Was the question which came to Father Wesley. Help, sure. He'd help with any situation if he were capable. But she was asking him to be understanding. He wasn't sure what to make of that request.

As they entered the kitchen he saw Heather sitting at the table with what looked like a body with a blanket draped over it. Whoever it was, was whimpering. Heather looked up from her sitting position, her eyes pleading for help while her arms sought to comfort the person under the blanket. Father Wesley turned to Maria and asked, "What's going on here?"

Maria took him by the arm and led him to the dining room, where they could be alone while she tried to explain. Maria had been stunned when she heard the story the person under the blanket had to tell.

"Father, this is going to be as great a shock to you as it was to us. The person in the kitchen is Rachel Travers. I found her on our back porch earlier this morning. She was huddled under some canvas we use to protect the patio furniture. She was crying and covered with blood. She kept saying something about her mother being stabbed. I can't quite determine if it was she or somebody else who did this alleged stabbing."

"Yes, Maria, her mother was stabbed. The police are trying to find Rachel right now. Our main concern was that Rachel may have stabbed her mother, and once she realized the severity of the act she had committed she might end up doing some harm to herself. Thank God you found her."

As he said the words Father Wesley prepared himself for the words he was going to need to hear. *Why had she come here?* There were plenty of other places to seek shelter. She could have gone to a friend's place. She could have gone on the run. But, no, Rachel chose the Castlemans' home to find safety. To anyone else it might not have made sense. For Father Wesley it did. Rachel being here was the answer to the question nagging him. If his suspicions were correct, now was the time to put aside whatever bitterness he had and be the man God had chosen him to be.

"Maria, why here? What prompted her to come to you for safety?"

"Because she claims to be our granddaughter." It was the booming voice of Frank Castleman answering the question, his large bulk taking up a good portion of the doorway he was standing in. "What she had to say is true, Maria. We have a kike for a granddaughter."

"Nice to see you haven't changed," Father Wesley blurted out. He had forgotten just how prejudiced Frank Castleman could be. He always referred to Jews as *kikes* or *Hebs*. Blacks were *niggers* or *spades*. Asians were *gooks*. Puerto Ricans were *spics*. Father Wesley now realized how much Frank's biased nature had not bothered him in the past, for he had been just as much a bigot as Frank Castleman. In fact, Frank Castleman once held Paul Wesley in high regard because of his hellacious ways, which Frank interpreted as being manly. Father Wesley now felt only shame, for he had reveled in Frank's adulation of him.

"And I see you have," Frank countered. "I suppose now that you hide behind the cassock of a priest you expect everything to be all right." Frank Castleman's rancorous statement sizzled with cynicism.

"Dad, stop it, right now!" Heather Castleman had entered the room and the conversation. "What did you find out? Explain it so Father Wesley understands." The Castleman's daughter was doing a good job of standing her ground.

Frank Castleman sneered at her. The memory was still fresh from fifteen years ago when his little girl of twelve was infatuated with this maverick from the beach, and how he had approved of her case of puppy love. Now, if given the chance, he would rip this man apart, limb from limb. No matter how much good Paul Wesley did for the rest of his life he would never earn Frank Castleman's forgiveness. Paul Wesley's recklessness had taken his son away from him and because of that injustice, Frank Castleman was incapable of changing the way he felt.

"Please, Dad, that young girl needs our help. If she is family, it's our duty to be there for her. What did you find out?"

Slowly, Frank Castleman shifted his attention back to Father Wesley, as though the priest had asked the question. "I just talked with Alan Travers in Florida. He reluctantly verified that Ruth Ann had a daughter by Billy. He and his wife are on their way here to be at their daughter's bedside."

Father Wesley remained silent for a moment. The truth was ripping his heart apart. His best friend and girl had betrayed him. All those years of guilt. All those years of blaming himself for not measuring up for Ruth Ann and being so trustworthy of Billy. He had been cheated by those who had meant the most to him. Now, for the first time since he had been ordained, he questioned his vocation. Had he taken on the ministry because he had been redirected in life? Or had he taken it on because he sought emotional refuge from a life he thought he was destroying with his wanton ways, only to discover the two people he trusted and loved the most had been disloyal to him? It was now time for the true Father Wesley to stand up and be counted. It was time for Father Wesley to forgive if he truly loved Ruth Ann and Billy as he claimed.

The troubled priest looked into the eyes of Maria. Her expression was one of sadness. She knew exactly how Father Wesley was feeling and she, in turn, was feeling sorry for him. He had paid a heavy price for an act of deception. An act of personal treason perpetrated by her son.

"Will you people stop feeling sorry for yourselves and do something to help this poor girl?" Again, it was the voice of Heather, the only voice of reason in the room.

"I think it's time I spoke to Rachel," Father Wesley told Maria. Turning to her husband he asked, "Have the police been notified?"

"No," a gruff Frank Castleman answered.

"Good. Don't call them until I tell you," an equally surly Father Wesley responded. "And when you do, call the State Police and see if a Richard Kilcullen is on duty. If he is, tell him Father Wesley of St. Theresa's needs to see him as soon as possible. Tell whomever you're talking to that I can be found here."

Without waiting for a reply Father Wesley marched past the three Castlemans and into the kitchen. He sat down next to Rachel and removed the blanket from her head. "Rachel, I'm Father Wesley. I am a friend of your mother and I was a friend of your father. I want to help you."

Rachel, her eyes swelled with tears, felt comfort in the company of the priest. "Yes, my mother told me about you. She said you were my father's best friend."

"That's right. Why don't you tell me what happened? Did you and your mother have an argument and it somehow got out of control?"

"Oh, no!" Rachel shrieked. "It wasn't me! It was that rotten pig down on the beach. He's the one who stabbed my mother. She's dead, isn't she?"

Father Wesley took her left hand in his hands. "I don't think so. Who's the pig on the beach? Exactly what happened?"

"My mother works nights at a twenty-four hour convenience store on the parkway. Last night I was home alone and fell asleep on the couch. I was awakened by a hand shaking my shoulder. It was the old guy from the beach. He must've followed me home and when he saw my mother wasn't there, he invited himself in." Rachel paused. What she had experienced was surreal, as if it hadn't really happened.

"So your mother wasn't home. What happened next?"

"You've got to understand something about this guy. He's always got something to say to the girls on the beach. He started with me so I played along with him. He wanted me to..." Rachel wasn't quite sure how to repeat what happened to a priest.

"He wanted you to do what, Rachel? Don't be afraid to say what has to be said. What did this old guy want from you? It was a sexual favor, wasn't it?" Father Wesley's voice carried a stern tone in it.

Rachel nodded her head, vigorously.

"Rachel, what did he want? Did he want you to perform oral sex on him?" The memory of Shagtyme chasing the pervert who had tried to violate Jenna Napoli was resurrected in his mind.

"YES!" she screamed. "But he didn't ask. He already had it out when he woke me up. He grabbed me by my hair and told me to start sucking. He said he had a gun and he would hurt me if I didn't do as I was told."

"So you were forced to perform oral sex on him?"

"Yeah. Only I bit him. He squealed like a pig. I made a run for the back door. But he caught up to me and pressed me against the floor. I could still feel his slimy...you know what...rubbing against me. Then my mother gets home early and sees the whole thing. She started screaming. The pervert panicked. He knew he was cooked. He grabbed a knife off the kitchen counter and went at my mother and stabbed her. Blood was gushing everywhere. I tried to pull him off her, but he said I was next. I ran for the door and never looked back. I assumed he was right behind me. Father, please say you believe me! Please!"

Father Wesley stroked the back of her head as he pressed it against his shoulder. The poor kid. If Rachel was telling the truth she had become a victim of this swine who was operating in the neighborhood. This time, he had gone too far.

"Everything is going to be okay, Rachel. But the police are going to want to talk to you about this guy from the beach. Are you up to it?"

Again she nodded.

"Rachel, why did you come here? How did you know the Castlemans were your grandparents? I heard the kids on the beach were giving you a rough time since you didn't know who your father was. Did that change? Did your mother tell you who your father was?"

"Yes, she did."

"So when did this all happen, your mother telling you who your father and grandparents are?"

"Just the other day."

"Father, aren't you getting off the subject?" It was once again the angry voice of Frank Castleman. He didn't realize how much this sudden revelation of the truth was hurting Father Wesley and how he needed to hear it. The priest had to find forgiveness in his heart, and the only way that was going to be accomplished was to know the truth. But Frank Castleman was right to a certain extent. The most important matter at the moment was to see that Rachel was exonerated from any wrongdoing, so the police could start tracking down the true assailant of Ruth Ann. Maybe later he'd have the chance to discuss with Ruth Ann the injustice she and Billy inflicted upon him.

"Shouldn't we be calling the police by now?" Maria asked.

"Yes." Father Wesley then looked at Frank and said, "Go ahead and call the State Police. Make sure you ask for Officer Kilcullen."

Frank Castleman walked away to make the call from the phone in the bedroom, mumbling under his breath as to who had died and made Father Wesley boss. The priest then turned his attention back to Rachel and the matter he intended to resolve on this day. Right now he wasn't thinking like a priest. He was thinking like the Paul Wesley of nearly two decades earlier. If he had a gripe in life, it was with Ruth Ann and Billy, not Rachel.

"Now, Rachel, once more, before the police arrive, tell me what you can about this man on the beach."

"He's always sitting on a bench. Him and a friend. I think his name is Sully."

SALVI! It had to be. Father Wesley could feel his blood pressure soaring. The frustrated hormones of an old man had imploded to the point where he might have killed someone. But that someone had been Ruth Ann. Despite the wrong she had done him, he still cared enough about her to avenge the act of malevolence which had been carried out against her and her child.

"Father, I'll accompany Rachel to the police station," Heather said, placing her hand on Father Wesley's left shoulder and snapping him out of his trance like state.

"I'll be going with her too," Maria added. She then called out to her husband, "Frank, I want you to call Jerry Brandt. Tell him to meet us at the State Police station. I don't want Rachel to be detained any longer than necessary."

"Just a minute—" Frank Castleman tried to respond to his wife's directive.

"No, you wait a minute," she curtly cut him off. "You tell Brandt to be at that police station as fast as possible. Rachel may need a lawyer and Brandt's our lawyer. Now, just do it!"

"I don't want him," Rachel declared, unexpectedly.

"Why not?" Heather asked as though she had been a caring aunt for years rather than just an hour.

"I just don't. I'll take any other lawyer but him," Rachel begged.

"But, Rachel, Jerry Brandt is our family attorney. He'll make sure that your rights are not violated. What you have to tell the police is very serious and you should have a lawyer present."

"It's not that," Rachel answered. She looked around at the three adults who until today had meant nothing to her. Now they were her lifeline. Being an adolescent, she had her priorities out of order. Hers was an infatuation period in life. Rachel feared rejection because of what had happened to her.

"Then what is it?" her grandmother asked.

"It's because of Freddy. If he finds out that sick bastard tried to do me he might not want to see me again. His father is Jerry Brandt, so he is going to find out if his dad is my lawyer."

"Freddy Brandt?" Father Wesley had to ask.

Rachel, with an intimidated look upon her face, knew she had to plead Freddy's case. "Father, I know what he did to your dog, and he's really sorry about it. He knows it was stupid and he'd never do it again," she lied.

"It was stupid, Rachel, but it's not the only stupid thing he's done in his life. He and his buddy—that Danny Corrigan—have been a thorn in my side since I've been at St. Theresa's. But that aside, he's got to be a good three or four years older than you."

"Now you sound like my mom. She says the same thing. She said she went out with an older boy when she was a kid and it was a mistake. I guess the older boy was my father since I came along as sort of a surprise. It just seems like Freddy's a lot older right now. In a couple of years it won't, and then it won't matter."

"Rachel, Freddy is going to find out one way or the other. We don't have the time to play games and pacify Freddy Brandt because you have a schoolgirl's crush on him. We have a bigger issue to deal with. You should be worrying about your mother and not the hurt feelings of a boyfriend you'll soon forget." Father Wesley knew of what he spoke.

Rachel bowed her head in shame. The priest was right. She should be concerned about her mother and not Freddy Brandt. At that moment Frank Castleman reentered the room.

"The police are here," he told them. "Two squad cars."

CHAPTER
THIRTY

"Any serious problems at the Castlemans' place?" Father Coniglio asked, as he looked up from the diocesan newspaper he was reading at the kitchen table.

"You don't want to know," a gruff Father Wesley answered as he slammed the kitchen door behind him and headed straight to his office, without uttering another word.

"I wonder what that was about?" Father Coniglio was forced to ask Shagtyme, his only company at the moment. "I think we'll let him cool off for a few minutes before asking what seems to be upsetting him."

Shagtyme wasn't waiting for anyone. The dog sensed a problem. The large canine raised himself off the floor and went to seek his master. The dog, through instinct, realized the priest needed a friend right now.

Father Wesley had left the door to his office slightly ajar. Shagtyme nuzzled it open with his nose and made his way around to the back of the desk where the priest sat. Father Wesley took notice of the animal and his loyalty to him. "At least I can count on you," he said as he rubbed the top of the dog's head. "You're about the only friend I have left," he went on.

"That's not quite true." It was Father Coniglio who had taken heed of Shagtyme's lead and followed the dog to Father Wesley's office.

"Something's troubling you and I'd like to be of help, if I can. But if not, just tell me to go away and I'll leave you to be by yourself."

A feeble smile came to Father Wesley's face. "And they tried to tell me you had lost something off your fastball," he tried to joke.

"Not yet," Father Coniglio replied as he made his way into the office and took a seat on the opposite side of the desk. "So, I gather, all is not well at the Castlemans."

Father Wesley leaned forward and began rubbing the nape of his neck. "No, things didn't go well. Rachel was there. She claims she didn't try to kill her mother. She said some pervert followed her home. The same pervert, in all likelihood, who tried to accost Jenna Napoli. According to Rachel it was this degenerate who stabbed Ruth Ann and then threatened to do her in. She ran like hell and hightailed it to the Castlemans."

Father Coniglio was relieved to hear what his fellow priest had to say about Rachel, but he was also somewhat confused. "It's good to know Rachel is safe and that she didn't try to kill her mother. Is her story believable?"

"Kilcullen was one of the cops who showed up to take her to the station. The police had no idea there was a third person involved and they'd have to check it out. I asked him what was going to happen to Rachel. He wasn't sure. I don't want to see her placed in some juvenile home. Maria and Heather followed the cops to the station and were to be joined by the Castlemans' attorney. Hopefully the police will grab the depraved swine that did this and Rachel can be released into the custody of the Castlemans. As for me, I believe what she had to say."

"Then that's good enough for me," Father Coniglio told him, hoping to boost his fellow priest's confidence. "What I don't understand, Father, is why did Rachel run to the Castlemans' home?"

"Because she claims the Castlemans are her grandparents."

"What? That means—"

"That means Billy Castleman, my good buddy, a person I could have entrusted my life to and he'd have seen I was taken care of, was a person I could not trust with my girl. What happened between them I don't know. Were Ruth Ann and Billy seeing each other behind my back? It's possible. Maybe Billy forced himself upon her, but I don't think so.

Billy wasn't a sleaze. He was a good friend and I think he and Ruth Ann just happened to fall in love. Only Ruth Ann can answer that question and right now she can't talk to anyone. But I do know this: on the night Billy died he stayed with me because we had something to talk over. We agreed to get good and drunk but then we were going to talk. But, now, as I recall, Billy had very little to drink that night. He was obviously trying to stay sober because he wanted to speak to me about a matter that was very serious, and he needed as clear a head as possible to do so."

Father Wesley drooped his head. He could feel he was on the verge of tears. He had ambivalent feelings, at the moment, towards Ruth Ann and Billy. "Why couldn't they have just been honest about the whole thing? They should have told me up front about their involvement and we would have all been the better because of it."

"Father, try to go easy on yourself. Hindsight only carries regret with it. It seems obvious to me that, through Billy, they were trying to reach you in a way that was going to minimize the hurt they knew they'd inflicted upon you. On that night the lives of three people changed, forever. Why such tragedy evolved from it, I don't know. But what I do know is we have to accept it. Stop thinking in terms of *what if.*"

Father Wesley raised his head, the sad expression still gracing his face. "You're right," he told the older priest. "But it's tough trying to be honest with yourself. What I found out today has me questioning my vocation."

"That too is to be expected," Father Coniglio quickly countered. "But don't dwell on that for too long, either. Father, you've proven to be a good priest. You've proven to be the elixir St. Theresa's needed."

That last remark by Father Coniglio certainly didn't make the younger priest feel any better. However, he could take solace in the fact that he had done what the cardinal had asked of him—despite the claims of Father Moore—and he managed to make the cardinal's secretary's life total frustration, when it came to St. Theresa's. Father Wesley truly believed he had managed to get a stay of execution for the tired old parish. The thought made the emotional weight preying against his heart a little less heavy.

"Now, Father, you must tell me of this degenerate person, the one Rachel claims stabbed her mother. The one you claim to be the pedophile that makes our neighborhood nervous, and makes men like us want to forget we are priests so we can vent our rage on this lecherous demon, whose satanic perversion imperils the children we strive so hard to protect."

Pretty strong language from a priest who went by the book concerning the Church's outlook on certain matters, Father Wesley thought. But telling Father Coniglio that Salvi was the suspect of those hideous acts had to be done tactfully. He wasn't sure what kind of person Father Coniglio had conjured up in his mind as being the perpetrator of the vile actions brought on Jenna Napoli and Rachel. But he knew Salvi wasn't included in the lot. Sure, everyone knew the guy tried to attract the attention of all the young ladies cavorting along the beach with his insensitive comments. He had been doing it for years. Everyone had come to accept it, never thinking he might actually snap.

The doorbell chimed. With any luck that would be someone here to speak with Father Coniglio, and Father Wesley would have the time to think of what to tell the old priest about a man he had known since his first day at St. Theresa's. A man the old cleric thought he had known. But Dame Fortune was not smiling on Father Wesley on this day.

"Father, this is not easy," the younger priest began. "Rachel claims a man from the beach must've followed her home and somehow gained entrance to the apartment Rachel shares with her mother. She claims to have known the man from his catcalls along the beach. Rachel wasn't sure of his name. She thought it was something like *Sully.*"

Father Wesley paused to see if Father Coniglio made the connection. The older priest had. His face suddenly became pallid. What Father Wesley had to say was something he never expected to hear. He didn't want to believe it, either. Although Salvi was just a sporadic churchgoer, Father Coniglio felt he knew the man.

"Sully," he said, slowly. "You mean it sounded like Sully but actually might have been…Salvi."

Father Wesley nodded. He knew this revelation was killing the old priest. A Catholic from his parish guilty of such depraved acts? The younger cleric was certain Father Coniglio was taking Salvi's fall—from what little grace the man had—as a reflection of his ministry being a

PRODIGAL PARISH

somewhat failed one. Father Coniglio was not good at taking bad news when it concerned one of his parishioners.

"And you say you believe Rachel?" Father Coniglio asked.

Father Wesley expected the question. The old priest was having a tough time coping with this horrible news. He had to be hoping against all odds that Rachel had been mistaken. However, the thought of her lying never entered the venerable old priest's mind.

"I do," Father Wesley responded.

"It's so sad," Father Coniglio murmured as he bowed his head and shook it in disbelief.

Father Wesley looked up to see Mildred and Officer Kilcullen standing in the doorway. It had to have been Kilcullen who had rang the doorbell.

"Fathers," Mildred said, "the officer here, has something to say to both of you." There was an air of curiosity in the housekeeper's eyes. She knew whatever had happened at the Castlemans' house was now taking on a life of its own.

Kilcullen, nervously twirling his cap in his hands, stepped into the office and stood at the corner of the desk so he could speak directly to both priests. "Father, does he know the whole story concerning Rachel Travers and what happened last night?" he asked Father Wesley while leaning his head towards Father Coniglio.

"He does," the curate answered.

"Okay. We followed up on what Rachel had to say and sent a squad car over to Salvi's place. What happened next wasn't pretty. Obviously, Salvi knew he'd be named and, I guess, the disgrace of it all did him in. He was ready and waiting for the officers when they arrived. He opened the door for them and simply stated: 'I'm sorry.' He had been holding a gun behind his back and once finishing what he had to say he quickly put its barrel under his chin, and before either officer could do a thing, he pulled the trigger. He's dead."

Father Wesley raised his right hand to cover his eyes and said a silent prayer for the repose of Salvi's troubled soul. Father Coniglio did something different. He rose to his feet and announced he was going for a walk. He needed some time to himself. Dejectedly, he made his way

267

out of the office. Shagtyme again sensed a problem and followed the old priest out of the room. The animal seemed to know when he was needed.

Officer Kilcullen solemnly nodded his head at what he was witnessing. "Pretty special dog you have there," he told Father Wesley.

"He's a priest's best friend," Father Wesley informed him.

268

CHAPTER
THIRTY-ONE

"You've got to be kidding me," was all Arthur Gregorio could say as one of his bar mates at Rose's informed him of the untimely demise of Salvi. The old horny rat had been his ace in the hole and now he was gone. The goose who had laid the golden egg had committed suicide and, in the process, severed Arthur Gregorio's lifeline.

Gregorio slammed his empty beer glass against the bar in frustration. "You all right over there?" Bryan Fogarty yelled across the bar. The expression on Arthur's face told it all. Whatever the reason, Salvi's death had Gregorio muttering to himself.

Gregorio just glared at the burly biker, as if to say: *stay clear of my business..*

Arthur stewed for a minute or two about his misfortune and then started thinking about ways to correct it. With Salvi now gone there was no way Alfredo was going to advance him any more money. Now he was going to have to wait for the go ahead to torch St. Theresa's, and he wasn't all that sure Alfredo intended to use him for the job since the Temple Beth Abraham fiasco. This was a very precarious situation he was in. He couldn't blow the whistle on his dealings with Alfredo and Salvi without incriminating himself. Arthur was angry. Without the largesse of Alfredo he was going to have to go back to work. It was a thought that didn't set well with him. He had to find another means of reaping benefits without lifting a finger for it.

There was another problem. His business with the pair had always gone through Salvi and had always been conducted at the park bench on the beach. Now with Salvi gone, and winter coming on, Gregorio had no idea as to how to get in touch with Alfredo. He could ask around but one of the agreements Salvi had made him swear by was that he was never to acknowledge any dealings with them. It was futile to break that pact since he knew Alfredo would enjoy—now that the tables had been turned—having him right where he wanted him. No Salvi meant no blackmail. No blackmail meant Arthur Gregorio was out of luck, and about to run out of money.

Arthur could feel himself drowning in frustration. His breathing became labored. He had to get out of Rose's and be by himself, so he could think. He wasn't about to let the good times come to an end. He enjoyed it too much.

He ambled across the parkway and sat on the seawall. With the chilling wind blowing in his face Gregorio took stock of the situation. He had to replace that lost income somehow.

The more he thought about it the more empty he came up. He was becoming more discouraged by the minute and his state of frustration was leading to desperation. The thoughts of becoming a petty thief entered his mind. But that wasn't good enough for Arthur Gregorio. He believed he had moved past the nickel and dime routine of a street smart looter. No, he had graduated. He should be able to pull off a job and sit idly by for an extended period, until another well-financed chore came his way. However, Salvi's cowardly decision to blow his head off had taken that away from him.

Just when he thought it was hopeless, he had what he considered a brainstorm. Why he hadn't thought of it before was beyond him. There was another cow to milk and it was an udder he should have been working all along. He came to the conclusion his thinking must have become distorted, because of the humiliating circumstances surrounding his sorry plight. But his thinking wasn't clouded now. He decided it was time for him to live off his wife, because of the disgraceful state she had placed him in.

As he figured it, Anna had worked as a dental hygienist for twelve years before they married. He knew she made good money over that period of time and she had to have saved a good portion of it. Anna had told him she had five grand in the bank but Arthur never bought off on that figure. He always thought it to be at least five times that amount. Anna claimed to have kept the account in her own name because she didn't trust him with the money. Even Arthur understood her reasoning. But he always thought someday he would get his hands on it. Now he wanted it more than ever. As he quickly did the math in his head, he came to realize the amount she claimed to have was far from what she actually had. That bitch!

Anna had lived at home until they were married. She always had an astute head on her shoulders, when it came to monetary matters, and never did any outlandish spending. If Arthur's estimate was right his wife was sitting on a six-figure bank account and he had been stupid to never realize it. He now intended to correct that oversight on his part. He was going to strong-arm his own wife. In his twisted way of thinking she owed it to him. He was going to be greedy. He wanted half of what she had.

—◆—

That evening, just after the dinner hour—the Grimaldi family always ate at six and Arthur knew it—he showed up at their front door. He was greeted by his father-in-law. Although Arthur didn't appear to be drunk he did smell of beer. If he was in an intoxicated state, Grimaldi knew they had a problem. He sensed trouble but he thought he could handle it.

"Good evening, Arturo. How can I help you?"

"Knock off the Arturo crap, will you. The name is Arthur. If I want to be known as Arturo I'll buy some sheep and head for the hills of Italy."

"As you wish," Grimaldi agreed. "Again, how can I help you?"

"I'm here to see my wife, if you don't mind. We have some business to discuss."

"Business? What kind of business?"

"None of your goddamn business! Now tell Anna I want to see her."

"Arturo—I'm sorry, Arthur—I can tell you've been drinking. I think it would be wise if you came back when you are sober."

"I'm not drunk, and you know it. You just don't want me to see my wife but I'm going to see her. Do you understand?"

"It's all right, Dad." It was Anna moving up behind her father. "I'll talk to him. We have some matters which need to be ironed out."

Grimaldi stared into the eyes of his daughter and then into the eyes of her husband. The warmth and compassion that had become so much a part of Anna's character could be seen in her eyes. In Arthur's eyes he saw terror. "I'm not so sure I approve," he told his daughter.

"Don't worry about it," she tried to assure her father. "Arthur, go into the living room. I'll join you there in a minute."

As Arthur walked past them, Grimaldi gave his daughter a skeptical look and said, "You don't suppose he knows about the baby's possible… you know…possible skin color, do you?"

"I doubt it. Not unless you and mom have been spreading the word."

"I assure you we haven't. Whatever you do, don't tell him the baby might be black. The crazy fool will cut your throat if he finds out."

Not wishing to upset her father any more than she had, Anna replied, "Don't worry. I just want to see why he's here. There's been a story circulating that he has been high rolling it of late. I'll bet he ran out of cash and is hoping he can get some from me."

"Don't you give him a nickel," Grimaldi warned her.

"I said I'll handle it." Anna's mind was not so much on the money but about the fact that Arthur was going to have to be told about the baby's possible skin pigmentation sooner or later. She decided, on the spot, that later was better.

As Anna retreated to the living room, Grimaldi decided it was time for Father Wesley to know how he sensed a real danger developing, for what he still considered the priest's ill-conceived advice.

"Okay, Arthur, what is it you want? I'm sure you're not here to inquire about my condition?" Anna asked her husband, who was sitting on the sofa, as she entered the living room.

An angry scowl found its way to Arthur's face. *You got that right, you miserable slut. Now you're going to pay for what you did to me,* was Arthur Gregorio's thinking.

"Anna, please sit. You want me out of your life, and believe me I can't wait to get out of it."

Anna, with hesitation, took a seat at the other end of the sofa. "All right, Arthur. Let's hear it. This is about money, isn't it? You want me to pay you to go away."

Now a satisfied smirk came to her husband's face. "You were always such a smart girl, did you know that?" was his observation.

"Spare me, please."

"Anna, my sweet, I think both of us will agree that you did the most disgraceful act that could be committed against any husband. I think you owe me for your…indiscretion."

"And how much is this act of repentance going to cost me?"

Now it was time for Arthur to find out exactly how much money his wife had socked away. If his calculations were correct—and he was fairly certain he was in the right ballpark—then he intended to zing her the way she had zinged him. She had robbed him of his pride, which he would freely admit he had very little. But a little or a lot, he felt he was owed many dollars from her concealed savings.

"Anna, I think you came into our marriage with a lot more money than you claimed. Let's face it, you've been living off your parents for years while making a decent salary. I think because of the embarrassment and hurt you brought my way you owe me some of it."

Anna looked at her husband, suspiciously. He had finally figured it out. Arthur was a schemer and she was astounded when he bought off on the figure of $5,000. Now she was thankful she had kept silent about the true amount.

"And how much am I supposedly worth? And how much do you think you deserve?" Anna was willing to be somewhat benevolent because of the way she had failed him as a wife.

"I say you're worth at least a hundred thousand. I want half."

"What!" she answered, hysterically. "Where in heaven's name did you come up with that figure?" Actually, Arthur wasn't that far off. She had amassed nearly $80,000 in her hidden bank account and Anna had no intention of parting with half of it. "Tell you what I'm going to do. I'll give you a thousand dollars and then I don't want to see or hear from you again."

"A thousand bucks? You can do better than that. If you don't, I'll make your life as miserable as you've made mine."

"Don't you threaten me." Anna was wondering how she never saw this side of the man when they were dating.

"And don't you insult me." Arthur was becoming more enraged with the thought his wife had lied to him. He was going to leave here with his rightful share.

"Arthur, I think you should go. We're through talking. Either you take what I offered or we'll settle this in court. I doubt you'll win there as well, when I describe how you drove me into the arms of another man."

"Why you miserable whore," Gregorio lashed back. "Do you think you're going to do that to me, and get away with it? I'll drag your sorry name through the streets. By the time I'm finished with you, the definition of Anna Grimaldi will be one of pure smut. People will come to see you as a slut! A whore! A cheat! Maybe I'll become a little creative and expose your love life for what it is: a sordid lust for blacks and Latinos to join you in your bed. Yeah, how do you like that? I'll tell the world you have been sleeping around with black men and their engorged endowments from the Almighty and have been doing it for years! I wonder how your old man will like hearing that in the streets. His sweet little girl is into blacks. I'll tell the world your baby is probably the end result of a very dark and lurid moment—and I assume you know what I mean by *dark*— that brought embarrassment and heartache, that can't be measured, to your faithful and loving husband." Arthur sat back, feeling fairly confident he had put the fear of Arthur Gregorio into her. He had no idea his racist threat was the truth.

Arthur was disappointed when he noticed Anna was taking what he had to say in stride. She actually looked relieved. And she was. It was time for her to admit to the sin she had committed that violated the wedding vows they had exchanged.

"Arthur, I didn't know how to put this to you, but you did it for me. You can't insult me or my baby. You see, Arthur, if it is your plan to disgrace me then you'll also be disgracing yourself. The chance is very good the baby inside of me is that of a black man. It happened at Kerry Whalen's bridal shower. They hired a black stripper to entertain the ladies and had a raffle for anyone who wanted to be with him. I won the raffle and I chose to be with the man, not because of any engorged penis as you planned to tell the world. Hell, no. I was with him because I was starving for physical passion. Passion you'd only commit to a Heineken bottle. So go ahead, Arthur, smear my name. You'll only be telling the truth. You'll be telling the world you weren't man enough to satisfy me."

Arthur immediately felt sick. He was unable to say a word. His cold steely glare did the talking for him. His lower lip began to quiver. He couldn't believe what he was hearing. His threat and lie was Anna's truth. Arthur Gregorio, the ultimate bigot, had been hit with the ultimate indignity.

"You son of a bitch," he finally muttered as he raised himself off the couch and went at her. Anna was going to pay for this degradation. He grabbed her by her white blouse and began to shake her, frantically.

"Arthur, please, the baby," she pleaded.

"Oh yeah. Like I care about the baby," he replied as he brought his right knee up and slammed it into her stomach and knocked her to the floor. "Take that you whore."

"Please, Arthur, no more. I'm going to lose the baby. Please."

"You should," he replied as he slammed his right foot into her bloated abdomen.

Grimaldi and his wife, Nanette, came running into the room upon hearing Anna's cry of anguish. Nanette froze at the sight of her daughter being beaten but Grimaldi came right at his son-in-law. "You miserable bastard," he said as he tried to push Arthur away from Anna. But Arthur swatted him aside as if he were an annoying bug.

An incensed Gregorio then made his retreat to the front door, but as he stepped on the porch he was met by Father Wesley, who was coming up the walk after taking heed of Grimaldi's phone call of concern regarding his daughter's well- being.

"Stop him, Father," Nanette screamed from inside the house. "Stop him. He's hurt Anna and my husband."

Gregorio made a quick glance back at the house and then looked at Father Wesley. "Don't even think of trying to stop me," he warned the priest.

"Arthur, what have you done?" Father Wesley wanted to know.

"I did what any self-respecting husband who had been betrayed by a jezebel of a wife would do. Now get the hell out of my way."

"You're not going anywhere until I know what's going on."

"Oh, is that right?" Gregorio then tried to cast a kickboxing move on Father Wesley but the priest was too quick afoot for Gregorio. He caught Arthur's foot as it came at him and flipped the man around so he lost his balance and fell, hitting his head on the top step leading from the porch.

"Take that," the priest berated his subdued opponent. He then grabbed Gregorio by the back of his shirt collar and began dragging him into the house while telling Nanette to call the police.

In the living room Father Wesley was shocked by what he saw. Grimaldi was crawling to his injured daughter who was down on the floor, on her knees, clutching her stomach. "Are you hurt?" the priest asked.

Anna looked up, her eyes filled with the sorrow of a mother who knew she was about to lose her child. "It's the baby," she groaned. "I think it's coming. Oh God, it's too early."

"Nanette!" the priest yelled. "Tell the police we need an ambulance and we need it fast!"

Father Wesley then peered down at the prostrate Arthur Gregorio. "You're going to pay for this. If I weren't a priest, I'd pound your miserable ass into a bloody mess until you pleaded for mercy."

Gregorio, grabbing hold of his bleeding head, managed a beleaguered laugh. "Pretty tough talk for a man of God. She got what she deserved and so will you."

THIRTY-TWO

"Bryan, do you have any idea how to get in touch with that bookmaker, Alfredo?" Johnny Rogers called out from behind the bar.

"Why? Who wants him?"

"I've got Arthur Gregorio on the phone. He's in jail and says he has to talk to Alfredo. Says it's important."

Wasn't this interesting, Fogarty mused. Why did Gregorio need to talk to Alfredo? He didn't know the two men knew each other. And what was Gregorio doing in jail? Fogarty had to find out.

"Let me talk to him," Fogarty said as he leaned over the bar and took the phone from Rogers' hand. "Arthur, this is Bryan. What the hell happened? Why are you in jail?"

"I don't have time for small talk, just find Alfredo and tell him I need his help. He'll understand."

"You and Alfredo tight? I didn't know you knew him."

"Fogarty, will you stop with the crap! They're not going to let me stay on this phone all night. Do you know how to find him?"

"Well, I have a friend who has a friend who has another friend—"

"Knock it off. You know how to get in touch with everyone on that beach. So skip the bull and just do it, you fat pig!"

"You keep insulting me like that and I won't give you the time of day. I'll let your ugly ass rot in that stinkin' jail cell before I lift a finger for you."

Gregorio didn't need to be hit over the head to realize he had better treat Fogarty with a little respect if he hoped to have him locate Alfredo. A more gentlemanly tact was necessary.

"Sorry about that, Fogarty. I didn't mean any disrespect. I've got to get out of here and Alfredo's the only one who can help me. I'll owe you one."

"Yeah, sure you will." Normally Fogarty wouldn't do a thing to help out Gregorio. But he felt this situation was different. If Alfredo was the only one who could bail him out then it meant Gregorio was working for him. It helped explain the source of his recent windfall. Fogarty needed to find out more and the only way that was going to happen was if he came to Gregorio's assistance.

"All right, Gregorio, I'll find Alfredo for you. But let me tell you one thing. This had better be legit. If I find out you're jerking me around or getting me involved in something...shall I say dishonorable...I'll hunt you down and make you pay."

"I swear to you, Fogarty, you're not going to be involved in anything dishonest. Just find Alfredo and tell him I need to see him as soon as possible. I've got to go now."

The hefty biker leaned over the bar and handed the phone back to Rogers. "So what's going on?" he asked as he took the phone from Fogarty.

"Gregorio needs to see Alfredo. I guess he's looking for that old bookie to get him out of whatever jam he's in. Something stinks about this whole mess."

"So, are you going to help him?"

"Yeah. It's the only way I'm going to find out what's going on. It's pretty obvious to me that Alfredo's been Gregorio's benefactor. You'd think it'd be Gregorio who was under Alfredo's thumb. Why do I feel it is just the opposite?"

"Bryan, do you think all the tough talk he's been spewing about getting even with Paulie finally went down and that's why he's in jail? If that's the case then I don't think you should help him."

"Johnny, with all the crap Father Paul has gone through since coming back here, I think if Gregorio got in his face Father Paul would forget who he was for a few minutes and beat him to a pulp. Gregorio wouldn't be in jail, he'd be in the hospital."

Johnny Rogers' face beamed with the thought. "So, how do you go about finding Alfredo? It's too cold to sit on that park bench and now that Salvi's gone he may never sit there again."

Fogarty gulped down what remained of his beer and let out a loud belch as he stood up to leave. "I'll find him," he promised Rogers as he headed towards the door.

"Do you think he can tell you what's going on?"

"Don't count on it. It looks to me as if Gregorio has something on Alfredo. If that is the case, and Alfredo does come to Gregorio's rescue, then that means something bad has gone down or is about to go down. I just want to make sure that whatever it is, it doesn't have an effect on anyone we know. Namely Father Paul."

Father Wesley paced the emergency room corridor at the Lutheran Hospital. Grimaldi and his wife were there with him and sat on an old wooden bench, looking as though their world had come to an end. Anna had gone into premature labor because of the beating she had taken by her irate husband. Arthur had been arrested but Father Wesley worried that his stay in jail was going to be a short one. Right now they had him on a domestic abuse charge and the priest knew—with the help of a slick attorney—he'd be back on the streets before noon tomorrow.

But, right now, Father Wesley had to place his concern about Arthur Gregorio aside. At this moment his thoughts and prayers did not go beyond these walls. In this hospital, in critical condition, were two women who had come to him for help and, it now seemed, he had failed them both. His ministry at St. Theresa's had taken a turn for the worse.

After waiting twenty minutes the Grimaldies were approached by a roly-poly man named Dr. Moraine who explained the complexities of the moment. The baby was coming on this night. The good doctor then cautioned Grimaldi and his wife that since Anna was only in her fifth month, there was a strong chance the baby was not going to survive and, if the newborn did make it, he was certain there were going to be complications. There was also the slight chance that toxemia might threaten Anna's life. The smallish and portly doctor looked Father Wesley's way and suggested a prayer or two at this moment wouldn't hurt.

Father Wesley forced a smile meant for encouragement, but at the moment, even he was not in the mood for praying. His concentration was shot. Right now he was an anxious man. He wasn't feeling like Father Paul Wesley but rather the Paul Wesley of old who knew only one way to settle a problem. But, right now, Grimaldi and Nanette needed a priest, and Father Wesley was the only one on the floor.

For the better part of an hour Father Wesley remained with Antonio and Nanette in the hospital chapel. He was there to be their beacon of light through this stormy period in their lives. But Anna's situation, although serious, wasn't the only one on Father Wesley's mind. Somewhere in this hospital Ruth Ann could also be found. Something was luring him to her. It was not the concerned feelings of a priest drawing on him. It was the tender and heart crushing emotions of a smitten lover.

He excused himself from the Grimaldies, without explaining where he was going or what he had to do. Father Wesley wandered aimlessly through the hospital corridors for a few minutes trying to sort things out. Just a few hours earlier he had been angry with Ruth Ann and Billy for the deceitful way they had played him. But he couldn't say the same now. The feeling he was fighting was much like the one he had experienced back on that fateful day when Ruth Ann removed him from her life, and the day on which Billy had died. It was a feeling he could do without. He was a better man now. He had made his decision in life and it was time to stand by it.

The priest found himself standing before the front desk. The attendant was a young brunette woman who looked at him as if she were trying to figure out how to help him without asking. He looked troubled.

"Father, may I be of some assistance?" she was finally forced to say.

"Yes," he replied, his voice sounding melancholy. "I'd like to check on the condition of a Ruth Ann Travers. She was a stabbing victim brought in yesterday."

The pretty young attendant nodded as she scanned the computer screen. Ten seconds later she looked back at Father Wesley and said, "She's currently in intensive care. If you take the elevator to the fourth floor you'll see the doors to the unit on the right. Currently Nurse Davis is on duty there. She'll help you. I'll call ahead to make sure there's no problem."

After thanking the young lady for her help, Father Wesley made his way slowly to the elevator doors. As a priest he owed it to Ruth Ann to be at her side. As a man he owed it to himself to be as far away from this place as possible. He could feel the *Big Hurt* coming his way again.

The doors to the intensive care unit were locked, admittance allowed to only those with the proper clearance. But a priest has a way of opening doors without saying a word, especially in a place such as this. Upon seeing him through the glass portion of the doors, Nurse Davis was of the assumption he was here on official business. She buzzed him in. Father Wesley entered with no fanfare whatsoever.

The eeriness of death seemed to careen off the walls. There was a certain finality about this place. A feeling of the expected but unwanted prevailed.

"Good evening, Father," the hydrant shaped, middle-aged nurse greeted him. "I'm told you wish to see Miss Travers. Are you here to administer the last rites? She's been heavily sedated and her wounds are severe but she is expected to survive. I'm sorry, I didn't know she was Catholic."

Interesting, Father Wesley thought. His clerical garb was making it easy for him to maneuver in this hospital. He could continue to use this ruse and nobody would be the wiser. But it was a Machiavellian stunt. He preferred to be honest and forthright about the entire situation.

"I'm sorry. I'm not here to administer the last rites to Miss Travers. She's not Catholic, but she is a friend. I was hoping I might look in on her."

"I see," the nurse responded. "Since you're not here to perform the last rites I'm expected to tell you that no one is to visit Miss Travers without the family's approval. But you did say you were a close friend, so I guess I never asked you about the last rites matter. My silly presumption just told me that's why you are here." She winked to let Father Wesley know she was also confessing to her lie as she committed it.

Father Wesley's smile suggested it was one of a forgiving nature. "Nurse Davis, thank you for bending the rules for me. I am grateful."

Nurse Davis returned the smile. "Ruth Ann's in there," she said, pointing at the room across the hall.

Seconds later Father Wesley found himself standing over the heavily sedated body of his former and unfaithful girlfriend. In addition to her stab wounds she had taken quite a beating. It was hard to believe that the frail Salvi had been capable of such violent behavior. It probably surprised him as well. The deplorable and shameful conduct he had exhibited had disgraced him in such a way that the only way out was to take his own life.

Father Wesley worked his way around the tubes and machines linked to Ruth Ann's body and sat on the edge of the bed. He took her limp hand in his own. He wasn't quite sure as to what to say. He wasn't sure if she could hear him. But he did know it was time for him to speak to her.

"Sorry, Ruth Ann. I'm sorry for ruining your life and ending Billy's. I'm sorry for putting so much fear into you. I was a young hotheaded punk whose only concern in life was what I could get out of it. It's not fair that I lived and Billy perished. It's not fair that I found my direction in life while you were left to struggle with yours, because of my insensitive and greedy ways. It's funny that I should be talking this way, because just a few hours ago I had developed a tremendous amount of disdain for you and Billy, because of what you did to me. Then I thought about what had happened and came to realize it was me, and not you and Billy, who was at fault. Thinking back on what I was like, I'll bet you thought I was going to use you and then dump you after I became bored with the experience. I honestly can't tell you what direction I was headed. But, with that being the thought, I understand how you found comfort in Billy's arms. Don't blame yourself for what happened between us on that day."

Father Wesley's eyes began to moisten but it didn't stop him. "I've met Rachel. She's a very pretty girl, much like her mother. I didn't find her to be the rebellious rapscallion you described for me. But, of course, I met her after the most traumatic event in her life, and yours too." The priest then placed his other hand over Ruth Ann's and clasped it firmly.

"Ruth Ann, I want you to know that Rachel is going to be fine. You did the right thing by telling her about the Castlemans. Maria and Heather are already doing what is necessary to make her life easier."

A slow clap of hands sounded. Father Wesley turned to see Alan Travers standing in the doorway. He looked much like Father Wesley remembered. He was still a tall and heavyset man with tussled hair which was now completely gray. He was leaning against the doorway to his daughter's hospital room.

"How long have you been standing there?" Father Wesley asked.

"Long enough to hear what you had to say," he answered as he pushed himself away from the doorway and walked to his daughter's bedside. "I was really touched by the *don't blame yourself for what happened between us* part."

"Are you trying to be sarcastic?" Father Wesley was not in a mood to have his emotions brought into question.

"On the contrary. I can't begin to tell you how much grief Ruth Ann laid on herself, and still carries with her today, because of what happened to you and Billy on that night. She'll never forgive herself for not coming right out and telling you what had developed between her and Billy. She's convinced herself if she had, then Billy would still be alive today."

"Young love. Sometimes it ends in such tragedy," Father Wesley lamented.

"Isn't it the truth," Alan Travers bemoaned, as he sadly turned his head and looked at his daughter. "And now this. Ruth Ann finally became the victim. It's as if she's been headed for this fate since that day. Thank God she's expected to survive. We're lucky in that respect."

The priest gave him a sorry smile. There was a certain amount of truth in what he said. "Alan, when did you get into town? Did you come alone?"

"I arrived about an hour ago. Came straight from the airport. As for Miriam, she's still pretty shaken up by the news. She's been staying with some friends while I came on ahead. I called her and told her Ruth Ann is expected to be okay. She'll be on the first plane out tomorrow."

"That's good."

"Another thing, Father."

"Yes."

"Thank you for looking out for Rachel. Frank Castleman told me what happened and how the police thought Rachel might be involved. She'd never do something like that. If there's anything I'm sure of in this world, it's that Rachel would never hurt her mother. Have the authorities found out anything else? Have they any idea who the scum is who did this to my little girl?" Alan Travers appeared ready to display his sorrow with a torrent of tears.

"They have. It was a man by the name of Salvi. He took his own life just as the police were about to arrest him."

Alan Travers was stunned by the news. It was unexpected, but it was a relief to know that this Salvi character's only escape was into the bowels of hell. Rachel was off the hook and Ruth Ann was going to survive; now that was good news. Sanity was finding a way back into his life.

Father Wesley decided it was time for him to leave. Alan Travers needed to spend some time with his daughter and say the things that probably should have been said years ago. The priest extended his hand in friendship. Alan seemed to understand. It was a strange setting for both men. Neither man ever thought they'd see the day when they would be drawing strength from one another.

Jerry Brandt sat at the desk in his den, working at his computer when the phone rang. It was Alfredo calling. "Jerry, I need you to do something for me," he told the attorney without identifying himself.

Recognizing his old friend's voice he replied, "Sure. I'll do what I can. What seems to be the problem?"

"I need you to get someone out of jail. Then I want you to bring him to me so I can make it perfectly clear to this buffoon that this is a one-time deal."

"And who might this person be?" Jerry Brandt was uneasy with the conversation. Alfredo's voice lacked its usual conviction. Instead, he sounded like a man being used.

"Arthur Gregorio," was the reply.

"And what did this Gregorio person do?"

"He gave his wife a beating. Something to do with his wife having another man's baby."

Damn! was the lawyer's thinking. A domestic abuse case. Jerry Brandt hated domestic abuse cases. "Gee, Alfredo, I'd like to help you out but right now I'm all tied up with this custody case involving the Castlemans and their granddaughter." Brandt stopped when he realized the Castlemans' granddaughter had originally been sought for the crime Alfredo's longtime associate had committed. "By the way, I'm sorry to hear about Salvi but I'm also shocked by it. I never thought he was that kind of person."

"Never mind what happened to Salvi. Right now I need your help with this Gregorio matter. You're the only lawyer I can trust. Do it!"

Brandt felt compelled to lend his hand to Alfredo's problem. When Jerry Brandt's parents needed money to finance his way through school, Alfredo had been there to help them out. It wasn't a loan shark transaction. Alfredo simply saw to it that Jerry received the money needed to finance his education, with no stringent terms attached as to how Alfredo was to be repaid. The debt had since been paid off, but Jerry still felt he owed the man.

"All right, Alfredo, I'll help you out if I can. Where is he being arraigned?"

"Right here in Paine. He'll be charged tomorrow."

"Okay, I'll meet the man there tomorrow morning just before court. I need to know the extent of the abuse he brought on his wife. It'll help me set up my game plan tonight and try and get it before the right judge, rather than have to do it at the last minute as we're going into court."

"He put her in the hospital," Alfredo answered, an unwavering pitch in his voice.

"Just what I didn't need to hear," was Brandt's reply.

CHAPTER

THIRTY-THREE

The following morning Father Wesley sat on the back bench in the decrepit old building that housed the District Court, and watched as Jerry Brandt displayed some nifty courtroom histrionics in securing the release of Arthur Gregorio on his own recognizance. The lawyer argued Gregorio's case convincingly, making it sound as though Arthur were the victim. There was to be a hearing on the matter in a month's time, but in order to move on with the case, Anna was going to have to file a complaint. Father Wesley felt there was little chance of that happening. There was no way Anna Gregorio was going to relive the story of her pregnancy. The day's outcome turned Father Wesley's stomach. The only sentence meted out was for Arthur Gregorio to attend some court appointed domestic abuse classes, and to adhere to a restraining order that prohibited him from coming within 100 feet of his wife until this matter was resolved.

As Arthur left the courtroom, he caught a glimpse of the priest and the two men locked eyes on each other. Gregorio had a contemptuous, self-satisfied smirk on his face. Father Wesley was furious with his mocking grin. Again, the priest wished he were free of his religious vows so he could reach out and pummel this impudent bastard into the ground.

Father Wesley allowed Arthur Gregorio and his attorney a few minutes so he wouldn't cross paths with them. He didn't trust his feeling that—if pushed— he might try and exact a little revenge for Grimaldi and his daughter. After all, it wasn't Arthur who was the loser in this scenario but rather Anna and her newborn baby boy, named Antonio after his grandfather. He checked into the world at the premature size of two pounds and eleven ounces just after midnight. As Anna had dreaded, the baby was half-black but the infant's skin color no longer seemed to be an issue, especially for Grimaldi. He was now a concerned father and grandfather and the color of the baby's skin failed to bring forth his wrath. His major worry at the moment was for little Antonio's survival.

"Don't look so down," the priest was greeted, as he stepped out of the court building into the crisp and sunny December morning. "That's the way the system works. How'd you get here?" It was Officer Kilcullen.

"Took the bus," Father Wesley answered as he turned up his collar to ward off the strong breeze lashing against the building.

"Well, let me give you a ride back to St. Theresa's. We can talk on the way."

"Talk? What's there to talk about?" Father Wesley asked.

"Something that might interest you. I know it interests me."

The police officer had the priest's attention. "So what is it?"

"Last night, as I was putting in some overtime, I bumped into your friend Fogarty as he was coming out of Rose's. He was headed towards that bike of his; I don't know how he can ride that thing in these cold temperatures. Well, anyway, he flags me down and asks me if I've seen you. I tell him about our meeting at the Castlemans' place and then he tells me he has a message for you and to pass it on, should I see you before he does."

"What's the message?"

"He was headed out to find Alfredo, you know that bookmaker who can usually be found sitting on the beach, Salvi's old buddy. So he tells me he's got to find Alfredo because Arthur Gregorio needs to speak to him. Now Arthur's in jail. So what do you think he needs Alfredo for?"

"To find him an attorney?"

"You got it."

"Maybe Gregorio and Alfredo are friends. Gregorio's desperate so he asks for Alfredo's help."

"Possibly, but I doubt it. According to Fogarty he didn't think Gregorio and Alfredo knew each other. Again, according to Fogarty, he got the sense that Gregorio had something on Alfredo. I didn't think much of it until seeing Gregorio get off with what amounts to nothing more than a slap on the wrist, thanks to Jerry Brandt's courtroom theatrics."

Father Wesley's mind was trying to put it together but was coming up empty. "Do you have any idea as to what Gregorio might have on Alfredo? Gregorio's been flashing wads of money around of late. Maybe he's now in Alfredo's employ?"

"I tend to doubt that as well," Kilcullen was quick to say. "Alfredo and Salvi always worked as a tandem. They supposedly were what you might call retired but then again, does anyone ever retire from that business. I just couldn't see them taking on a third partner, especially someone so penniless as Gregorio."

"Were they strictly into bookmaking?" Father Wesley asked.

"I believe so, but I could be wrong. I'll do some checking into it and I'll get back to you as soon as I find something to suggest otherwise."

"I want to speak to Alfredo. Do you know where he lives?"

"And what's that going to accomplish, Father? He's not going to tell you anything. He'll probably claim he and Gregorio are long lost cousins."

"Still, I don't think it would hurt to talk to the man."

"Father, let's wait and see if I can uncover anything else about Alfredo and Salvi's business dealings. Okay?"

"All right," Father Wesley agreed, reluctantly.

—ɯ—

Once finished with Arthur Gregorio's day in court, Jerry Brandt informed his client he'd be giving him a ride back to the beach. What Brandt didn't tell him was they were going to meet Alfredo. Brandt assured the old bookmaker he'd have Gregorio out of court by ten. Alfredo was on the park bench waiting.

At 10:30 Jerry Brandt's white Mercedes sedan came racing down the parkway and came to a halt across from where Alfredo was sitting. "Get out!" Brandt demanded of his passenger.

Gregorio glanced at Brandt and then across the street to where Alfredo was seated. "What's going on?" he insisted on knowing.

"Alfredo wants to see you," the attorney answered as he tilted his head in the direction of Gregorio's benefactor.

"What about?"

"How do I know. Just get out."

As Arthur emerged from the automobile, he thought he had a fairly good idea as to what Alfredo wanted to talk about. Gregorio was now indebted to the man for coming to his rescue. But in his warped way of thinking, Arthur believed Alfredo owed it to him. If Alfredo thought he was going to run him off so easily he had better start thinking again.

As Brandt's Mercedes sped away, Gregorio found himself standing on the edge of the road staring at Alfredo. The old man on the other side was doing the same. As he made his way across the parkway, Gregorio wondered if the death of Salvi had taken something out of Alfredo. They were a team, and a finely tuned one at that. Arthur wasn't sure what Alfredo was made of; his dealings had always been through Salvi with Alfredo monitoring the situation from afar.

"Arthur, my boy, please, sit." Alfredo was sounding a little too jovial for Gregorio's liking. If there was one thing Arthur was good at, it was smelling a rat. Alfredo's congenial tone was not fooling him. Nevertheless, he did as Alfredo asked.

"Alfredo, I'm sorry. I didn't mean to drag you into this mess, but I somewhat overdid it with my wife. I needed your help to get me out of that jam and I'm grateful you came through."

"Overdid it, you say? Is that what they're calling a senseless beating these days?"

Arthur cowered as though he were a reprimanded child. "Alfredo, I said I'm sorry. What more do you want to hear from me?"

"Actually, nothing," Alfredo was happy to tell him. "Arthur, I'm telling you this, so listen. Today was the final payment on everything you were owed. The slate is now clean between us. Don't think for a second you can lean on me for another cent or favor. Do we have an understanding?"

"Wait a minute," Gregorio countered. "What about St. Theresa's? Don't tell me you're abandoning the project. Or do you have another boy to fill your needs? If you do then you can count on me not to be sitting idly by. I'll sing, Alfredo. I'll sing. That's a promise."

"Don't you threaten me," Alfredo replied, harshly. "You're not going to sing to anyone. If you do, you'll be the only one the authorities will be looking into. Now, I did you a favor by getting you out of that sticky situation you managed to get yourself in. If I were you, I'd think about running. You're in a no win situation, pal."

"You think so?"

"I know so. If that wife of yours decides to make a case against you, you're a goner. But let's say something happens to the infant, such as dying. You'll really be up that proverbial creek without any oars should that occur."

"Then I'll sell out and take my chances. I'll tell the powers that be you paid me to burn Temple Beth Abraham and you wanted me to burn St. Theresa's. If I'm going down, then so are you."

"Don't get too confident. No one is going to be coming after me. Any direct link to me will be absorbed by our late and dearly departed friend, Salvi. Poor soul was really pitiful as the years went by. I tried to help him, I really did. But, you know, Arthur, the poor guy became dispirited by his sorry lot in life and blamed it on the good Lord. That's why he had you burn Temple Beth Abraham. Poor bastard's mind had become a real mishmash of contradiction. He also blamed the Lord above for not allowing him to control his sexual anxieties. How does that story sound to you, Arthur?"

"You think that will stick?"

"I know it will. You see, I've got a good high-priced attorney to see that it does. What do you have, Arthur? A public defender? Arthur, run while you can. It's the only way you're going to save your sorry ass."

Gregorio knew it was futile to think he was going to bring Alfredo around to his way of thinking. Maybe a little pleading could do the trick. "You're right, Alfredo. But just give me enough to do in St.

Theresa's, and then I'll be long gone and hard to find. You can take my word on it."

"Arthur, I wouldn't take your word if you swore on a stack of bibles. Don't worry about St. Theresa's. It's not going to happen. Because of your blundering initiative to burn Temple Beth Abraham, St. Theresa's has gained a second life."

"You're lying," Arthur claimed.

"No, I'm not. It's unfortunate because it promised to be a big money winner. Arthur, if it were going down I would use you. Not because I like you but because I don't like too many fingers in the pie. Maybe that thought will help you sleep at night."

"What are you, a comedian?"

Alfredo raised himself from the bench and tightened the collar of his overcoat to fend off the wind. "Arthur, this is good-bye," he said as he turned and began walking away.

Gregorio stayed seated on the bench for a few more minutes, ruing the stupid decision he had made to burn Temple Beth Abraham, thereby killing off the chance to burn St. Theresa's. Well, he just might burn St. Theresa's for the hell of it. It was a good way to straighten out that priest who wanted to pound his sorry ass into a bloody mess.

—⁓—

Later that evening, after the dinner hour, Father Wesley sat alone in his office still trying to get a grip on the sorry happenings of the past thirty-six hours. It happened so fast, it all seemed surreal. His concentration was interrupted when he looked up and saw Father Coniglio and Officer Kilcullen standing at the entrance to the office. The disturbed look on Kilcullen's face told him that he was here as the bearer of bad news. There did not seem to be an end to this run of bad times.

"Father, do you mind if we come in and talk?" Father Coniglio asked.

Father Wesley did not say a word, simply nodding his okay. The two men entered and sat in the two chairs in front of the desk. There was a sense of remorse hovering in the air. Kilcullen spoke, getting right to the crux of the matter.

"Father, Anna's baby died less than an hour ago. His lungs were underdeveloped and he succumbed to a respiratory condition. Anna is in a state of shock and Grimaldi is swearing he's going to hunt down his son-in-law and kill him."

Father Wesley shook his head, but it was news he was expecting. He knew the odds were not in little Antonio's favor. He looked to Father Coniglio for support but the older priest's face was expressionless, apparently trying to mask the pain he was experiencing. He then looked at Kilcullen and asked: "Gregorio. What happens to him? Does he still get to walk the streets? Is he still just guilty of a little domestic strife?"

"Father, it's hard for me to call this good news, but the answer to that question is *no*. He's now wanted on a possible manslaughter charge. Anna now wants to fight him for what he did to her. It's going to be a tough battle for the woman since she is destroyed by her loss. I'm not sure if she'll be able to hold up, considering what she is going to be asked to go through. But she's willing to give it a try."

"You'll never catch him," a doleful Father Wesley replied. "He'll get wind that you're looking for him and he'll hide. I don't consider him to be a risk to Anna any longer. He's the type of guy who'll do whatever it takes to save his own ass. Unless you put out a major dragnet, then consider him gone and hard to find."

Kilcullen had to agree with the priest. Locating Gregorio would be a major concern for about the next forty-eight hours. Then, if there were no leads, the case would find its way to the back burner. After that it was going to require a little luck to nail him; good fortune such as a friend turning on him or should he be stopped for a traffic violation.

Father Wesley redirected his attention to Father Coniglio. "Father, it'd be good for you to look in on Grimaldi. If he's blind with rage right now, it could end up getting him hurt. He's just as much a victim as his daughter. His hot Sicilian blood is only going to make him do something rash and it's going to get him into trouble. Or he could end up getting his brains bashed in. I saw what his son-in-law is capable of doing."

"I'll do that," Father Coniglio assured him.

"Father, there's another thing concerning Grimaldi," Kilcullen went on as he spoke to Father Wesley while glancing Father Coniglio's way. "If my read on the man is correct—and I'm sure Father Coniglio can verify whether it is or not— he might be angry with himself. The money you talked about. The money Gregorio's been spending like a drunken sailor. It might have been Grimaldi who pointed him in the direction that brought Gregorio his good fortune and everybody else misery."

Father Wesley bowed his head while covering his eyes and shaking his head. Why wouldn't the pain racking the Grimaldi family just cease. It had done its damage. Now it was time for it to go, time for it to go far away.

"Fathers, according to some of the guys at the station house, when Anna married Arthur Gregorio her father started asking people on the beach if there was anything they could do for his new son-in-law. Apparently, Grimaldi didn't think Gregorio had much of a future as a used car salesman. A fellow officer claims to have seen Gregorio, on two occasions, talking to Salvi and Alfredo on the bench where those two elderly gentlemen conduct their business. Now it's just a hunch on my part but I think Gregorio was working for them."

"Doing what?" Father Coniglio asked. "I've known those two men for years. Yes, their business is illegal but they've always been a two-man operation. They've always been kind of mellow as bookies go. They have a regular roster of clientele and wouldn't think of welching on their bets, knowing it would become common knowledge on the beach and a source of embarrassment to the guilty parties. It was a nice and quiet business they had going, not to mention profitable. It's been that way for years. What could Arthur Gregorio possibly bring to their daily operation? They couldn't possibly be thinking of expanding their base, not at their ages."

Father Wesley had a gut feeling the police had unearthed something new on a possible Salvi and Alfredo alliance with Gregorio. He was eager to hear what it might be. "Father, I don't think Officer Kilcullen is talking about bookmaking. Let's hear what he has to say."

"Thank you, Father. A couple of summers ago a bar on the parkway known as the Beachhead burned to the ground. The place once had a solid reputation, but over the years it became a hangout for the riffraff or lesser likes of life. The owners wanted to refurbish the place; you know, bring back the more refined patronage. But to give the place the look they wanted then the joint was going to have to be razed. That costs money. Money you don't have to take out of your own pocket if the place burns down. Insurance covers it. Fathers, two of the major owners of the Beachhead were Alfredo and Salvi."

Father Coniglio was aghast. "Are you saying Arthur Gregorio burned the place to the ground?"

Father Wesley put his hand in the air, indicating he had something to say. "I know the place. I was there the day it burned down. It's where I found Shagtyme. It was also the day Anna and Arthur were married right here at St. Theresa's."

Now it was Officer Kilcullen's turn to put his hand in the air to alert the priests to slow down. The story was about to develop an interesting twist. "As it turns out the Beachhead was not a set fire, at least according to the insurance company. But I wonder if Alfredo and Salvi found a new line of business because of this stroke of good fortune which came their way."

Both priests developed puzzled looks. However, they were anxious to hear where Officer Kilcullen was headed.

"A company by the name of Old Colony Real Estate moved in and took care of clearing the site and then building a new Beachhead—."

The mere mention of Old Colony Real Estate piqued Father Wesley's interest.

"—Now, upon finding out about the possible involvement of Alfredo, Salvi and Gregorio, I decided to do a little investigation of my own. Old Colony Real Estate had approached the good rabbi at Temple Beth Abraham about buying his place, since there was some talk that they were thinking of constructing a new temple and made him a good offer too. But Rabbi Zuckerman, as you well know, was not interested. Soon thereafter, Temple Beth Abraham burns to the ground and it's obvious it is the work of an arsonist. Old Colony Real Estate was thought to be implicated in the burning but a subsequent investigation exonerates them. But after hearing all this, I can't help but wonder if the burning of Temple Beth Abraham has something to do with Alfredo and Salvi. It was right around that time that Arthur Gregorio becomes Mister Moneybags."

"Do you really think that's possible?" Father Coniglio asked, an incredulous look on his face.

"Absolutely," Kilcullen told him. The police officer then looked at Father Wesley and asked, "What do you think?"

Father Wesley knew better than to elaborate on what he knew about Old Colony Real Estate, and their possible involvement to some other house of worship fires. But Temple Beth Abraham he couldn't figure out. However, one thing he could figure out was to be on alert from now on. It was no longer Father Moore who loomed as St. Theresa's greatest foe. It was now Arthur Gregorio.

As for Kilcullen's reasoning, Father Wesley believed the police officer was on to something. Old Colony could have subcontracted the job out and Arthur Gregorio, petty thief, moved into the major leagues when he became the *hired gun.* Father Wesley believed he had removed St. Theresa's from the endangered species list with his discovery of Father Moore's association to Old Colony Real Estate. But now the little church on Everton Street was right back on it. If the stories were true that Arthur Gregorio had it out for him, then the priest knew burning St. Theresa's was the best way to get back at him.

"Well, Father, what do you think?" Kilcullen asked again.

Father Wesley snapped himself out of his semi-trance. "Ah... yeah...I think you might have something there," he stammered.

"OH MY GOD!" was the shriek heard from the other room. It was Mildred. The three men rushed to see what was wrong. Mildred was standing in front of the television, her hands covering her mouth. There was a news reporter, a talking head, on the screen.

"What is it?" Father Coniglio asked as he approached the woman and placed his arms around her.

With a nervous twitch of her right arm, the housekeeper pointed at the television screen. "It's the cardinal," she said through her tears. "They're saying he's suffered a fatal heart attack."

Father Wesley dropped into the easy chair he was standing aside. St. Theresa's saving grace was gone. The little church on Everton Street had just run out of miracles.

CHAPTER

THIRTY-FOUR

Father Wesley spent the next two hours locked in his room, the television set on only one channel, the New England Cable News Network. They were providing in depth coverage of the cardinal's passing and Father Wesley was hanging on every word.

The gist of the story was that Cardinal Burke had suffered a major heart attack as he was preparing to sit down for dinner at his residence. He was pronounced dead upon arrival at St. Elizabeth's Hospital in Brighton. The paramedics had worked diligently trying to resuscitate him en route but their efforts were in vain. Cardinal Burke was dead just ten days shy of his seventieth birthday.

The cardinal's passing was a loss for all of the two million Catholics in the archdiocese of Boston. But the one who felt the loss, perhaps the most, had to be Father Wesley. He was convinced he and the cardinal had an understanding in regard to St. Theresa's. If he had the place running on a semblance of spiritual and monetary continuity then the parish was safe until the passing or retirement of Father Coniglio. The thought of Cardinal Burke dying had never crossed the mind of Father Wesley.

It was reported the cardinal's physicians had recently warned him about the severity of his weight problem. His Eminence was deemed to be more than one hundred pounds overweight and unless he immediately started losing some of the poundage, he was placing himself at risk. The cardinal's love affair with good food was believed to be the source of his sudden demise.

Father Wesley was bewildered by the string of tragedies which had suddenly become a part of his life. The events of the past two days seemed unreal but they weren't. As he continued to watch the newscast the priest was looking for just one tidbit of information. When he heard the news he had been hoping to avoid he thought he was going to become ill.

The day-to-day operation of the archdiocese was to be run in part by Bishop David Sasso of Worcester and Bishop Humberto Santos of Fall River. They were to tend to the spiritual needs of the Boston archdiocese faithful, until the Holy See had decided on a successor to Cardinal Burke. It was thought the entire process could take up to four months.

As for the daily business operation of the archdiocese, it was now in the capable hands of Cardinal Burke's longtime personal assistant, Father John Moore. The mere mention of the prelate's name seemed to cut Father Wesley off at the knees.

The dispirited priest did not desire to hear anymore. He took the remote in his hand and flicked off the TV. He had prayed that this day would never come but now it was here. He considered whatever abstract pact he had with the cardinal to now be null and void. He stood no chance of keeping the same covenant with Father Moore. Father Wesley felt it was his responsibility to caution Father Coniglio as to what to expect, now that Father Moore could wheel and deal without the intervention of the cardinal.

It was growing late but Father Wesley did not think he could put this matter off until morning. He made his way down the dark hallway to the bedroom at the far end. It was unusual for Father Coniglio to stay up later than ten. It was now eleven but as Father Wesley approached the door he saw a light shining from the crack at the foot of the door.

It was Father Wesley's deduction that the old priest was unable to find sleep on this night, due to the passing of a friend of fifty years. He gently rapped on the door as he tried to put together the medley of thoughts and emotions ravaging him.

"Come in," the voice called out.

Father Wesley slowly opened the door and popped his head in. What he saw was Father Coniglio sitting up in bed, a school yearbook—a memento from his seminary days—opened before him. "Trouble falling asleep?" he asked.

Father Coniglio nodded. "I'm finding this hard to comprehend. He was so...so...vibrant. He seemed indestructible, impervious to the ruination and immorality which mortality inherits and brings to all our lives."

"I know what you mean," Father Wesley answered as he stealthily made his way into the room and sat in the chair opposite Father Coniglio's bed. "Father," he continued, "there is something we need to talk about, and the sooner the better."

"Oh my, this sounds serious."

"It is. It's very serious." Father Wesley thought the time was right for him to expose himself for the fraud he believed he was.

"You mean like counting down the days St. Theresa's has before she becomes part of St. Matthew's?"

"Huh?" Father Wesley muttered. "You knew St. Theresa's was going to run into immediate trouble with the cardinal's passing?"

"Let's say, I had a hunch. Father, I may be old but I'm not stupid. When the cardinal visited me a few months before your arrival he did so with my best interests at heart."

Father Coniglio raised the yearbook off his tired legs and pointed it at the younger priest. "Father, in the seminary, the cardinal—or as he insisted I call him, Carroll—was not the smartest of the students; in fact I had to help him on numerous occasions with his studies. But what he lacked academically he made up with in charm. He was the most engaging person you could imagine, when around other people. A few minutes with Carroll and he had you under his spell. But, in addition to being a gracious individual, he was loyal to a fault. Following his visit to St. Theresa's, I knew he was not going to allow my church to go quietly into the darkness of the night. He thought too much of me as a friend to allow such a thing to happen. I knew he was getting pressure from that skinny priest, who was with him that day, to throw sentiment aside and bring in the wrecking ball and put it to our church."

"You mean Father Moore," Father Wesley was forced to say, the name leaving a bitter taste in his mouth.

"Yes, Father Moore. I had heard some awful things about the man. Once I met him I knew the S-O-B couldn't be trusted. I have to admit, at the time, I wondered how much influence he wielded over the cardinal. When Carroll left without saying a word about a gloomy future for St. Theresa's, then I knew he had none in this instance. All I had to do, after that, was resign myself to the fact I'd have to share my parish with another priest. I'll admit I was inflexible when you first arrived here, and for that I apologize. You took some getting used to. But you've been good for this church and parish. Real good. How much weight do you think this Father Moore can toss around now that the cardinal is gone?"

"Plenty."

"That's not good."

"Father, I was assigned here with the understanding I was to watch over the parish and report back to the chancery on a regular basis, as to the status of the parish and the status of your health. The cardinal was worried about you. Father Moore, on the other hand, wasn't. He was more in a rush to see you…"

"Die?"

"That's one way of putting it."

"I sure am happy I disappointed him."

"We all are," Father Wesley responded through an awkward snicker.

"So what can we expect next?"

"We can expect Father Moore to move swiftly. He wants the land this church sits on, and he wants it bad. The man's a manipulator. He's been given carte blanche with the death of the cardinal. Father, our little church is now like a duck on the pond and Father Moore is standing on the shore with the rifle pointed in our direction, with the intention of blowing us out of the water. By the time Rome appoints and installs a new archbishop, he'll have the so-called wrecking ball in place, ready to level St. Theresa's. He'll convince the new bishop that the destruction of St. Theresa's was the next order of business for Cardinal Burke, only to be interrupted by his passing."

"Sounds as though St. Theresa's has used up all of her lives," Father Coniglio commented sadly.

"She has," Father Wesley was forced to admit.

"Father, call me naive, but you don't suppose the cardinal left instructions that St. Theresa's was to be spared the Grim Reaper should he die, do you?" The old priest was now grasping for straws.

"No, I don't," Father Wesley answered as he sadly shook his head. "Even if such a thought occurred to him, he'd have run it past Father Moore and Father Moore, being the person he is, would see to it that the cardinal's request went to the grave with him."

"So what do we do now?"

"We wait, and as we wait, we die the slowest death possible. Father, St. Theresa's is now at the mercy of Father Moore and he's not going to be showing any."

—⋘—

Cardinal Burke hadn't been dead five minutes when Father Moore started getting a satisfied feeling in his gut. The debacle surrounding St. Theresa's and the cardinal's sentimentality concerning an old friend was over. St. Theresa's was now back on Father Moore's *hit list* and this time the *prodigal parish* was going to stay there. However, the disposal of the place had to be handled differently. He had to circumvent that troublesome Father Wesley. There was to be no drastic action taken. No convenient fires which made the job at hand a little easier. The parish of St. Theresa's was going to fade into history in the proper protocol as adhered to by the archdiocese.

Father Moore didn't think Father Wesley would be much of an obstacle if the matter was taken care of in this manner. It was public knowledge the church was downsizing, so the Catholic population was aware of the closing of certain churches. Father Wesley had managed to fend off the demise of St. Theresa's by figuring out the fires at St. Kevin's and the Sacred Heart might be linked to Old Colony Real Estate. The only reason Father Moore had allowed Father Wesley so much leeway with his accusations was that it might have gotten back to the cardinal, thus spurring a possible investigation.

But what Father Wesley had was nothing more than a well thought out theory. His only sounding board at the time was the cardinal, and now he was gone. Father Wesley had a helluva lot of conjecture but no *smoking gun*. If he threatened to open his mouth now, Father Moore was prepared to assure him that by doing so he would be impugning the good name of the late cardinal. Without the proverbial *smoking gun*, any outrage by Father Wesley would only dishonor the name of a man who had come to respect and admire him for the work he had accomplished at the impoverished parish of St. Theresa.

Father Moore had it planned out. He was even ready to take a hit in the closing of St. Theresa's. He intended to be there to make sure the passing of the parish was done in style. St. Theresa's was to be given a sendoff unlike any parish had before. It was necessary for Father Moore to see that the spirit of the Church of St. Theresa lived on in its merger with the Church of St. Matthew.

Now all he had to do was inform his brother to make sure no criminal damage came St. Theresa's way. The least little incident against the small church on Everton Street could prove to be calamitous. St. Theresa's had to sail into the sunset on a calm sea, not a violent ocean.

In the stillness of his office Father Moore picked up the phone and punched his brother's number on the keypad. It was now closing in on midnight, but Father Moore didn't care. He believed in dealing promptly with the situation at hand.

A sleepy-eyed James Moore picked up the phone at the other end. "Hello?" he mumbled.

"James, it's your brother."

There was a brief moment of silence. Then James Moore spoke. "John, do you realize what time it is? What do you want?"

"Since when do you go to bed before midnight?"

"Since I started getting old, that's when."

"Well, I want you to know, I've got St. Theresa's back in my grasp now that the cardinal's dead," he said with satisfaction.

"It's too bad about the old guy. He was a pretty good archbishop."

"Yeah, sure he was. Well, he's gone and that's good news for us and the family business. Now, the reason I'm calling is to make sure those dogs you hired are called off. St. Theresa's is not to go up in flames.

I'm going to close the place as quickly as I can, so I don't want anyone getting curious as to what is going on by some obvious distraction, if you know what I mean."

"You're sure you want to do it this way? A fire accelerates the process and gets us rolling."

"Make sure it doesn't happen! I have my reasons and I don't have the time to go into it. I just want you to make sure all parties are satisfied so there are no…no incidents by some unsatisfied…employees, shall we say."

"Yeah, I'll take care of it. But it's going to cost us a few bucks to pay off that guy Alfredo for some of the cleanup work he had to do and for the money he's going to lose."

"How much do you think?"

"Ah…he's a pretty even keeled individual. I'd say he'd accept ten cents on the dollar, considering nothing was done. Call it ten grand."

"Then do it. What about the guy with the match? Will Alfredo take care of him?"

"He already has. He jettisoned that moron with a fabricated story about St. Theresa's being granted a pass, because of his bumbling attempt to impress us by burning the Jewish temple. Alfredo will make sure that jackass doesn't know a thing about this transaction."

"Good. Then I guess we're back in business. I want to rid ourselves of this St. Theresa's problem as quickly as possible, without arousing suspicion, and then move on. You can go back to sleep now. Just make sure there are no loose ends when we get back into this."

"I'll handle it starting tomorrow," James said before hanging up.

Father Moore leaned over and put the phone down before opening the top drawer of his desk and removing an aging manila folder from it. Inside its covers was the proper documentation for the closing of St. Theresa's, complete with Cardinal Burke's signature. His Eminence had signed it just hours before his death, or so Father Moore would have the world believe.

THIRTY-FIVE

Ten days passed and neither Father Wesley nor Father Coniglio had heard a word from the chancery concerning the fate of St. Theresa's. In those ten days Cardinal Burke, little Antonio Gregorio and Salvi had been buried, a deeply depressed Anna Gregorio had been released from the hospital, and Ruth Ann was out of intensive care and scheduled to come home any day. Meanwhile, Rachel was living with the Castlemans and Arthur Gregorio had vanished off the face of the earth. It had been a ten-day span unlike any other in St. Theresa's history.

Despite the impending doom they knew to be headed their way, Father Wesley and Father Coniglio put up a brave front, not tipping their hands to what the future held. It was the Christmas season and like the year before, the priests were trying to keep the spirit alive and the parishioners were cooperating. There was hope by the faithful to raise enough money to stage another Christmas party for the children on Christmas Eve.

Unfortunately, this time around, Father Wesley was unable to hold up the chancery for the necessary funding. Father Coniglio had already decided to put what little money the church had towards the yuletide event. If he was to believe that Father Wesley was correct about the dire future for St. Theresa's, then the little church on Everton Street would see its life end the way it had lived—poor.

On that tenth day, a gray and dismal one, the black Audi rolled up in front of St. Theresa's. Father Moore was showing up unannounced. In his possession was the document with the late cardinal's signature on it for the closing of St. Theresa's. Although he had been looking forward to this day, Father Moore was feeling just a wee bit apprehensive as he made his way up the walkway to the rectory. In his two previous trips to this parish he had come away from the place dissatisfied. First, there was the cardinal and his unexpected sentimentality for an old friend. On the second visit, there was the confrontation when Father Wesley let the cardinal's associate know he had come across what he considered damaging information that could prove to be injurious to his relationship with the cardinal. In order to keep this alliance intact he had permitted Father Wesley to hustle and embarrass him. Father Moore didn't have much regard for Father Wesley, but he did admire the man for his guts. He could say that now since he had his fellow priest at *his* mercy.

Standing before the front door, he glanced around prior to ringing the bell. There was no one in sight. Not even the large dog. Uneasiness prevailed.

Mildred was alone inside, doing her housework, when the doorbell rang. As usual she became irritated by the intrusion. However, she became alarmed when she opened the door and saw who was standing before her. She never felt comfortable around Father Moore and now that the cardinal was dead, she was feeling downright panicky in his presence. For the first time in her memory, she could feel the life of St. Theresa's being sucked out of the small church.

"Good afternoon, Mrs. Fortnat. It's nice to see you again." There was a singsong cadence to Father Moore's voice.

Now that was a bad sign, thought Mildred. The fact Father Moore remembered her name had to stand for something—something bad! She had never taken to the priest since he had a personality of a cold and calculating menace. Now he was standing before her trying to be charming. But Mildred felt she was seeing right through his poorly portrayed façade of good tidings. No, behind that smiling face was the greed of the devil.

"Father, I'm sorry. I didn't know you were coming. Neither Father Coniglio nor Father Wesley informed me."

"Nor should they," he countered in his breezy monotone. "Neither one of them knew I was coming. I hope I didn't make a mistake by showing up when neither one is around."

"No, Father, they're here," she said, with reservation. "They're in the church trying to come to some kind of compromise for this year's Christmas party for the children of the parish."

"Ah, yes, St. Theresa's surprise Christmas party. How are the fathers doing this year for cash? I seem to remember last year's bash being quite the success."

"Well, this year's not quite the same, Father. Last year Father Wesley found money somewhere. Nobody knows how he came by it and nobody asked. This year he's not having the same run of good luck."

"That's too bad," the priest said as though he meant it. "I think I'll just wander on over to the church to see my two fellow priests."

—⁂—

Father Coniglio and Father Wesley were sitting in the front pew of the church discussing the frustrations of planning the Christmas party. Stretched out in the center aisle was Shagtyme. Father Coniglio was using the topic of the Christmas party as a way to block out the inevitable. Father Wesley, however, was being more pragmatic. He couldn't see the Christmas party happening unless they came up with more funding—much more.

"Father, I think we should just forget about the whole idea," a disillusioned Father Wesley was saying.

"Father, do you think your friend Mr. Fogarty will once again play the role of Santa Claus?" Father Coniglio was turning a deaf ear to any disheartening talk by Father Wesley.

"Father, I'm sure he will, but in order to do so he needs some gifts to hand out. Right now we don't have enough money to feed that horde, let alone buy presents. You make it sound like we're dealing with the loaves and fishes here."

"Father, last year we started with seventy dollars and made it work. Who's to say we can't make it happen again this year?"

"I say it can't happen again," a frustrated Father Wesley reiterated. "Last year I managed to get the money from the chancery. I can virtually guarantee it is not going to happen again."

"Why not?" Father Coniglio asked, as if he expected a plausible answer.

"Because he was told it was a one shot deal," the voice called out before Father Wesley was able to respond. Both priests looked to the back of the church and saw Father Moore headed their way. They instantly looked back at each other and realized St. Theresa's final hour was at hand.

"That's a hearty looking dog you have there," Father Moore went on as he approached the two priests. Shagtyme sat up and Father Wesley had to command him to stay. The canine was confused since the man approaching was dressed like the two men the dog knew best.

"We've been awaiting your arrival, Father. To be honest with you, I thought you'd be here a lot sooner." Father Wesley wasn't mincing any words.

"Father, your rankling does nothing to dismay me," Father Moore continued as he took a seat in the pew behind the two fellow priests. "As you seem to have expected, I'm here on official business for the archdiocese. In the name of the late Cardinal Burke, I should add."

"Sure you are," Father Wesley just had to say.

"I am here to inform the two of you that as of July 1st the Church of St. Theresa will close its doors." As he spoke the words, Father Moore took the document from his vest pocket and handed it to Father Coniglio.

"What about Father Coniglio?" an incensed Father Wesley demanded to know. "You'll never convince me the cardinal had a change of heart concerning his old friend's future without saying something to the man himself."

"Father, this document has the cardinal's signature on it," a bewildered Father Coniglio said to his associate.

"Of course it does," a still irate Father Wesley continued. "I imagine Father Moore here has a desk full of blank papers with the cardinal's signature on it."

Nice deduction, Father Moore thought. But this time Father Wesley didn't have a prayer of using it against him, and he was going to let him know that. "I'm sorry, Fathers, but the cardinal changed his mind about St. Theresa's. It had been his intention to come here and inform both of you, personally, but unfortunately he passed on before getting the opportunity."

"You're lying, you piss poor excuse for a priest!" an enraged Father Wesley screamed back at him.

"Father, please, calm down," Father Coniglio implored his colleague. He then turned to look at Father Moore and asked, "What becomes of us?"

"Father, you'll be asked to take your retirement. We have a wonderful facility in Malden, St. Joseph's. It's a retirement home for priests. It was one of the pet projects of the cardinal and because of his sustained interest it has proven to be a success. As for Father Wesley, he'll be reassigned in the next six months."

"And St. Theresa's becomes what? The church itself, I mean," Father Coniglio asked warily.

"I'll tell you what becomes of it," Father Wesley interjected. "The church and the rectory will be leveled to make room for a high-rise retirement and disability home. Correct me if I'm wrong?" he slyly added for Father Moore's agitation.

Father Moore was now becoming annoyed with Father Wesley's tone. At least he wasn't letting Father Coniglio in on what he now considered their little secret. He'd play the word game Father Wesley was proposing.

"Yes, St. Theresa's will give way to a retirement home. But, Fathers, let's face it, St. Theresa's has had a good run. Her life span may not have been a monetary success but it has been a spiritual one." Father Moore then focused his stare on Father Coniglio. "Father, you should be proud of St. Theresa's and the way you ministered to her parishioners needs. Your entire congregation owes you a heartfelt thank you."

"They owe me nothing," Father Coniglio corrected him. "I understand the financial crunch the archdiocese is enduring because of the glut of churches and the shortage of priests. In business theory what you're doing makes sense. In the ways of God, it does not. This tiny church, as impoverished as it may be, has a far greater wealth that cannot be measured in dollars and cents. St. Theresa's will not die by the swing of your wrecking ball. Her legacy will live on and St. Matthew's will never be able to replace what this church has given so many."

"Very eloquently put," Father Moore replied. *Now spare me the rest of your pontifical rhetoric,* was his follow up thought. "I want to see that St. Theresa's has a grand sendoff." He then reached into the inside pocket of his black coat and produced another envelope which he gave to Father Coniglio. "Open it," he instructed the priest.

Father Coniglio did so. After seeing the contents of the envelope he turned to Father Wesley. "Father, it's a check for $10,000."

"Is it blood money?" Father Wesley asked of Father Moore.

"No," he answered emphatically. "Like I said, I want St. Theresa's to have a grand sendoff. I'm sure that's the way Cardinal Burke would have wanted it to be as well. I know you need the money for your Christmas party. Please, take it. Do what is good for the children of St. Theresa's. Now, I must get going. I'm sorry St. Theresa's has to go but in the end it will all work out. Fathers, have a good day."

As Father Moore was leaving the church Father Wesley turned to Father Coniglio and said, "Not much of a reward for all those years of hard work. I'm sorry it came down to such an unjust ending."

"It could have been worse," the old priest told him. "Now, I have something to ask of you."

"What is it?"

"Could you call Mr. Fogarty and see if he will once again participate as Santa Claus at the St. Theresa's Christmas party?"

A weak smile creased the face of Father Wesley. "I'd be happy to," he answered, somewhat solemnly.

LEO F. WHITE

At precisely the same time, down at the beach, Father Moore's brother was meeting Alfredo at his office on the park bench. As was the case at the church, a transaction was taking place concerning the fate of St. Theresa's. The Brothers Moore were in a very giving nature on this day. James Moore handed Alfredo an envelope with one hundred $100 bills in it.

"Sorry you have to take such a hit," James Moore said as Alfredo took the envelope from his hand and placed it in his coat pocket without checking the amount. "It might have been a different story if it wasn't for that bozo burning down the synagogue."

"I understand," Alfredo told him. "In a way I'm relieved. I realized the church had to go anyway so why not make a buck out of it. But I've seen the old place make such a comeback in the past year, and it was making me feel guilty to be involved in such a plot against it. I'm not the greatest practicing Catholic but that church is the only one I've ever attended. Since the death of my pal Salvi I've been forced to take a good look at my life and I've decided to make some amends. I guess I fear such things as mortality now. I look back on agreeing to burn that church and think what a heretic I've been. It's as if I looked into the face of God and told him to *go take a flying leap*. I'm telling you, it leaves one with a very unsettled feeling. I'm glad it's over."

James was somewhat surprised by what he was hearing. He had never envisioned Alfredo as being such a sentimental old fool. It might have been a good thing the St. Theresa's job had gone by the boards, or else the old softhearted gentleman might suffer such a guilt trip he'd do them all in. But there was one other thing he had to be certain about.

"Alfredo, assure me we have no other problems to speak of. I assume you know what I mean?"

Alfredo nodded, vigorously. "My former business associate made a very poor choice when selecting our fire man. Don't worry about him. The man has been more than compensated for his ineptitude".

"Good to hear. I guess it is now safe to say our business is complete."

"Yes, it is," Alfredo told James while trying to convince himself Arthur Gregorio was no longer a player in a game that was concluded.

310

CHAPTER

THIRTY-SIX

Arthur Gregorio may have been on the lam but he hadn't run very far. He was hiding out in the city of Lye, which was located just north of Paine. He was living in a flop house, an old three story brick building located on Munro Street, which was on the poorer side of the commuter rail tracks which ran straight through the city. Arthur was running low on cash and this place only cost him $300 a month. But even this dump would soon be out of range. He was down to $279. He needed some kind of bankroll to enable him to get out of New England.

Arthur had altered his appearance. His head was now clean shaven and he saw to it he had at least a day's growth on his face when he ventured out. He kept his eyes hidden by an ever present pair of sunglasses. Living like this was killing him and he was becoming more pissed off by the day because of the opportunity missed.

On a cold mid-December day he sat in his room, a six-pack of Heineken chilling in the filthy porcelain sink. He was skimming through the newspaper, *The Lye Item*, when an article in the Metro section caught his attention. It read: *Fabled Paine Church to Close*.

He didn't want to believe what he was reading. Whatever dwindling hopes he had for torching St. Theresa's for money were now gone. But despite his disappointment, something was wrong. The idea had been to burn the church so it could be closed. But now it was closing anyway.

311

Somebody had scared Alfredo and Salvi away from seeing that the job be completed. It wasn't adding up. If the church was going to close, then why burn it?

Now, as he remembered it, St. Theresa's had always been rumored to be on the verge of being shut down. That is until the annoying Father Wesley showed up. He gave the parish of St. Theresa's a second wind and with it, a second life. A second life that was threatening to render Arthur Gregorio indigent.

Arthur had to get up and walk around for a minute. He needed to put his sorry lot in life together in his head. He popped open a Heineken and leaned against the sink. The barrage of thoughts concerning the run of bad luck that had come his way made his head ache. He wanted to lash out at the world as he had never done in the past. He sat down and began to read the rest of the article about St. Theresa's. Maybe there were some answers for him in the news piece.

Gregorio became engrossed in the newspaper article. The story went on to document the three-decade tenure of Father Coniglio and how, despite the church's monetary failure, the little church on Everton Street had reaped huge spiritual gains. The article explained how the St. Theresa's annual Christmas party for the children of the parish was still scheduled for Christmas Eve, despite the sudden demise of the church.

What a crock, Gregorio mused. The so-called little church on Everton Street had been both a financial and spiritual disaster until that Father Wesley came along. It was also Father Wesley who had instituted St. Theresa's so-called annual Christmas party.

Gregorio didn't have time to dwell on such banalities. He read on and learned something which infuriated him even more. There were people involved in this plot against St. Theresa's who were going to earn extensive returns, if not immediately, then in the near future. It was all spelled out in black and white.

The land on which St. Theresa's was located was to be redeveloped and a fourteen-story retirement and disability home would be constructed. However, the loyal congregation of St. Theresa's were prepared to go to court to save their church. There was also talk of a parishioner sit-in at St. Theresa's for as long as it took to rescue their house of worship from the wrecking ball.

312

There it was, Gregorio thought. *The burning of St. Theresa's was meant to quell parishioner protest.* With the actual structure gone, then there was no church to fight over, no protest to mount. He had been hired to do the dirty work for the hierarchy in the Church, but when he decided to torch Temple Beth Abraham he made a major mistake. One fire would draw some attention, but a second fire against another house of worship, in the same neighborhood, would draw greater attention. Whoever was paying Alfredo and Salvi to take care of the dirty work suddenly realized they had a problem. It was someone who had a lot to lose, someone close to the situation at hand who understood the ramifications involved. It had to be someone inside the Church. The news story went on to explain how the entire phase of the redevelopment and future management of the property was to be handled by the Old Colony Real Estate Planning and Developing Company. If Arthur was right, he could definitely use this information to his advantage.

Gregorio let the newspaper drop on the table. He didn't need to know who was calling the shots at Old Colony and who the perpetrator of malfeasance was inside the archdiocese. All he had to do was make Alfredo think he knew. He also figured if he mentioned Temple Beth Abraham and Old Colony in the same sentence, it might provoke a rise out of Alfredo. Gregorio was now convinced that the party Salvi had mentioned as being interested in Temple Beth Abraham had to have been Old Colony Real Estate. Old Colony Real Estate, and whomever they were working with inside the chancery, had both developed great patience because they were now ready to take a more orderly route to the completion of their task.

Gregorio tossed his empty beer bottle in the trash basket next to the sink and popped open another. He was feeling rather good, confident he could squeeze more cash out of Alfredo, and whoever else was involved in this immoral act of corruption. Gregorio decided to splurge a little on this night. He was going to buy another six-pack to enjoy, as he drafted a plan to extort from Alfredo the cash, he believed was owed him.

"Hey, look who's here. I'll be damned," Johnny Rogers said as he stood behind the bar at Rose's. "Did you happen to bring that big dog of yours with you? He has some responsibilities to meet," he joked.

Father Wesley stood in the entrance to Rose's. It was his first visit to the place since his return to St. Theresa's. "No, I didn't," he replied to the question. He then glanced around the place and immediately felt the sting of pain his memories invoked. "It's nice to see you, Johnny. I should have dropped by to say hello long before today."

"Better late than never. So, tell me, what brings you here?"

"I came to see Bryan," he nodded as Fogarty approached the priest, adjusting his fly, upon exiting the restroom.

"Father Paul. What are you doing here?" a surprised Fogarty called out.

"I came to see you," as a mischievous smile invaded the priest's face.

"Let me guess. St. Theresa's is going to have another Christmas party before she goes out of business and you want me to play Santa Claus again."

"You're so perceptive. But, I should add, you are the kids' favorite." Father Wesley moved to a bar stool and sat down.

"Yeah, sure I am."

"What can I get you?" Rogers asked.

"Ginger ale. I don't think it would be proper for me to be setting a bad example," the priest scoffed.

"Understood," Rogers answered, playing along with Father Wesley's little game. "I wouldn't want to be the one responsible for your fall from grace."

A manufactured smile flashed across Father Wesley's face. He was finding this meeting of three old cronies to be a bit awkward.

"Father, I have this feeling you are here for something else, other than to ask me to play Santa Claus." Fogarty was right on top of the situation.

"You're right. I came here to ask you, Johnny and whoever else is left from the old gang to be a friend again for Ruth Ann. She's getting out of the hospital in a couple of days, but she's still going to require care on a daily basis as she undergoes her rehabilitation. Her parents want her to go home with them to Florida but Ruth Ann said *no*.. As a result, her mother is going to stay up here and tend to her until Ruth Ann is able to go it again on her own. In the meantime, Rachel is going to be staying with the Castlemans. They've really warmed up to her. Even Frank has come around to accepting her as his granddaughter. This whole tragedy now has a chance to have a happy ending, so I am determined to see that it does."

"That's very understanding of you, considering…well…considering what happened to you…and her," said Rogers.

"She's still a friend to us all and that's where you, Bryan, Sharon and whoever else you can dredge up can really help. Since the death of Billy, poor Ruth Ann has had to shoulder all the guilt. I guess she figured the best way to accomplish such a task was to ostracize herself from all her friends. In doing so, though, she was killing herself from within. It wasn't right. I intend to help her right that wrong, but I have a feeling as soon as the New Year rolls around I'll be reassigned, and I don't want to leave Ruth Ann foundering. She's going to need all her old friends to be coming around and rallying by her side. That's the real reason I came to see the two of you."

"So you want us to be demonstrative. As if the years had never gone by," Bryan added to the conversation.

"Very good, Bryan. I know it sounds foolish and perhaps romantically whimsy. We can never recapture what we've lost. But I think in Ruth Ann's case, a little of living in the past might make living in the present somewhat tolerable."

"You can count on us," Fogarty told him while smiling in the direction of Rogers.

"Yeah, you can count on us," Rogers went on. "Whatever it takes to get Ruth Ann back on track, we'll be there for her. But what about you? I know you're a strong-willed individual, but everybody has a breaking point. Finding out Rachel's not your daughter but Billy's must be killing you. I think you're going to need our help as well."

"We have to be more concerned with Ruth Ann. I'm coming to grips with what happened, and I no longer consider what she and Billy did a betrayal of me. At least in my case it's out in the open. If I feel like screaming my brains out because of what happened I can do so. Ruth Ann didn't have that chance. She had to live with her dark secret for what…fourteen years. Once Billy was gone she was alone. Living in that kind of a vacuum can swallow you whole."

"All right, Father," Bryan acquiesced. "Maybe you should have her and Rachel attend St. Theresa's Christmas bash. That might get her juices flowing in the right direction."

"I intend to do just that, if she's up to it."

"Now that we solved the Ruth Ann problem what about the other one you have? You know, the one concerning the Grimaldies and their family favorite, Arthur Gregorio," Bryan had to ask.

"Good question. That situation is totally different. Anna is still very depressed, and her father is still angry and vowing to get even with his son-in-law, if he can ever find him. Have you heard anything about him?"

"Nothing," Fogarty had to tell him. "But, don't worry, he'll resurface. I'd still like to know what his connection is with Alfredo. But that old bookmaker's not saying anything. He's not fooling me though. I'm still convinced Gregorio was on his payroll."

"So am I," Father Wesley agreed. "Now, Johnny, what's this I hear about my dog becoming a father?" he went on, turning his attention to Rogers.

"That's right. If you want, I'll give you one of the litter but the rest I'm going to sell. A German shepherd pup can bring a pretty good return these days."

"You always were one with a keen eye for making a buck," the priest said.

Rogers winked with delight at his old friend's remark.

Less than an hour after Father Wesley departed from Rose's, the bar phone rang. The call was for Bryan Fogarty. It was Arthur Gregorio on the line.

Gregorio had left his squalid little room to go out and pick up another six-pack. On the way he made a stop at a pay phone, in the debris littered courtyard in Lye's Central Square. He had decided to call Fogarty, wanting him to again get in touch with Alfredo.

"Yeah, is this you again, Arthur?" Bryan said as he took the phone from Rogers.

"It is. I need your help again."

"Oh, I bet you do."

"I want you to find Alfredo and tell him I need to speak with him. Tell him it's important, very important. Tell him I've got the whole thing figured out. Let him know I have nothing to lose at this point, so he had better talk to me."

"Arthur, where the hell are you?"

"None of your goddamn business. And don't give me the crap about having to be nice to you or you won't help me. If you don't get through to Alfredo for me then some bad things are going to happen. Some very bad things."

Until now, Bryan Fogarty had never taken anything Gregorio had to say seriously. But now, for some reason, he had cause to believe Gregorio meant every word he was saying. If he could just get Gregorio to loosen up a bit and tell him a little something, as to why he needed to see Alfredo, then maybe, he might be able to figure out what the man meant when he said: *some bad things are going to happen.*

"Arthur, I'll try, but what if Alfredo says he won't help you. The last time you had me track him down he was pretty emphatic about not hearing from you again."

"If you tell him what I just told you, he'll hear me out."

Fogarty was beginning to feel uneasy. He couldn't put his finger on it but something was wrong. Fogarty now realized Arthur Gregorio had turned into a desperate man, and a desperate man was capable of doing some strange things. He had to play along with him and find Alfredo and, hopefully, start to unravel this mystery that seemed so threatening.

"All right, Arthur, I'll do what I can to find Alfredo. How do you propose he get in touch with you?"

"I'll get in touch with him. You just tell him to be at Rose's tomorrow night at seven. I'll contact him then. And, Fogarty, remind him this is serious business we're getting into, and if he doesn't come around then I'll expose him and his partners for the criminals they are." Gregorio then abruptly hung up.

317

CHAPTER

THIRTY-SEVEN

Less than a mile from Rose's, on the parkway, overlooking the beach, stood a twelve-story building with the grandiose appearance of a luxury hotel. It was the Court of St. Andrew Condominiums and it was where Alfredo called home.

He had lived at the Court of St. Andrew for the past ten years, or since the passing of his wife. It was a solitary existence which he had come to appreciate. But now, as he stood at the glass balcony doors, peering out at the dark sea, a glass of red wine in his right hand, Alfredo was finding his precious private time being disrupted to the point of aggravation. He wasn't going to put up with much more. Arthur Gregorio had become a major nuisance in his life.

Alfredo had just spoken to Fogarty regarding the situation involving Gregorio. Alfredo was blunt, explaining to Bryan he had no intention of listening to anything Arthur Gregorio had to say. Bryan tried to push the issue and uncover more on the relationship between Arthur and Alfredo, but he came up with a big *fat* zero. The old bookmaker wasn't saying anything of substance. Alfredo simply dismissed his dealings with Gregorio as being the payment of a long overdue debt he had to work out with the man, a professional interchange over a bet Alfredo had been unable to cover, and Gregorio had been gracious enough to see the man had some time to make good on the money he was owed.

According to Alfredo their dealings were now complete and he owed Gregorio nothing else. Fogarty didn't believe a word. He had never heard any stories of Alfredo ever being unable to cover a bet. Bryan was well aware of the fact that Alfredo was a shrewd businessman when it came to bookmaking.

Now Alfredo had to decide if Gregorio was simply blowing smoke or was he truly onto something and intended to carry out his threat. He knew the man was unnerved and was not afraid of putting the match to St. Theresa's. The question now lurking about was quite simple: *was Arthur's lack of funds and his belief he was being shortchanged clouding his mind enough to allow him to make such a drastic move?* Alfredo had to believe the answer was *yes*.

Alfredo had to figure out how to deal with the matter. How did he go about warning the priests of St. Theresa's that their church was in peril without implicating himself? Then it came to him. Tomorrow was Saturday, one week before Christmas. Thank God for those guilt trips the Catholic Church perpetrated on its faithful.

—m—

Following his conversation with Alfredo, Fogarty made a beeline to the rectory. He had to warn his old friend that Arthur Gregorio was now a hopeless soul and had sworn to take his vengeance on someone or something now that Alfredo had refused to offer him any help. It was Bryan's opinion that Gregorio's target for revenge was Father Wesley.

When Fogarty arrived at the rectory he found both Father Coniglio and Father Wesley sitting in the living room discussing the details for the Christmas party. It didn't take much persuasion from Fogarty to put the party talk on hold for the moment. What he had to discuss was of a serious nature.

After explaining his earlier conversations with Gregorio and Alfredo, Fogarty made an impassioned plea to Father Wesley to be cautious. Bryan expressed concern that Gregorio now intended to make good on his threat and that Father Wesley was, in all likelihood, his intended target.

A somber air hung over the room. Father Coniglio looked over at his young associate and said, "Father, should Mr. Fogarty be right, it might be wise for you to keep a low profile. I don't mean to sound like an alarmist but if Arthur Gregorio does blame you for his problems, then why hasten trouble."

"And what do you suggest I do? Stay in the rectory for the rest of my days here at St. Theresa's?" an exasperated Father Wesley asked.

"No, Father, I don't. I suggest we contact Father Moore, explain our dilemma to him, and have you transferred as soon as possible."

Father Wesley shifted his stare at Fogarty. "And you, Bryan. What do you think?"

Fogarty shrugged his shoulders. "Father, I just don't want to see you get blindsided. Gregorio's no fool. He knows there's a chance you just might forget you're a priest long enough to give him the beating of his life. It's that cowardice factor that scares me. A man who is frightened becomes dangerous because his reaction is unpredictable."

"Well, I'm not going to hide because Arthur Gregorio refuses to recognize his shortcomings in life. I'll be ready for whatever ambush he has planned."

Fogarty and Father Coniglio could only stare at each other. Both men came to the conclusion that Father Wesley was not going to allow Arthur Gregorio to intimidate him. A noble quality, without a doubt. Father Coniglio only hoped it did not prove to be a foolish decision on his associate's part.

Bryan Fogarty, however, sensed something different. With all the sad incidents surrounding St. Theresa's in her waning days, it would not surprise Fogarty if Father Wesley's nerves were becoming a bit frayed. He believed his close friend was now itching for a fight.

—◆—

"Watch it with the mustard and relish," Freddy Brandt screamed at Danny Corrigan. The two teens were sitting in Freddy's new van—a combination birthday and Christmas present from his parents—which was parked along the seawall. They had each purchased a hot dog at the Banana Boat and were wolfing them down. Danny was being a slob about it.

He gave Freddy an incredulous stare. "What are you turning into, some kind of neat freak because you have some new wheels?"

"No," Freddy answered, cynically. "But I'm not going to just sit here and watch you drip that stuff all over my upholstery."

Danny took a paper napkin and wiped the mess from between his legs. "There," he answered with a degree of cynicism of his own. "It's all clean."

"Don't be a wiseass," Freddy countered. "I've got some big plans for this van, so I don't need you turning it into a pig sty."

"What are you talking about? What kind of big plans?"

"Look around. I'm thinking of tossing a mattress in the back and calling this van *Freddy's House of Ill Repute* on wheels. What do you think about that? Can make a lot of money that way."

"You're crazy, do you know that? Who are you going to get to serve as your *Midnight Lady*? Rachel? Boy, you already screwed-up big time with her."

"How was I to know the old man's junk was going to explode at the sight of her? He wanted to hear some stories about how she liked to mess around in a not so ladylike way. He paid us off in beer, so what do you care. I had no idea he was gonna follow her home only to find out she was nothing more than a tease. It's not my fault he blew his brains out over the thought of getting caught."

"Well, your traveling whorehouse idea is not going to come true any time soon, either. So you can forget about writing this van off as a business expense. Do you have any other lamebrain ideas?"

"I sure do, and this one is going to reap us dividends, immediately."

"All right, let's hear it," Danny said with a trace of skepticism in his voice.

"I want to steal a dog."

"WHAT?" Danny yelled. "We already tried that one, you donkey. Don't you remember? It almost backfired on us, big time."

"I'm not talking about that dog. Besides this time it's going to be different. The last time it was your idea. This time it's my idea, and I intend to make some money out of it."

"How?" Danny asked, still skeptical.

"The dog they keep at Rose's, you know, the big German shepherd. She's about to have puppies. She's as big as a house. She's going to become a mother any day now. Do you know how much those pups can get us?"

"No," Danny answered, although he had a fairly good idea,

"I'll tell you how much. Anywhere from a hundred and fifty to two hundred bucks a pup, that's how much."

"And how, may I ask, are we going to kidnap this dog? There's always some kind of activity going on in the place, unless you're planning on stealing the mutt at four in the morning. Also, it's a watchdog, you idiot. This isn't like the priest's dog that proved to be a big, lovable, slobbering pain in the derriere after he got drunk."

"Don't put too much stock into that watchdog thing," Freddy corrected him. "She's pretty friendly, and they don't use her much as a watchdog anymore since she became pregnant. We'll do it the same way we did it with the priest's dog. We'll get her drunk and lead her to the van and be off with her. We can do it on Christmas Eve. The dog sleeps in a heated shed behind the place and Rose's will be closing about nine that night. By nine-thirty there won't be a soul around except for you, me and Miss Love Muffin."

"And once we have the dog, what do we do with her?" Danny still couldn't see this happening.

"That's where you come in, my friend. That big empty garage behind your grandmother's house is a perfect spot to hide her until she gives birth."

"And what do we tell my grandmother? Do we tell her we bought a pregnant dog?" By now Danny was sure Freddy had this plan well thought out and would have an answer to his question.

"No, you nitwit. We tell her the dog was being abused so we freed her. We convince the old girl that she can't tell anyone about the dog, including your parents, because people will be looking for the mutt. Your grandmother's an old sentimental fool. She'll go along with it, I'm sure. Once Love Muffin has her pups we let her nurse them until the appropriate time and then we sell them. At the same time we bring

Love Muffin back to where we found her and tell your grandmother she ran away. I honestly think we can pull it off."

Danny pondered the idea for a minute. The plan wasn't as lame as he originally thought. "You know, you might be onto something," he had to admit. The two juvenile delinquents then exchanged a high five that served as their gentlemen's agreement to be business partners.

CHAPTER
THIRTY-EIGHT

Alfredo rarely left his condo when the weather made the outside conditions unbearable, and this day was bitterly cold. But the frigid conditions were not going to deter him from the purpose this day brought with it. His decision to alert the priests at St. Theresa's of the danger Arthur Gregorio presented, had Alfredo feeling good about himself. It was as if he were atoning for the unfortunate burning of Temple Beth Abraham. The feeling masked his true desire to do in Gregorio.

Alfredo was still having a problem understanding Gregorio's thinking. Yes, he was able to comprehend Gregorio's taking a shot at trying to extort more money from him with some veiled threats. It was worth the try. But his shakedown routine had failed, and if he did attempt to burn down St. Theresa's to achieve his revenge, the only harm he was doing was to himself. There was no way Alfredo was going to allow Gregorio to succeed in implicating him, or the dearly departed Salvi into what was now solely Arthur's plot against the small church on Everton Street. If the man took such a route, then Alfredo would have the world believing Gregorio had gone mad with rancor towards the Church because of what he believed to be the faith's meddling in his personal matters. Alfredo was prepared to feign ignorance should the question be put to him about his and Salvi's dealings with Gregorio.

The old bookmaker was willing to go so far as to say a series of poorly placed bets had caused the man to experience disfavor towards himself and Salvi. Those things often happened between the bettor and the ungracious bookmaker, and that argument should be enough to convince whoever needed to be sold on the fact. Alfredo had no qualms about rolling over Arthur Gregorio.

As he stepped out of the entrance to the condominium complex, the stark reality of the atmospheric conditions hit him in the face. There was brilliant sunshine all around but the temperature couldn't have been more than twenty degrees. Throw in the stiff wind off the ocean and you had arctic conditions. Up went the coat collar to protect a neck that was already fighting off the bitter effects of the day under a finely woven Nordic scarf. Alfredo donned some fur lined gloves and began the ten minute walk to St. Theresa's.

As he entered the church Alfredo counted nine people sitting or kneeling in the pews. It was about what he expected. He then summoned from his memory the last time he had graced this holy building. It had been the wedding between Anna Grimaldi and Arthur Gregorio. How ironic, he thought, that he should now return to do trade with the God above on the soul of the same Arthur Gregorio.

Alfredo walked down the side aisle and sat in an unoccupied pew. He did not know any of the nine people in the church and that suited him just fine. He leaned forward and asked the young Asian woman sitting in the pew in front of him as to who was hearing confessions on this cold afternoon.

"Why, Father Wesley," she answered, with what seemed to be a tone of indignation. "He's the only one who ever hears confessions."

"Is that so," his snide reply a clear indication of his displeasure to her answer of his simple question. *How was I to know,* he wanted to tell the young lady. The last time he had confessed his sins, the gleam in the eyes of the young girl's granddaddy had yet to have its day. It had been a long time.

Now came the insufferable period of waiting. Alfredo was not good at it. Yet, on this day, he was prepared to match the patience of Job. He waited nearly a half hour before it was his turn to enter the confessional.

In the dark and cramped area Alfredo knelt. He was uncomfortable and his knees began to hurt almost immediately. *How did he ever do this as a boy?* He wasn't sure he'd be able to get up. But he had to go through with this geriatric agony. In a few minutes he was going to deliver to Father Wesley a fitting trophy to mark his days at St. Theresa's. The way Alfredo looked at it was that Arthur Gregorio only proposed to play deceitful games, unlike himself who was prepared to play a game of his own. He was going to sell out the man who intended to sell him out.

Although Alfredo hadn't practiced his faith since his schoolboy days he was certain the rules were basically the same. He was aware of the moderate changes the Church had implemented in the past few decades. But he knew the sanctity of the confessional remained the same. It was much like the lawyer-client privilege or the doctor-patient bond. Those ties were bound by secrecy and so were those of the sinner and his Father Confessor. The confessor was there to grant absolution to the sinner for the wrong committed and wouldn't do so unless the sinner was truly contrite. Alfredo, however, was not seeking absolution. The sin he was here to confess had yet to be committed.

After a short amount of time the side panel of the confessional opened. Instead of beginning with the standard: *Bless me Father for I have sinned,* Alfredo said, "Bless me Father for I come here to report a sin yet to be committed, but a sin so grievous in nature that it warrants my intervention…and yours."

Father Wesley was caught by surprise. He had never heard of anyone confessing a sin before it was committed. He wasn't sure of the voice. It didn't belong to a regular. The voices of many of the parishioners were readily recognizable to him. He was unable to put a face to this voice.

"This sin you speak of. Is it to be committed by you?"

"No, Father, it is not."

"Why are you so eager to confess the sin of another person? A sin you say has yet to be committed. Are you a concerned individual or do you have it in for someone?"

"Father, the sin I am trying to prevent is a sin against the Church of St. Theresa. Father, this church stands in danger. That danger has nothing to do with the archdiocese's intention to close it down. This has to do with a man who holds you and the Church you represent in disdain. He is a snake of a human being who moves against your church and brings with him the fire of hell."

Arthur Gregorio immediately came to Father Wesley's mind. The voice was that of an older man and he was here not to confess but to warn. It had to be Alfredo, the priest surmised. He knew of Gregorio's intention and he was using the secrecy and anonymity of the confessional to deliver his message.

"When will this sin against St. Theresa's be carried out?"

"Soon," the voice told him. "Now I must go."

"Wait," Father Wesley implored the informant.

"Yes."

"I thank you for bringing this…this deplorable act to my attention."

"Father, when I die I'm going to go before our Maker, and he's going to have a long list before him of the wrongs I did in my life. I guess it's time I started doing something right."

"I'll say this. You have certainly taken a step in that direction."

Later that evening, Arthur Gregorio stood in the courtyard of Lye's Central Square, phone in hand, not quite believing what he had heard. Bryan Fogarty had informed him Alfredo refused to speak with him and had told Bryan to relate to Gregorio that any foolish act on his behalf would be his to regret and his only.

Alfredo was playing him for a fool and that fact made Gregorio's blood run hot. If Alfredo thought he was bluffing, then the man was going to find out he wasn't.

Quickly, Arthur brought his thoughts together. The time to strike was now. What was it he read about St. Theresa's? Oh, yes, the Christmas party for the children of the parish.

"It's not gonna happen," he mumbled to himself in the frosty night air. St. Theresa's was not going to make it through the night, he decided. He hurried back to his room to gather what he needed.

Once finished talking to Gregorio, Fogarty made another trip to the rectory to inform the priests of the conversation and how Alfredo was not going to play ball with the man. Once there he found Father Coniglio and Father Wesley in deep conversation with Officer Kilcullen about a possible arson attempt against St. Theresa's. The information they had come by, piqued Fogarty's interest. All he knew was that Gregorio might be thinking of performing some irrational act. But the priests and the police officer were talking of an arson attempt against the church as though it were a done deal.

Father Wesley quickly brought Bryan up to speed. He informed his friend of the anonymous tip that had been passed on to him in the confessional. The priest admitted he was not one to speculate or blindly point an accusing finger at an unsuspecting individual. But, in this instance, he was going to be more discerning. Father Wesley believed what the man in the confessional had to say, and he believed that man to be Alfredo. Thus, he was placing the onus squarely on the head of Arthur Gregorio. Now they had to put their heads together and figure out how to stop the man.

It was Bryan's turn to relate the conversation he had with Arthur Gregorio less than an hour ago. What he told the group convinced them that the arsonist was Arthur and, now being so frustrated and disillusioned, he was apt to strike any day. When the name of Alfredo was brought into Bryan's story, Kilcullen became determined to talk to the man about his association with Gregorio. Now that they were fairly certain Gregorio was planning an arson attempt against the church, it made sense that Grimaldi's attempt to improve his son-in-law's lot in life took him in a criminal direction. Kilcullen was sure, with a little digging, he might be able to bring the whole thing together and, in the process, bring to justice whomever was responsible for the burning of Temple Beth Abraham.

"Fogarty, just what do you know about Gregorio and Alfredo's dealings?" the police officer asked.

"It's a big mystery. I've tried and tried but I can't seem to come across anyone who knows a thing. However, I did find out that his dealings had more to do with Salvi than Alfredo."

"Maybe I can give you an answer to that one," Father Coniglio said.

"And?" Kilcullen prodded him.

"As we discussed before, I spoke to Grimaldi about him trying to get Arthur into a more prosperous and stable line of work. He admitted speaking to both Alfredo and Salvi about it and they told him to send his son-in-law down to the beach to see them. Where it went from there, Grimaldi didn't know."

"And neither does Anna,," Father Wesley added.

"But Alfredo and Salvi are bookies. What kind of work could they pass his way? If he were collecting bets or serving as muscle we'd know about it." Kilcullen was willing to wager that the two old bookmakers had expanded their business and had gone into something far more serious and dangerous.

"They have connections," the elder priest countered.

"Yes, but what kind of connections?" Kilcullen pressed.

"What are you getting at?" Fogarty wanted to know.

Kilcullen found himself pleased to answer the question and having the chance to throw out his theory. "You'd have to call Alfredo and Salvi small potato operators at best, at least on the surface. But perhaps there is, or was in Salvi's case, a more sinister side to them."

"Where are you going with this?" Now it was Father Wesley becoming intrigued.

"This is where I'm going. Alfredo and Salvi, admitted small-time operators, do have the connections for bigger and more profitable enterprises. I mean, what could they possibly use Gregorio for; except to take care of some dirty business. Business that would leave their hands clean. So, they put Gregorio on the payroll to take care of said *dirty work*, but then something goes wrong, and their plans have to be put on hold. In the meantime, Gregorio goes out and gets into a jam that lands him in jail and he needs money to get out of it. Alfredo does help him out but the guy comes back again, figuring he can squeeze some more cash out of him. Gregorio's got something on Alfredo and he figures he can put the tap on him for more money just to keep him quiet. But Alfredo draws the line and doesn't pay, so Gregorio figures he's going to show him a thing or two by finishing the job he had been hired to do, money or no money. That is burn down a house of worship and even the score in the process. What do you think, Father?" Kilcullen's question was directed to Father Wesley.

The priest answered the cop's question with a question of his own. "In a roundabout way, are you suggesting Arthur Gregorio burned down Temple Beth Abraham? That the burning of the Jewish synagogue was what went wrong?"

"That makes sense to me," Kilcullen responded.

"Wow," Fogarty exclaimed. "I never thought Alfredo and Salvi were capable of such a thing."

"It's strictly a theory, Bryan," Father Wesley reminded the biker. But Father Wesley knew better. Alfredo and Salvi were the men James Moore hired to see that St. Theresa's burned to the ground but, for some reason, Gregorio burned Temple Beth Abraham. That's where Alfredo reenters the picture. Gregorio wanted to finish off the job, but the cardinal's death and the fact that he was onto Father Moore prohibited the torching of St. Theresa's. It was the small Catholic church and not the Jewish synagogue that promised to bring the big pay day. Gregorio found himself being stiffed but may have decided to finish off the job anyway. It was his way of getting back at everyone who had made his life miserable. Father Wesley had a feeling that it was no longer a question of whether Arthur Gregorio would try to burn St. Theresa's, but when.

"I know this," Officer Kilcullen went on. "I want to talk to Alfredo. Does anybody know how to get in touch with the man? The only place I've ever seen him is on that bench on the beach and I won't find him there this time of the year. Does anyone know where he lives?"

"I would think Grimaldi does," Father Coniglio said.

"He used to live down at Paine Point, but after his wife died he moved. I think he now lives in one of those condos on the beach. But he's not going to be of much help," Fogarty added. "Maybe we should concentrate more on Arthur Gregorio than Alfredo," he went on.

"Trust me, I'm not forgetting about Gregorio," Kilcullen assured the group. "Unfortunately, at the moment, we don't know where to find him. At least we can track down Alfredo."

"What about the church?" Father Coniglio postured. "She's the one at risk right now."

"My suggestion is to keep the church locked at all times. If Gregorio wants to burn it, he can probably figure out a way. What has to be done is to make it as difficult as possible for him to get at it. Should he somehow manage to get a fire started keep the damage as minimal as possible." Kilcullen now seemed antsy, as if he were in a hurry to go find Alfredo.

"I'm not very keen on that idea; I've always prided myself on the church being available to any soul who needed it. Now you're asking me to lock it up as if it were my own prized little kingdom. It saddens and angers me to put my church through this ordeal." Father Coniglio was not too happy with what was being asked of him.

"Sorry, Father, but as long as Arthur Gregorio is on the loose I suggest you conduct business in this manner. If you don't, your church will be closing a lot sooner than you expected," said Kilcullen.

"Father, I guess we should start tonight," Father Wesley suggested. "Grimaldi usually locks the church around eight every night and opens it at seven in the morning," he said for the benefit of Fogarty and Kilcullen. "I assume it will have to be locked at all times, unless there is a service going on."

"That's what I suggest," Kilcullen told him. "I'll see to it that a squad car checks on the church every half hour or so or until Gregorio is apprehended."

"Or until he burns the place down," Fogarty chimed in with an impending sense of doom.

THIRTY-NINE

As Arthur Gregorio made a vigorous walk back to his dingy rented room, following his phone conversation with Fogarty, his decision to burn St. Theresa's on this night became more firmly committed in his mind. He figured Fogarty was probably now running to Father Wesley to let him know he was up to something. If he decided to wait, he might never get the chance.

Gregorio needed just a few simple items to get the job done. He took a half filled plastic gallon jug of water from the dormitory size refrigerator in his room and dumped the contents into the sink. He then made a siphoning hose out of some rubber tubing from an air pump. Finally, he took a bed sheet and ripped it to shreds. These were the rudimentary elements for the fire bomb he was planning to make. Gregorio placed the items in a brown paper shopping bag.

A quick glance at the clock told him he had roughly five minutes to make it to the bus stop and catch the 449. Five minutes after that he would be back in Paine. A half hour later St. Theresa's would be a rising plume of holy smoke, its flames reaching high into the sky on a cold winter's night. The thought of accomplishing this feat was exciting Gregorio as though it were an erotic experience.

—ᴔ—

Less than fifteen minutes later, after the bus crossed the causeway separating Lye from Paine, Arthur Gregorio stepped off the bus onto the shoulder of a dimly lit section of North Shore Road. Immediately before him was the marsh, a vast wetland, which on a night such as this made the environment seem colder and more bitter than it was. Behind him was the ocean, and he could feel the chill wind on the back of his neck. But on this evening Gregorio was generating his own heat. His compulsion to finish off St. Theresa's was still giving him a sensation that needed to be satisfied.

Gregorio needed one component to complete his arson kit—gasoline! He began to make the 200 foot trek towards the corner of Everton Street and North Shore Road, where he would be free from the harshness of the open marsh and he would have access to the much needed petroleum. On the corner was a used car lot, closed for the night. He looked around to see if there were any witnesses to what he was about to do. He then slithered his way to the back of the lot. It was here that he found what he was looking for—a twelve-year-old Honda Civic.

Gregorio squatted low and popped the lock before removing the gas cap. The car was parked in such a way that it was virtually impossible to see him unless someone was standing within ten feet of the vehicle. Gregorio took a much needed breath of fresh air. Within seconds he had his siphoning hose operating and soon the plastic jug was full.

Gregorio exited the car lot, keeping to the dark end, away from the street corner. He waited until there was a break in the rush of automobiles making their way down the highway before stepping out of the shadows. So far, so good. Once he was out of the used car lot, Gregorio began what looked like a leisurely stroll. With his shopping bag in hand, he gave the appearance of a man returning home with a bag of groceries or gifts.

As he began the walk up Everton Street he noticed the police car across from the rectory. The sight of the vehicle gave Gregorio an uneasy feeling, but it also seemed to boost his determination. He didn't see Fogarty's motorcycle, but the temperature was in the teens, so the chances were good he was not riding it on such a frigid night. But Gregorio was certain the biker was inside the rectory with the cop and the priests, plotting their strategy to stop whatever they thought he was going to do. Gregorio smiled. He was way ahead of them. They weren't going to ambush him; he was going to bushwhack them.

The street was quiet. All the parts were coming together and seemed to be working to Gregorio's advantage. He quickened his pace and walked to the front door of the church. He made a fast jerk of the door handle, not knowing whether the door was open or locked. It was open. He was in and the place was empty, not a soul to be seen. This was perfect. Inside the church he leaned back against the door to catch his breath and contemplate his next move.

—m—

Ninety seconds after Arthur Gregorio entered the church the front door of the rectory opened. Fogarty and Kilcullen were leaving. Standing at the door, the police officer kept emphasizing the importance of seeing that the church was locked. Gregorio, leaning against the door inside the vestibule, could barely hear what was being discussed. He pushed the door open a crack, just enough to give him a line on what was being said.

"Father, please make sure the church is locked, and do it as soon as possible. If you want I'll wait around and go into the church with you to see that everything is all right."

"Officer, please don't get paranoid on us. We're grown men. We can handle the situation," Father Coniglio assured him.

"Well, then make sure Father Wesley is with you when you lock the place." Kilcullen didn't want the old priest confronting Gregorio on his own.

"Good call," Fogarty whispered into the cop's ear. "Unless Gregorio is planning on shooting Father Wesley, the guy doesn't stand a chance against him. I'm beginning to think he's tired of acting like a priest."

Kilcullen forced a weak smile. "Fogarty, for once I hope you are right."

Once Fogarty and Kilcullen had left, Father Coniglio turned to Father Wesley and said: "You don't have to go with me. I can lock the place by myself. Why don't you call Grimaldi and tell him we're securing the church early tonight and that he doesn't need to do it.

But, please, don't tell him why. Considering all that poor man and his family have gone through, I don't want him knowing we are bracing for another vicious attack by his son-in-law."

"I'll do so, Father, but please wait for me. I don't want you doing this on your own."

Just then Father Wesley's office phone rang. He rushed to answer it, Father Coniglio following behind. It was Father Moore. Father Wesley cupped his hand and said it would be just a few minutes.

But the mention of Father Moore's name made Father Coniglio fidgety. He had had it up to his eyeballs with the man. He had no intention of listening to what the two men had to discuss. He was going to lock his church and protect it from the harm that now threatened it.

"Father, you do what you have to do with Father Moore. As for me, I'm going over to the church. I'll be back in a few minutes."

Father Wesley, his hand still covering the phone mouthpiece, called to the old priest. "Father, if you're in such a rush then at least take Shagtyme with you. It would make me feel better."

"If it'll ease your mind, I will. Shagtyme!" he called out.

—m—

Gregorio now realized he had just a few precious minutes to complete the arson attack on St. Theresa's. The best and most ideal way to torch the place was to come through the roof. That's the way he had done Temple Beth Abraham. But Arthur didn't have the necessary time in this instance. He had to do the greatest amount of damage possible with a very small time frame of opportunity.

He also would have liked to have started the fire at the altar. The white linen and Christmas tree, which was set before the steps leading to the altar, provided an excellent propellant for his planned inferno. But now time was working against him as far as that plan was concerned. Arthur decided he was going to set the blaze in the sacristy. That part of the building also offered him egress out of the place. There was a door leading to the backyard of the rectory. From there he needed to negotiate a few other backyards and the edge of the marsh, and he'd be gone.

Inside the sacristy Gregorio found exactly what he wanted and then some. He found a number of cassocks and surplices. These garments would greatly enhance the blaze once he got it started. Then he found a closet where Grimaldi kept cleaning ingredients. Included in the lot was a large container of kerosene. *Leave it to my father-in-law,* he thought, *to have this stuff lying around as a cleaning agent.* What he found was gold. He quickly began splashing the kerosene and gasoline around the sacristy. This place was going to go up like a Roman candle.

Arthur set the gallon jug of gasoline in the center of the room, under one of the surplices. He attached his fuse made out of the torn bed sheet to the plastic jug and its remaining contents. Except for the time restraint he was working against, everything was going his way. Holding the end of the tattered bed sheet, Arthur fumbled through his pockets looking for his lighter.

As Father Coniglio entered the church with Shagtyme, the dog's snout immediately thrust forward. Shagtyme's reaction did not go unnoticed by the elderly priest. Someone was in the church. He looked around and saw no one. But the old priest knew Arthur Gregorio was in the place. The thought brought a sick feeling to the pit of his stomach.

He thought of going back to get Father Wesley but then decided he was not going to allow Gregorio any extra time to burn St. Theresa's, and reduce his beloved church to cinders. He leaned over and unleashed Shagtyme. As he was doing so he whispered in the dog's ear, "Go get him."

Shagtyme sprinted down the side aisle and came to the door of the sacristy. The door was on a swing hinge and the dog was aware of it. Shagtyme stood on his hind legs and let his body fall forward.

Gregorio had backed away and allowed himself the luxury of a few seconds to admire his firestorm. He loved these old buildings. No sprinkler system, and in the corner rested a dusty fire extinguisher which Gregorio was willing to bet hadn't been tested in years. Then he heard a fire alarm go off. This building wasn't as antiquated as he thought. It was time for him to make his exit. It was at this time Shagtyme came crashing through the door.

Damnit, he thought. He had not factored the dog into the equation. The animal could prove to be a problem.

Shagtyme bared his teeth, and Gregorio glanced hurriedly to his left. Next to the fire extinguisher was a large candelabra. Arthur needed something to ward off the dog and he needed it now. The sacristy was already a ball of fire. He reached out and grabbed his only weapon of choice.

As Shagtyme and Gregorio were facing off in the sacristy, Father Coniglio was trying to race down the side aisle. Between his age and the agitation the situation presented he was beginning to feel strange. He could feel himself becoming winded, and his head started feeling woozy. The heat emanating from the sacristy wasn't helping matters, and the dark smoke starting to make its way underneath the sacristy door was making it hard for him to see and breathe. After somewhat awkwardly making his way down the side aisle, the old priest stumbled forward towards the sacristy. His breathing was labored. As he reached the sacristy door he felt a sharp pain in his chest. Immediately a stinging sensation struck at the base of his brain, and he collapsed in a heap. He was gone in a matter of seconds. Father Coniglio had suffered a fatal heart attack.

Gregorio tried to make a dash for the back door but Shagtyme leaped at him and forced him to retreat to the edge of the flames. He was now trying to beat off Shagtyme with the candelabra, but it was to no avail. The dog blocked his access to the rear door. His only other choice was to go out the front entrance of the church. He made a charge at the sacristy door. As he slammed into it, he was repelled as the door only moved an inch or so. The dead body of Father Coniglio was slumped against it. Since the door had no handle, Gregorio was unable to open it inwardly. It was going to require a couple of forceful shoves to dislodge the dead priest's body. But he had to contend with this damn dog. Gregorio had a decision to make. He dropped the candelabra and concentrated on moving the body blocking the door.

As Gregorio did so, Shagtyme dug his teeth into Arthur's left wrist. The pain the bite inflicted was difficult for Gregorio to tolerate. But he was now in a life or death situation. Using just his right shoulder, Arthur kept ramming against the door while Shagtyme was trying to pull him in the opposite direction. Finally the body of Father Coniglio moved just enough for Gregorio to make his escape. By this time the sacristy was completely engulfed in flames. The fire had moved rapidly across the ceiling and was beginning to burn in the main part of the church.

Now Gregorio had to free his wrist from the grip of the dog's teeth. The candelabra he had hoped to use to bash Shagtyme's skull was now out of his reach. He was going to have to use his right fist to pound over the dog's head, and he wasn't sure if it would be enough. Then he began to smell it. A nanosecond later he saw it.

Shagtyme's coat was beginning to smolder. The dog was on fire! Gregorio was wild with joy. Surely this beast would be more concerned with saving his own hide and release his wrist. Gregorio looked over his shoulder and could see the near side of the church turning into another wall of flames. There was no longer a second to spare. It was now or never. Gregorio made one mighty jerk, and the dog's teeth slipped down to his hand. Shagtyme had him by the thumb and had tightened his bite. Gregorio knew one more pull and he would be free of the dog's locking teeth.

He gave it one more yank. His hand came free as the scream he cried out reverberated off the burning walls.

CHAPTER
FORTY

Father Wesley was becoming increasingly annoyed with Father Moore's phone call. The message imparted was to simply inform him that he was to be reassigned to St. Monica's Church in South Boston once St. Theresa's closed down. Father Moore was prolonging the conversation and seemed to be enjoying the experience. It was Father Moore's chafing way of wishing his adversary a not so *Merry Christmas.*

Under normal circumstances Father Wesley would be required to grin and bear it. Father Moore was his superior and according to the unwritten rules, Father Wesley was to be at his mercy. But these were not normal circumstances. The perilous situation facing St. Theresa's superseded whatever mundane chatter his priestly rival had to rain down on him. If there was anything to feel good about on this night, it was the satisfied feeling Father Wesley would gain by cutting the man short. He informed him of the strange warning he received in the confessional about an arson attempt against St. Theresa's.

The silence he received from the other end of the line was chilling. It made Father Wesley realize it was not inconceivable for Father Moore to know about Arthur Gregorio. The thought brought him back to Kilcullen and his assertion that Arthur Gregorio may have been responsible for the burning of Temple Beth Abraham. Father Wesley had the urge to cross examine his fellow priest but he didn't get the chance. The church alarm and blaring sirens he was now hearing was alerting him to the fact the impending danger they feared was now at hand.

"Father, I've got to go," a panic stricken Father Wesley said.

Father Moore picked up on the urgency in his voice and instantly knew what the problem was. He also knew the burning of St. Theresa's could spell trouble for him and his brother, with Father Wesley knowing what he did. "Father, is there a problem with the church?" he asked. Father Moore's voice had a helpless sound to it.

"I believe so," an anxious Father Wesley responded before slamming the receiver down.

—m—

The street, which had been quiet for most of the evening, was now abuzz with curiosity and frenzy. There were two fire trucks in front of the church and several firefighters were busy rushing into the building. Smoke was billowing out of the place, and the air was filled with the fetid stench a major fire brings with it.

As Father Wesley ran out of the rectory, he could see through the stained glass windows that the fire was concentrated in the rear of the building. His heart began to race. Where were Father Coniglio and Shagtyme? Could they possibly have escaped the inferno? He quickly made the sign of the cross, praying they had managed to get out. He never gave a thought to the survival of Arthur Gregorio.

"Father," Grimaldi screamed as he came running towards the prelate, heavy plumes of breath rising from his rapid breathing into the night air. "What's happened?"

Father Wesley turned to look at him. The priest's eyes were black, his heart aching at what he feared would be his and the parishioners of St. Theresa's loss. "The church is on fire. I can't locate Father Coniglio. I think he might be trapped in that blaze."

"Oh, no," Grimaldi cried out. He immediately dropped to one knee and made the sign of the cross, as he too uttered a prayer for Father Coniglio's safety.

Father Wesley rushed to the street and tried to make his way into the building. A firefighter stopped him. "Sorry, Father. Not right now. It's too dangerous," he was told.

"But I believe Father Coniglio and my dog are in there. You've got to help them." As he said the words he could hear someone screaming from inside the burning House of God. It was the shrill of someone hopelessly trapped.

"We'll do what we can do to get them out," was all the firefighter could say.

The priest felt a hand on his shoulder. It was Kilcullen, who returned as soon as he heard the report of the fire over his car radio. "The bastard must have been in the church while we were discussing what our plan of action should be," the police officer's voice steeped with disbelief.

"I know," a sad Father Wesley replied. "I feel so helpless. They won't let me in there. It's my fault. I never should've allowed Father Coniglio to lock the church by himself."

"Father Coniglio's in there?" a stunned Kilcullen asked.

"I think so. He and Shagtyme went to lock the church as soon as you and Bryan left. I asked him to wait for me, but he wouldn't. I should have made him." The priest was on the verge of tears.

"It's not your fault," Kilcullen responded, trying to console him. "And what about Gregorio? Is he in there?"

"I don't know."

"Arturo? Is Arturo in there? Is he responsible for this?" Grimaldi had overheard what Officer Kilcullen asked.

Both Father Wesley and Kilcullen looked at each other. Grimaldi had to be told. The priest took the initiative. "Yes, we believe so. I'm sorry, Grimaldi. I know how much of a disappointment the man has been to you and now to add this on top of it…well…it just doesn't seem fair."

Suddenly there was the horrible sound of something collapsing. The flames and sparks from the falling debris jettisoned even higher into the night air. "The back of the building is caving in," one of the firefighters called out.

"Oh God," was all a despondent Father Wesley could say. The tears he had been trying to quell were now falling down his cheeks.

"Jesus, this is terrible," Frank Castleman said as he came up alongside the priest. "How did it happen?"

Father Wesley turned to see him with his wife, daughter and granddaughter in his wake. Father Wesley found a semblance of solace in seeing Rachel. He prayed the spirit of Billy was with her on this awful night to give him strength.

"Oh no, this can't be happening," Fogarty uttered as he too returned, having heard the news of the burning church down on the beach. "Tell me that sorry bastard didn't get away?"

"We don't know." This time it was Officer Kilcullen doing the explaining. "What we do know is that Father Coniglio and Shagtyme are probably in there."

Fogarty closed his eyes and tilted his head skyward. "Noooooo!" he screamed at the top of his lungs.

"Good Lord," George Napoli said, his eyes transfixed on the roaring blaze. He was holding the hands of his daughter and son. Jenna broke free of her father's grasp and tugged on Father Wesley's pants, her eyes filled with tears. "Father, someone said Shagtyme is in there. Please say it isn't so. Please," she pleaded.

Father Wesley looked down at his dog's favorite playmate. He didn't know what to say. He pressed her head against his side. "Shagtyme's in there trying to protect Father Coniglio. They'll be all right," he told her, knowing what he said had little chance of being true.

Father Wesley turned to his right and watched as a man he vaguely remembered approached him. "Father," the man said as he came near. "Sorry we have to meet again under such terrible circumstances. In case you don't remember, I'm Father Emilio Torrez, the fire chaplain."

Father Wesley remembered him and how they had met. It was at the Beachhead Lounge the day it burned down.

"Father, I understand Father Coniglio might be in the church."

"There's no might about it," Father Wesley told him. "He went in there with the dog we have here at St. Theresa's. God, I feel so helpless."

"Father, they'll get them out. Try to think positively." The fire chaplain then stared at the burning church. He was trying to be upbeat but even he knew, as he gazed at the roaring inferno, that if there was to be any good news they would have heard it by now.

Father Torrez stepped away from the others and moved towards the church. He also was feeling helpless. There was a fellow priest inside the building. A priest who, according to the stories he had heard, epitomized what it meant to be a parish clergyman. Now it was becoming clear he was gone.

The fire chaplain looked back at the crowd behind him. The parishioners continued to gather in the street, and the crowd was swelling. They gathered around Father Wesley. The forlorn little church on Everton Street was showing her strength. In order for them to carry on Father Coniglio's spirit they would now have to place their trust in Father Wesley. The compassion the venerable old priest had exhibited as their pastor was showing in their numbers.

As Father Torrez peered back at the crowd he noticed that although Father Wesley looked sad, he also appeared determined. Since he had first met the priest, the fire chaplain had been told Father Wesley had been the mover and shaker behind St. Theresa's revitalization. It had also been rumored that what he had accomplished at St. Theresa's had been done in direct defiance of his instructions from the chancery. Whatever he had brought to St. Theresa's had been contagious. His strong will and resolution had been imparted to the poor but faithful parishioners of the small church. Father Torrez knew the demise of St. Theresa's was not to be. Her hardcore faithful would refuse to accept defeat.

An hour later the fire was basically extinguished but the crowd, which had been pushed back to the other side of the street, had not dispersed. There was a sickening feeling among those who stood in the frosty conditions that what they were witnessing was, indeed, the end of their church. The word had spread that Father Coniglio had been in the building when the blaze started. Many of those people refusing to leave wept. Some were in constant prayer. Others refused to believe he was gone, hoping against the greatest of odds. Rabbi Zuckerman, who had joined the vigil, was stunned, unable to speak. Mildred, when told of the loss, fainted. Phu Luong stood off from the others, shocked by what he was witnessing. The crowd, their teeth chattering and bodies shivering, stayed behind because they had to. They stayed for the inevitable.

Father Torrez, who had not been seen for the past half hour, emerged from the ashes and rubble and again approached Father Wesley. The lone surviving clergy member of St. Theresa's knew what to expect.

"Father, they have recovered a body they believe is Father Coniglio. It's badly charred. He was found near the sacristy door."

Father Wesley drew a deep breath and the crowd gave off a mournful wail as the latest news passed amongst them. "I'd like to see for myself," the priest insisted.

"It's still dangerous in there. Why don't you wait until they move him."

"No, I'm going in there," Father Wesley demanded as he moved past his fellow priest.

Kilcullen accompanied the two priests as they entered the ruins of the church. The heavy smell of smoke was still in the air, and ice was forming where the heat had ceased to exist. Father Torrez led them down the side aisle to the spot where the body was located. Amidst an assembly of firefighters, Father Wesley stood over the remains. Although badly burned, the body was not beyond recognition. He turned to Father Torrez and said, "It's him."

Kilcullen broke away from the gathering in front of the burned out sacristy and walked to the center aisle and conversed with some other firefighters. Another body had been found. "Fathers, over here," he called out while waving for the two priests to join him.

The two priests ambled over to the spot where the cop was standing. At his feet were the scorched remains of Shagtyme. The dog's coat was badly burned. But there was something about the location of the carcass which disturbed Father Wesley. The dog and Father Coniglio had become so close it was unlikely Shagtyme would have deserted the old priest. The fire had been concentrated near the back of the church, by the altar. If Shagtyme had been trying to flee the flames he had been headed in the wrong direction. Something didn't make sense.

"Have you found any other bodies?" Father Wesley asked one of the firefighters.

The man looked around for some of his fellow firefighters. "Have we found any other bodies?" he yelled.

The answer was *no*. The firefighter then bent over the dead dog before looking up at the priest. "There's blood running down the side of his mouth," he said. He proceeded to run his fingers along Shagtyme's throat. There was something lodged in it.

"What is it?" Father Wesley asked.

The firefighter continued to fidget with the dog's mouth before pulling the obstruction from the animal's throat. "This," he answered. "I think he might have choked on this thing before the fire had a chance to kill him." The firefighter held in his hand a thumb. The left hand thumb of Arthur Gregorio.

Father Wesley looked up and tried to figure where Shagtyme had been headed. It appeared to be the confessional, which was still intact. He hurried through the debris, splashing his way through the soot and filthy water, to the confessional door and opened it. The priest had to take a deep breath and shook his head. In the confessional he found the slumped body of Arthur Gregorio.

The firefighter rushed past him. "Hey, Ralph, we've got another one," he called out to another firefighter.

"Is he alive?" Father Wesley asked.

The firefighter was feeling for a pulse. There was none. "No," he finally said. "I think the smoke and the bleeding was too much for the poor bastard. Between the fire and the dog he must've got trapped and the confessional was his only hope for safety. Is he the perpetrator?"

"I believe so," Father Wesley answered.

Father Wesley left the church alone. It was his responsibility to inform the parishioners of the deaths of their beloved Father Coniglio and Shagtyme. As he reemerged from the charred ruins he was met by Father Moore on the steps of the church.

"Father, I got here as fast as possible. I heard something about Father Coniglio being trapped in the fire. Is it true?"

"It is. He's dead. Everything you've been hoping for has come your way. St. Theresa's has burned to the ground, and Father Coniglio is gone. I guess you received your Christmas present a little early this year."

"Father, that's uncalled for. I had nothing to do with the fire. I swear."

Father Wesley looked back at the now sorry looking building before staring back into the eyes of Father Moore. "I believe you," he said. "But I think the man who started the blaze was once in your employ, so to speak. His name was Arthur Gregorio. Did you know him?"

"No, I did not," Father Moore answered honestly.

"I believe that as well. Let me ask you this: do you know of a man named Alfredo?"

Father Moore did not answer. His silence was answer enough.

"I thought so. Father, I'd probably have a tough time proving it but I believe you, your brother, and two men named Salvi and Alfredo were responsible for the burning of Temple Beth Abraham. The man actually responsible for setting the fire was Arthur Gregorio, and his body can be found inside the scorched walls of this church. I believe Arthur Gregorio was hired to burn St. Theresa's, but first burned Temple Beth Abraham when he heard the place might be up for sale. He was hoping to give our Jewish friends a bit of an incentive to move in that direction. How am I doing so far?" There was an unappreciative glare in Father Moore's eyes at what Father Wesley had to say.

"You're right. You'd have a tough time proving it."

"Then I'm prepared to do what no other priest would do."

"Such as?" Father Moore knew he didn't want to hear what it was.

"I'm prepared to violate the sanctity of the confessional. You see, it was Alfredo, I believe, under the guise of confession, who alerted me to Arthur Gregorio and what the man was planning. I imagine what I'm proposing to do wouldn't be admissible in a court of law; then again it might be. It wasn't an actual confession. But I do know one thing."

"And that is?" Father Moore knew he didn't want to hear anymore.

"Whatever I said would be enough to drag you, your brother, and Alfredo down. It's like I told you once before: *screwing around with someone's house of worship is like screwing around with their family.* I'm sure Rabbi Zuckerman and his congregation wouldn't take kindly to this information."

Father Moore could sense a bit of horse trading on Father Wesley's part. "Okay. What do you want from me?"

"Not much. It was inevitable you were going to get your hands on St. Theresa's, and now you have. When do you think you'll be starting construction on the high-rise retirement home you have planned for this plot of land?"

"You're pretty sure about yourself, aren't you? What if I were to tell you there are no plans for a...retirement home."

"I'd say, *I don't believe it*. Father, don't force me to call you a liar. You don't have the time nor the inclination to wait on this land. A new archbishop might mean the end to the role you now play in the archdiocese. It's best for you to get this plan moving before it's too late, considering what your family business has to lose."

"Okay, Father, I get your point. What is it you're trying to get from me?"

"When you proceed with your elaborate retirement home there will be a change in the configuration of the building. On the first floor—and I'm talking about the first floor and not the basement—a church, not a chapel, will be built. Those retirees and disabled who will call it home in your new and financially rewarding building, will also have a new church in which to worship. It will be the new St. Theresa's, and the new church will serve not only the people of your building, but also those people of the parish who strived to save the St. Theresa's that has burned down tonight. By doing so, Father, we have resolved the issue of whether St. Theresa's should close or not. You get your way and the parishioners of St. Theresa's get theirs."

A contemptible, but in a way, admiring look crossed the face of Father Moore. "You think I'm an evil man. But, you are somewhat evil yourself. Father, you're practicing extortion."

"Am I? Well, let's say, I'd rather be guilty of extortion than the carnage you helped perpetrate on this day."

"I see. Are there any other contingencies you want me to know about?" Father Moore asked, a touch of cynicism in his voice.

"Yes, there is. The church will still be known as St. Theresa's and the parish remains intact. The retirement home will be named in honor of the late Father Ronald Coniglio. And, on a personal note, if you ever think of torching a church again I'll expose you and your brother for the frauds you are."

Father Moore fired a cold stare Father Wesley's way for several seconds. "You know, I'll have to run your proposals past the new archbishop. I don't make these decisions by myself."

"You are a very persuasive person, Father. I'm sure you'll be just as convincing with the new archbishop as you were with Cardinal Burke. For your own sake, you better be."

Father Wesley left Father Moore alone on the steps of the church and walked off in the direction of the crowd. He was now forced to confirm the news they feared.

CHAPTER

FORTY-ONE

The parkway was deserted; except for Freddy Brandt's van. It was just after 9:30 on the night of Christmas Eve. It was another cold night, but the weather was not going to deter Freddy and Danny from the task at hand. The two young delinquents were out doing some last minute Christmas shopping. They were out to kidnap Love Muffin.

"All right," Freddy said to Danny. "I think the time is now."

"I hope you're right about this," Danny responded, the blade cutters in hand. "Do you think she's drunk? We only slipped the booze under the fence ten minutes ago."

"She's drunk," Freddy insisted as he jumped out of the van from the driver's side. "Let's get this whole thing over with. I've got four people lined up waiting for a pup."

"What if she doesn't have a litter that big?" Danny reasoned.

"She better," was all Freddy had to say to the question.

The two absconders made their way over to the fence. Rose's had been closed for a half hour. The bar regulars were gone, off to celebrate Christmas in some other place than their usual watering hole. Johnny Rogers had locked the bar five minutes earlier and departed.

"Damn," Freddy cried out as they approached the fence. Love Muffin had not touched the bowl of gin Freddy had left.

"What do we do now?" Danny wanted to know.

349

"We take our chances," Freddy answered without reservation.

"I think we have a problem," Danny replied. "This dog's not going to be so easy to take."

"Will you knock off the whining. I don't think we need the booze. I've been befriending this pooch for two weeks. Look, she's as friendly as can be."

Love Muffin had made her way over to the fence and did seem captivated by the presence of Freddy and Danny. But as Danny looked at the dog, he voiced another concern.

"She doesn't look too good. She looks like she might have her puppies right here and now."

"You really think so? That'd be fantastic," Freddy clamored. "Let's get her outta here and put her in the van. Put those cutters to good use."

A couple of hardy snips and Danny had the chain severed. They almost had her. Almost.

As Freddy prepared to open the seven foot high chain link gate, a police car came cruising down the parkway. Danny put the blade cutters out of sight but the cop in the cruiser still eyed them suspiciously as he drove by. Freddy and Danny hadn't counted on this happening.

"Let's get out of here before he decides to come back and check us out," Freddy said, hurriedly.

"What about the dog?" Danny asked.

"We'll come back and get her later. We'll park further up the beach and come back and get her. Let's give it about an hour."

"Come back later," Danny protested. "Goddamn it, Freddy, it's Christmas Eve."

"So what. Do you have to get home and get to bed before Santa Claus shows up?"

"No," Danny replied, somewhat bothered by Freddy's perception of him still being a child. "I'll be right back here with you in an hour," he went on, trying to reestablish his manliness.

—⟨m⟩—

Once they were gone there was an eerie stillness to the night. It was the only time of the year Paine Beach was this quiet. Love Muffin nudged her nose against the chain link gate. It opened, slightly, so she gave it a more forceful shove. Love Muffin had never been off the premises of Rose's but as she exited out onto the sidewalk, she did so with what seemed to be a purpose of knowing where she was headed. There was a bright moon to guide her.

On this Christmas Eve Father Wesley sat alone in the living room of the rectory, sipping on a glass of Merlot. His reassignment, for the moment, was incomplete. He was now the guardian of a parish without a church. Earlier in the day, he had seen to the burial of Father Coniglio and now he was feeling down. The emptiness which enveloped the place was unsettling. Father Wesley was feeling lonely and was again questioning his call to the priesthood.

He had spent the evening hours looking in on some of the parishioners, who were still dazed by the occurrences of the past few days. Father Wesley was there for them to lean on, and he could feel the weight the faithful were disbursing. He wanted to be their crutch, but his vocation had taken a hit. Father Wesley needed help on this Christmas Eve. He needed a friend.

Love Muffin made her way up Everton Street and—with some adventure to it—crossed North Shore Road before stopping at the rubble which was now the Church of St. Theresa. Her gestation period had made her a weak dog. Yet, it seemed only proper that she deliver her puppies here. Love Muffin seemed to be responding to her animal instinct. Or was it a call from a higher power? A wind began to howl.

Her agility had become severely limited the past few weeks but she was determined it would not serve as a deterrent on this night. She climbed the few steps leading to St. Theresa's before collapsing in the ruins of the drafty vestibule. This was as far as Love Muffin could go.

The loneliness of the night was destroying Father Wesley. His thoughts drifted back to the prior Christmas and how St. Theresa's had been such a vibrant and happy place to be. Now there was this.

The sudden wind outside rattled the windows, and the rectory became drafty. But Father Wesley had no inclination to get up and raise the heat. Instead, he reached over and took the bottle of wine from the coffee table, pouring himself another glass. "Terrible way to spend Christmas," he lamented to himself. He then raised the glass to give a salutation. "To you, Father Coniglio. I wish you a Merry Christmas. Wherever you are, I know it's a lot better than being here." The priest then took a sip.

He raised the glass a second time. "And to you my faithful friend, Shagtyme. Unfortunately, dog heaven only exists in our dreams. But your life was not without meaning. It was every bit as important as anyone else who has ever walked this earth." He took another sip and his eyes became moist.

A howl permeated the night air. The wind, he thought. It's howl eerily reminded him of Shagtyme.

It howled again, only louder. Freakish, he thought. He salutes his dead dog and the wind began to bay.

Another howl of wind and this time Father Wesley found himself checking the window. It wasn't possible for a dog to be a ghost. At least that's what he thought.

Again, another wail of wind. It had to be the wine, he reasoned. Yet, he was sure he heard something else in the gusts. A squeal? Must be somebody snooping around in the church seeing if there was something else they could salvage from the burnt out shell. Father Wesley found himself at the closet, his top coat in hand, ready to explore the source of the squeal.

As he stepped outside, Father Wesley listened attentively for the sound. He attributed whatever he was hearing to the wind. Perhaps the Merlot was not such a good choice of beverage for him on this mournful night. The spirits from the bottle were wreaking havoc with his mind.

Despite the frigid bite the wind brought with it, Father Wesley had to admit it felt refreshing. He took a pair of black fur lined gloves from his coat pocket and began walking towards the church. The noise he was hearing seemed to be emanating from the entrance to the place.

The sound was of something young or weak. He stepped over the sagging and, in places, unfettered police tape which flapped about in the stiff night breeze. The tape delivered a conspicuous warning that nothing good could be found from this point on. Except for the brilliant moonlight, Father Wesley had nothing else to guide him as he entered the ruins of what was once his church.

He was gaining on the sound. In the black ash residue Father Wesley could see the imprints of paws. *Had an animal come here to die?* It would certainly seem fitting, should that be the case, considering the downward spiral the fortunes of St. Theresa's had taken.

Another step and Father Wesley saw from where the sound was coming. In the corner of the vestibule rested a German shepherd. She had given birth to three pups. The three tykes were suckling.

Love Muffin raised her tired head and stared directly at the priest. She seemed to welcome his presence. Some force had driven her here for the sake of her young, and she somehow realized that in the shell of this place, she had found safety. Love Muffin allowed her head to drop back and the wind howled, as though a blessing was being imparted on the moment.

Father Wesley knelt down next to the prostrate dog's head. There was a chain around her neck. With a degree of caution he took note of the inscription on the medallion. It read: Love Muffin. Immediately the priest knew this to be the watchdog at Rose's. It was the dog Shagtyme had come to know. In his presence was their offspring.

One of the puppies crawled over and climbed onto Father Wesley's right shoe. The priest took the newborn dog in his hand and raised the animal above his head. It was a male. He cradled the young pup against his chest and felt his heartbeat over the wet coat of afterbirth. The puppy had the same markings Shagtyme had shown when Father Wesley found him at the Beachhead Lounge fire. The priest's heart felt uplifted. He had found the friend he needed on this night. Shagtyme had not left him alone.

Father Wesley removed his coat and tucked it against Love Muffin's drained body to provide warmth for mother and her pups. He took a step back and marveled at the beauty of life, realizing there was no room in his heart for despair, no place in his being for self-pity. It had become quite clear to him that there was no simplicity to life. Living was complex, and questions were to be asked which could never be clearly answered.

Suddenly the wind subsided and a cold but comforting calm prevailed. The troubled priest looked skyward at the cloud bank which, uncannily, was shaped in the image of a dog's head, as it passed before the full moon.

"Shagtyme, you were a good dog," he said, as a sense of peace settled over him.

THE END